UNDERSTANDING
ALICE WALKER

UNDERSTANDING CONTEMPORARY AMERICAN LITERATURE

Matthew J. Bruccoli, Founding Editor

Linda Wagner-Martin, Series Editor

Also of Interest

Understanding Colson Whitehead, Derek C. Maus

Understanding David Foster Wallace, Marshall Boswell

Understanding James Baldwin, Marc Dudley

Understanding Jennifer Egan, Alexander Moran

Understanding John Edgar Wideman, Quentin D. Miller

Understanding John Rechy, María DeGuzmán

Understanding Karen Tei Yamashita, Jolie Scheffer

Understanding Randall Kenan, James A. Crank

Understanding Stewart O'Nan, Heike Paul

Understanding William S. Burroughs, Gerald Alva Miller, Jr.

UNDERSTANDING
ALICE WALKER

Thadious M. Davis

THE UNIVERSITY OF
SOUTH CAROLINA PRESS

Published by the University of South Carolina Press
Columbia, South Carolina 29208

www.uscpress.com

Manufactured in the United States of America

30 29 28 27 26 25 24 23 22
10 9 8 7 6 5 4 3 2

Library of Congress Cataloging-in-Publication Data
can be found at http://catalog.loc.gov/.

ISBN 978-1-64336-237-3 (hardcover)
ISBN 978-1-64336-238-0 (paperback)
ISBN 978-1-64336-239-7 (ebook)

In memory of
my mother Helen, who always laughed, and
my gift Hatim, who always loved.

CONTENTS

Series Editor's Preface ix

Acknowledgments xi

Chapter 1
Understanding Alice Walker: The Sign of the Family 1

Chapter 2
The Sight of the Familiar: "I Love Myself . . ." 33

Chapter 3
The Work of the Woman: Coloring Purple 61

Chapter 4
The World of the Word: Mediating Self 99

Notes 137

Selected Bibliography 147

Index 155

SERIES EDITOR'S PREFACE

The Understanding Contemporary American Literature series was founded by the estimable Matthew J. Bruccoli (1931–2008), who envisioned these volumes as guides or companions for both students and good nonacademic readers, a legacy that will continue as new volumes are developed to fill in gaps among the nearly one hundred series volumes published to date and to embrace a host of new writers only now making their marks on our literature.

As Professor Bruccoli explained in his preface to the volumes he edited, because much influential contemporary literature makes special demands, "the word *understanding* in the titles was chosen deliberately. Many willing readers lack an adequate understanding of how contemporary literature works; that is, of what the author is attempting to express and the means by which it is conveyed." Aimed at fostering this understanding of good literature and good writers, the criticism and analysis in the series provide instruction in how to read certain contemporary writers—explicating their material, language, structures, themes, and perspectives—and facilitate a more profitable experience of the works under discussion.

In the twenty-first century, Professor Bruccoli's prescience gives us an avenue to publish expert critiques of significant contemporary American writing. The series continues to map the literary landscape and to provide both instruction and enjoyment. Future volumes will seek to introduce new voices alongside canonized favorites, to chronicle the changing literature of our times, and to remain, as Professor Bruccoli conceived, contemporary in the best sense of the word.

Linda Wagner-Martin, Series Editor

ACKNOWLEDGMENTS

Writing this book required reading again Alice Walker's earliest work, especially *Once*, and following through to her latest meditations, all the while embarking on an exercise in remembering my own path as a daughter of the South moving out of that South, a perpetual nomad, a Fulani heart. I remember the mentors showing the way: Blyden Jackson and Richard Barksdale, teacher-scholars; and Pinkie Gordon Lane and Arthenia Bates Millican, creative writers. I remember with gratitude: the models—Emily Dalgarno, Millicent Bell, Adelaide Cromwell, Sam Allen; the poetic guides—David Eberly, Rick Shaner, Connie Veenendaal; the friends—Nellie McKay, Marilyn Richardson, Fahamisha Shariat, Claudia Tate; the fellow-travelers—Michael Harper, Aishah Rahman, Dorothy Denniston, Barton St. Armand; and the bonding sisters—Gamma Sigma Sigmas and Delta Sigma Thetas.

I thank Alice Walker for her writings and travels, and for this gift of my remembering all those who once made a difference in my path. Although so many have now passed on, they all continue to radiate light and ignite laughter to mark my journeying.

My sincere thanks to Linda Wagner-Martin, prodigious scholar and incomparable editor, who asked me to write this book and never gave up on my getting around to it, and to Simba and Pushkin, my almost indomitable last boys, who tried their best to see me finish it.

CHAPTER 1

Understanding Alice Walker
The Sign of the Family

> "Mommy, there's a world in your eye. . . . Mommy, where did you get that world in your eye?"
>
> —Alice Walker, "Beauty: When the Other Dancer Is the Self" (1983)

Alice Walker, Pulitzer Prize and National Book Award winner, has been publishing poetry, fiction, and essays since the 1960s. Throughout her long career and from multiple ideological and spatial locations, she has committed to writing narratives of the hope and transformation possible within the human condition. In the process, she has demonstrated the aesthetic and political power of the word. Her art has turned increasingly to a pronounced spirituality that combines her inherently activist stance with an encompassing global vision of goodness and peace. Her unwavering attention to feminist causes, to anti-war discourses, to environmental issues, and to human rights struggles within the United States and around the world has infused her art with passion. It has also marked her work as constantly evolving, transforming itself and refusing to remain situated within any narrowly defined racial or ideological location. That very passion for standing up for causes she understands as ethical and just has often proven to be controversial, particularly in the politically contentious twenty-first century. Over the past fifty years and despite setbacks and obstacles, personal and professional, Alice Walker has persisted in writing poetry and fiction, along with autobiography, criticism, and meditative and political essays. Hers is a remarkable achievement well worth reconsidering for a twenty-first-century audience.

Walker is, arguably, the premiere African American Southern author of her generation, those writers born in the period of World War II and coming of age in the 1960s. The apex of her critical reception was the publication of *The Color Purple* (1982), winner of the National Book Award and the Pulitzer Prize for Fiction. In more recent years, she has privileged poetry along with nonfiction prose, publishing both frequently and primarily in small volumes addressing critical issues in a changing world. Her global politics, her taking on issues of political prisoners in many nations, her expressing outrage at the continuation of female genital mutilation, or another issue of pressing moral significance, sometimes obscures how her upbringing as a child in the rural, segregated South of specific social mores, racial culture, and political histories has influenced her work. She has steadily drawn upon her formative experiences to enlighten and empower her understanding of the wider world in which she now moves.

Walker's introverted, serious inspection of the interior of hearts and minds from her now-transnational and expansive worldview developed out of the emblematic and transformative aspects of her early life that have shaped her specific way of being in the world. What distinguishes her prolific artistic production is her way of seeing herself and her world. While Alice Walker has not been a subject within Disabilities Studies, her injury as a child, causing the loss of sight in an eye and a visible scarring, suggests that she could well be. Her writing underscores her attention to debilitating injury, inner vision, and spiritual awareness that attends to the wounded, the lost, the oppressed, the dismissed, the maligned, and the invisible.

Alice Malsenior Walker came into the world on February 9, 1944, the last child in a large Southern Black family.[1] As the youngest of Minnie Tallulah ("Lou") and Willie Lee Walker's eight children, Walker had siblings who were already adults and living away from home during her childhood. The oldest of her five brothers, Willie Fred, born in 1930, was the most unlike his father and brothers (William Henry, born 1934; James Thomas, born 1935; Robert Louis, born 1940; and Curtis Ulysses, born 1942) who observed a strict sense of masculine behavior and dominance. Her bothers Robert and Curtis were closer in age to Alice than her two sisters (Minnie Lee, born 1932; and Annie Ruth, born 1937); as a result, they became playmates for the tomboy Alice. The siblings, like their hardworking sharecropper parents and several generations of the family in Putnam County and Eatonton, Georgia, attended Wards Chapel, an African Methodist Episcopal church still in existence today.

Walker's childhood home in rural Georgia was where she experienced mid-twentieth-century Southern life still closely linked to segregation and the social reality of the past. Sharecropping defined the economic condition of her material world, just as legal segregation and its sanctioned customs under Jim Crow delimited her social world. As a child of field workers dependent upon the vicissitudes of crops, Walker spent her youth in poverty. Even with a good harvest, her father earned under $300 a year, and her mother's efforts to supplement the income with domestic work often netted only seventy-five cents a day. The family's economic hardships magnified the inequities of segregation that impacted work and domestic life in her formative years. Positioned within a rigid racial and social hierarchy, the family defied segregation and poverty by aspiring to a better life. Walker's parents helped to start the East Putnam Consolidated School in their community and made certain that Alice attended the elementary and middle school there beginning when she was four years old. Walker herself commemorated in a poem the economic progress her parents had made by the time of her birth when they paid the midwife three dollars cash for delivering Baby Alice instead of selecting a pig for payment.[2]

When she was eight years old, Walker suffered the traumatic injury that caused her to experience isolation and depression. During a game of cowboys and Indians with Bobby and Curtis, who were the cowboys with new BB guns, and Alice the Indian with a bow and arrow, Curtis aimed and fired his BB gun at Alice. The pellet entered her right eye. Her parents initially assumed she had fallen and injured her eye or stepped on a wire that hit her face in the story her brothers concocted, so they used homemade remedies to treat the wound. Only when it did not heal did they discover the extent of the injury. Unfortunately, not only did she lose her eyesight, but she also developed a disfiguring scar tissue on her eye. She revealed an additional aspect of the traumatic event years later when she recounted that her brothers had asked her to lie about what happened, how the injury had occurred, and she had agreed to protect them: "I was left feeling a great deal of pain and loss and forced to think I had somehow brought it on myself. It was like a rape. It was the first time I abandoned myself, by lying. . . . It is also the root of my need to tell the truth, always, because I experienced, very early, the pain of telling a lie."[3] This awareness of self and accountability, despite gender discrimination, forwarded her determination to being truthful to one's self which became a fundamental value in her writing.

The blinding wound caused even greater damage to Walker's youthful spirit. Ashamed of her appearance and fearful of losing her other eye, she retreated into herself and avoided contact with others. By the time she turned twelve, Walker believed that she was ugly and an outcast. The trauma of being wounded resulted in a hypersensitive awareness of her disability and self-consciousness about the scar tissue covering her eye. She remembered responding to the wounded eye with abuse: "I rant and rave at it, in front of the mirror. I plead with it to clear up before morning. I tell it I hate and despise it.

I do not pray for sight. I pray for beauty."[4] Moreover, she dreamed of death as a release, and later recounted her childhood fantasies of self-destruction: "falling on swords, of putting guns to my heart or head, of slashing my wrists with a razor."[5] Instead of suicide, she chose to become an observer and recorder of life around her. Already precocious, she became from the age of eight to fourteen more studious and retiring, yet also developing a type of second sight, an almost-psychic attention to details within her family and culture. Marred herself by physical and psychological scarring, she trained a watchful lens on her immediate community, particularly its suffering. Staving off loneliness, she filled her solitude by reading stories, keeping a scrapbook, and writing poems, much of which she preserved in a scrapbook now held in the collection of her papers at Emory University that includes her poetry entitled "Poems of a Childhood Poetess."

In almost storybook fashion, Walker emerged at fourteen years old from plastic surgery to become an attractive high school student. Cosmetic surgery, paid for by her brother Bill, not only removed the disfiguring scar tissue from her right eye but also lifted her out of isolation. Bill, who after her initial injury had borrowed $250 to take Alice to a doctor in Macon, had never given up hope for his baby sister's eye. He later left Georgia for Boston and with his wife Gaye arranged Alice's surgery at Massachusetts General Hospital during a summer visit. The operation facilitated her emergence from depression.[6] The transformation in her appearance enabled a new sense of her social self and brought about a different subject position after the surgery: "Almost immediately I become a different person from the girl who does not raise her head. Or so I think. . . . Now that I've raised my head I have plenty of friends."[7] Walker, permanently blind in one eye, flowered into a "most popular" student at Eatonton's Butler-Baker High School where she was valedictorian and homecoming queen of her senior class. This extraordinary set of transfigurations with its enduring legacy of disability mixed with celebratory triumph over that disability helped to produce early on a mature attention to a visionary ontology in Walker's writing and with it a sustained epistemology of difference in her ideology. As a result, her writing upholds an ethic of care and potential change for human beings, whether wounded or well, and for their habitat, the often-endangered earth. Concomitantly, her literary voice encourages a search for joy as a transformative value in living.

Although she has recalled feeing intensely alienated because of the disfiguring injury, Walker has also pointed out the pivotal role played by her mother and women teachers who encouraged her ability as a student, particularly after her injury. Perhaps the most inspirational was Trellie Jeffers, her seventh-grade teacher who empathized with her student because, having lost an eye as a child, she wore a prosthesis. Jeffers demonstrated by her presence in the classroom that having only one sighted eye did not prevent Alice Walker from fully developing her own talents. Years later, Jeffers recalled from memory the words, "You are my knight in shining armor," the first line of a poem that Walker wrote for her.[8]

Consistent in acknowledging role models, Walker drew the most encouragement from her mother, who knew and told the history of the people, events, and places of their community.[9] Minnie Lou Walker engaged her daughter's imagination with stories about her own past and that of their family, but moreover, she empowered her daughter with the freedom to become a storyteller herself. Somehow her mother managed to save enough to purchase three gifts for Walker's departure for college and her journey toward a different life: a suitcase, a sewing machine, and a typewriter. Walker acknowledged them as "the three magical gifts I needed to escape the poverty of my hometown and that [my] mother purchased while earning less than twenty dollars a week."[10] The three represented freedom from dependency. The gift of a typewriter signaled a mother's faith in a daughter's creativity and potential. Symbolically, the typewriter was part of a mother's permission for her daughter to be a writer, as Mary Helen Washington has suggested; it marked "the transference of authority and power" over stories from one generation to the next and from the oral to the written tradition.[11]

Walker, however, was not immediately reconciled to her blind eye. She fretted over its appearing unfocused if she were tired or how it would look to those who stared into her face or how it would attract the camera lens in photographs. It was not until her child Rebecca looked at her and saw a "world" in her eye that Walker fully accepted her eye: "Yes indeed, I realized looking into the mirror. There was a world in my eye. And I saw that it was possible to love it: that in fact, for all it had taught me of shame and anger and inner voice, I *did* love it."[12]

Written in 1983, "Beauty: When the Other Dancer Is the Self," detailing her loss of being pretty and cute at the age of eight when her brother shot her in the eye and her recovery of her sense of attractiveness once a surgeon removed the scar tissue from her sightless eye, ends with Walker's understanding of her wellness as a whole person. With the recognition that the dancer she dreams of is her own self, she felt "beautiful, whole and free."[13] Here Walker, as Kevin Everod Quashie theorizes on girlhood selfhood: "unites with her other self, a self she experiences spiritually but also materially. This meeting of the self is joyous, an act of mutuality that suggests that the human yearning for companionship is fulfilled in the meeting of a self that is one's self but also not oneself—the other dancer is both a distinct self from Walker but also her."[14]

Walker's 1980s essay remains pivotal in comprehending her insistent writing about self, but it also signifies her ability to see in a wholly visionary manner. The beauty of wholeness of self, along with its joy so much in evidence in her early publications, reverberates throughout her career. She carried forward the discovered freedom to be herself and with it the right to be happy. Walker's travels from Eatonton through the world have been marked by a spiritual quest for a wholeness of self and a physical alignment with a nurturing environment. Enlightenment in her journey toward how to live on the earth and with herself has remained a constant goal, a way to move onward and a source of joy.

That journey has not been easy. The beginning of her career as a published writer emanated from another awakening to the reality of trauma and pain, physical and emotional. Upon graduating at the head of her class, Walker received a scholarship to Spelman College in Atlanta. During her two years (1961–1963) as a student at the private African American women's college, she witnessed the emergent civil rights movement and experienced its impact on a generation of young African Americans who, in recovering their racial past, discovered their individual power to transform their collective future. In struggling against segregationist laws and practices in the South, Walker and the Atlanta students realized a fierce determination to affect political and social change in the world they inhabited. They also demonstrated the ability of individuals not only to empower an oppressed race but also to change themselves.

One of Walker's Spelman teachers, historian Howard Zinn became a mentor who exemplified commitment to ethical stances, just causes, and political activism. Decades later, Walker and Zinn recounted their initial meeting during her freshman year and her enrollment the next year in his Russian history course that mixed literature, language, and art. While mainly quiet in the class, she wrote a remarkable paper on Tolstoy and Dostoyevsky that Zinn shared with a colleague who found it inconceivable that she could be the author, to which Zinn responded: "There's nobody around who can write like this."[15] The 1996 Zinn-Walker exchange also revealed that Walker had arrived at Spelman from "Deep country," as she interjected, but following her first year of college, she traveled to Russia and brought back to Eatonton not merely nesting dolls and embroidered shawls, but much more: "I was always trying to bring the world back to my family and to my little town. . . . you bring back what you find. I loved doing it, especially doing it with my mother, and just try to make the world bigger for her."[16] In sharing, Walker differentiated herself from her brilliant, educated sister Minnie Lee who years before had experienced other worlds that she tried to share with her county family but in frustration had finally given up on returning home as Walker referenced in her poignant and wise poem "For My Sister Molly Who in the Fifties."[17] Walker's generous sharing of the bigger world along with her meditative and intellectual reflections on it is one of the most sustained characteristics of her written work.

When Walker transferred to Sarah Lawrence College in Bronxville, New York, for her junior year, she left the South with an awakened political and racial consciousness. Her gender consciousness would develop exponentially during her senior year. She had spent the summer in East Africa as part of the Experiment in International Living but returned to college and discovered that she was pregnant. She described the traumatic experience of being at the mercy of both her own body and social definitions of proper behavior as provoking not only an understanding of "how alone woman is, because of her body," but also a reconsideration of suicide, a reconsideration which led her to conclude that to take one's own life was not "frightening or even odd—but only inevitable."[18] During that physical ordeal in 1965, she was emotionally exhausted by the dilemma she faced: causing her family pain if she killed herself or shame if she bore the child. Though she once again dreamed of suicide as she had after her eye injury and kept a razor blade under her pillow for slicing her wrists, she retained hope that her college friends would locate an abortionist. Fortunately, her friends rallied, contributed financial and emotional support, and found an abortionist. The experience of waiting—suspended between life and death—and of finding sudden release spilled out in one week of nonstop writing of poems.

During this period of dread and suspension of normalcy, Walker wrote poems that would constitute her first book, *Once*. The poetry recapitulated her travelogue experiences in Kenya and Uganda, beginning with the opening poem "African Images, Glimpses from a Tiger's Back" which in forty-five short stanzas delves deep into the beauty and contradiction of an African American girl encountering Africa. The last stanza is evocative of the breath and elusiveness of the experience: "in my journal / I thought I could / capture / everything. . . . / Listen! / the soft wings of cranes / sifting the salt sea / air."[19] Walker further signals the autobiographical input in the Kikuyu name "Wangari," given to the first-person narrator, a young African American college student in the poetic sequence questioning how to reclaim an alien heritage. Wangari, the Kikuyu name that Walker received as an honorary member of the Leopard Clan during her sojourn in Kenya, later became the name her future husband used to address her in letters when they were apart.

In addition to Africa, Walker reimagined the South and her civil rights struggle there, especially in the long free-verse title poem, "Once." Importantly, too, she wrote love poems (for example, "Johann" and "Mornings"), and a sequence of suicide poems, including the longer poems "Ballad of a Brown Girl," "To Die Before One Wakes Must Be Glad," and "Exercises on Themes of Life."

In "Ballad of the Brown Girl," the residual effect of a pregnancy from an interracial love affair lingers in a recast version of parental disapproval that Walker herself had faced: "the next morning / her slender/neck broken/ her note short / and of cryptic/collegiate make— / just / 'Question—. / did ever brown/daughter to black / father a white/baby / take—?'"[20] In formal aspects, these poems show the influence of both Japanese haiku and Zen epigrams, which Walker said influenced her respect for short forms: "I was delighted to learn that in three or four lines a poet can express mystery, evoke beauty and pleasure, paint a picture—and not dissect or analyze in any way."[21] All of the poems in *Once*, however, focus on understanding and exploring a young woman's physical and psychological responses to her shifting experiential reality.

Walker recreated her varied actual and imagined experience in urgent poetic sequences that she presented to Muriel Rukeyser, one of her teachers at Sarah Lawrence. She acknowledged how Rukeyser, who "taught by the courage of her own life," sustained her: "Afraid of little, intimidated by none, Muriel Rukeyser the Poet and Muriel Rukeyser the Prophet-person and Truth-doer . . . taught me that it *is* possible to live in this world on your own terms."[22] Rukeyser encouraged Walker and championed her poetry by sending the poems to her own agent. Three years later, those poems would appear in *Once*.

Rukeyser was not alone in mentoring Walker during her senior year. In speaking at Sarah Lawrence's 1972 convocation, Walker singled out Jane Cooper and Helen Merrell Lynd, along with Rukeyser, as "gifts" to her as a woman and a writer. Her usage of "gifts" is reminiscent of her remarking her mother's three gifts when she left home. The surrogates taught Walker that "each woman is capable of truly bringing another into the world."[23] Cooper's "magic" instruction and her "true" ability to offer "listening" and "peace" and Merrell Lynd's capacity to render "philosophy understandable and the study of it natural" were valuable life models.[24] Merrell Lynd helped Walker understand her recent life experiences in broader contexts by showing her "for the first time, how life and suffering are always teachers, or, as with Camus, life and suffering *and* joy."[25] Walker made the philosophical connections to her own life explicit from her studying with Merrell Lynd: "Like Rilke, I came to understand that even loneliness has a use, and that sadness is positively the wellspring of creativity. Since studying with her, all of life, the sadness as well as the joy, has its magnificence, its meaning, and its *use*."[26] These teachers, much like her supportive ones in Georgia, assisted Walker in making sense of her experiences and in laying intellectual foundations for her writing.

Walker's distinctly female dilemma and the concomitant dependence upon women for a solution produced an acute awareness of her gendered self and of her love of life. "Writing poetry," she concluded, "is my way of celebrating with the world that I have not committed suicide the night before."[27] At the same time, she acknowledged that for her "Poems—even happy ones—emerge from an accumulation of sadness."[28] Writing poetry became her way of connecting her survival to the diverse experiences of all the women in her life, a family of women as it were, and of establishing the ground for her commitment to women's rights and feminist issues.

Walker further signaled the infusion of autobiography in the dedication and epigraph of *Once*. Dedicated to Howard Zinn, her Spelman teacher whose politics epitomized activism, *Once* is a courageous book for a young writer. It lays bare the anxiety in longing and love when race and nationality complicate interpersonal relationships. Along with the pain of social discrimination under regimes of segregation, it channels the costly but necessary struggle for political rights and freedom. The epigraph is from Albert Camus, *De l'envers et l'endroit* (1937): "Poverty was not a calamity for me. It was always balanced by the richness of light . . . circumstances helped me. To correct a natural indifference I was placed half-way between misery and the sun. Misery kept me from believing that all was well under the sun, and the sun taught me that history wasn't everything." Walker equated Camus's assessment of his experience to her growing up in Georgia and her lessons learned during her traumatic year at Sarah Lawrence. The French Algerian Nobel Laureate's words resonated deeply with Walker, whose senior honors thesis was "Albert Camus: The Development of His Philosophical Position as Reflected in His Novels and Plays," written under the supervision of Helen Merrell Lynd.[29] This conjoining of political and philosophical reflection opening Walker's first book would become one of her hallmarks.

Not surprisingly, Walker reiterated Camus's words from the epigraph of *Once* in one of her earliest published essays, "The Black Writer and the Southern Experience" (1970), which shed light on how she positioned herself as a writer in relation to both her Georgia upbringing and her philosophical education. She briefly discussed her mother's experience with a dismissive White woman working for the Red Cross during the Depression, and the lesson her mother conveyed to her young daughter about the ability of poor Black neighbors to share what each had to survive. Her mother's story taught a lesson about racial strength, which Walker used to delve further into the inherited resources of Black writers from the South: "solidarity and sharing [that] a modest existence can sometimes bring" and dependence upon "one another without shame."[30]

At the same time by incorporating Camus, Walker resisted romanticizing Black country life. She acknowledged hating much of it: "The hard work in the fields, the shabby houses, the evil greedy men who worked my father to death and almost broke the courage of that strong woman, my mother. . . . Southern black writers, like most writers, have a heritage of love and hate, but . . . also have enormous richness and beauty to draw from. And, having been placed, as Camus says, 'halfway between misery and the sun,' they, too, know that 'though all is not well under the sun, history is not everything.'"[31] Walker posited Camus's approach to his background as central to her mature understanding of her complex "advantageous heritage": "a compassion for the earth, a trust in humanity beyond our knowledge of evil, and an abiding love of justice. We inherit a great responsibility . . . for we must give voice to centuries not only of silent bitterness and hate but also of neighborly kindness and sustaining love."[32]

What precipitated this remarkable awareness of self and subject matter in relation to the South and Black Southerners was a return to her native region shortly after graduating from Sarah Lawrence in 1966. That year would prove to be fast paced in changes to Walker's life and writing. She worked briefly as a caseworker for the New York City Department of Welfare, but her talent for writing was recognized by the Bread Loaf Writers' Conference, which encouraged her writing poetry and prose simultaneously, a practice consistent throughout her career. In short order, she received a position in Jackson, Mississippi, for the Legal Defense and Educational Fund of the NAACP and departed New York for the residency in Mississippi that would change the course of her personal and professional life.

The civil rights effort she first encountered in Atlanta was in full force in Jackson where she worked under the supervision of Marian Wright Edelman, a Spelman and Yale Law graduate who later founded the Children's Defense Fund. Among the young people working in Jackson was Melvyn R. Leventhal, a law student at New York University and intern for the Law Students Civil Rights Research Council, who was assigned with Walker to the Greenwood project monitoring and recording retaliatory actions taken against Black residents who tried to register to vote. Leventhal would become Walker's husband the next year, 1967, when they returned to New York where interracial marriage was legal and where he would complete his law degree. Walker's initial stint in Mississippi and her assignment taking depositions from Greenwood sharecroppers evicted for attempting to vote infused her creative writing with new voices and subjects. Returning to New York, however, enabled her publishing. She completed "The Civil Rights Movement: What Good Was It?" for a contest in *The American Scholar*; it won a $300 first prize and publication, and increased recognition. She received a residency at the MacDowell Colony, where she continued to write poetry while also working on what would become *The Third Life of Grange Copeland*, a novel fueled by her engagement with

Mississippi sharecroppers. During this period, Walker published her first story, "To Hell with Dying," written while she was still a student at Sarah Lawrence but selected in 1967 for *The Best Short Stories by Negro Writers*.

Walker had already committed to becoming a writer and to asserting a moral function of art when she completed her undergraduate degree. Out of her personal experience, she had come to believe that art saved lives, and that her purpose as a writer was to maintain the connections among the personal, political, and social aspects of art. Her return to Mississippi in 1967 with her husband only strengthened her resolve to write out of a social and moral consciousness and out of a heightened political awareness of racial inequality. Because interracial marriage was not legal in Mississippi, they faced physical danger added to the disapproval they already endured from both family and friends. She admitted in a journal entry from 1966 that she had first gone to Mississippi "to 'tirelessly observe it' to kill the fear it engendered" for its "terrifyingly hard, pitifully cheap" treatment of Black life; however, she adjusted her rationale for returning to live there again because "'the stories were knee-deep'" and she was "in a fever to get everything down. . . . It was a period of constant revelation, when mysteries not understood during my Southern childhood came naked to me to be embraced. I grew to adulthood in Mississippi."[33]

During her second stay in Mississippi, Walker worked again in voter registration while writing fiction along with poetry, but she also held a job conducting workshops in Black history for the teachers of the Head Start Friends of the Children of Mississippi Program. She developed a reading list of Black history materials that she herself had not encountered in college. At the same time, inspired by the stories she had recorded and those of the ninety Black women in her workshop, she started collecting African American folklore. Her varied activities brought her into contact with Black women from across the state, who like her mother, had stories to tell. These women ranged from public school teachers to maids and fieldworkers. They quilted, canned, and cooked, but also taught the children in Head Start and worked to forward racial progress. Mrs. Winson Hudson, for example, was not only director of the Head Start Program where Walker worked but was also writing her autobiography which Walker was reading and typing.[34] These women reminded Walker of her mother and grandmothers, but at the same time, they evoked the Black literary foremothers that she was discovering in reading and preparing her classes. Mississippi, seen through the eyes of these women, was at once familiar and revelatory. These experiences became a productive incubator for expanding Walker's art, even though she lost her job, ironically because the Office of Economic Opportunity which paid her salary did not approve of teaching Black studies to Head Start teachers.[35]

Walker began her work as a novelist by listening to the stories of Black Mississippi women that reminded her of her own family's history in Georgia. Their experiences enabled her to ascertain the complexities of race and gender in their lives and hers. With them, she witnessed firsthand the impact of the movement on African Americans of all ages, and not merely on the young as she had seen in the student-led struggle in Atlanta. She observed the transformation of older Blacks who discovered the potential of political agency and who, despite immediate danger, acted upon their individual power to transform their racial and collective future. She explained that "in Mississippi, it seems I sometimes relive my Georgia childhood. I see the same faces, hear the same soft voices, take a nip, once in a while, of the same rich mellow corn, or wine. And when I write about the people there, in the strangest way it is as if I am not writing about them at all but about myself."[36] Walker's innate habit of observation helped her empathize with Black Mississippians, who, much like her own family, had for generations endured oppressive and dehumanizing conditions that had sometimes led to abjection and self-destruction. She realized from watching and listening that these individuals were forwarding change in personal as well as public arenas.

The Third Life of Grange Copeland (1970) drew upon Walker's expanding appreciation for how the civil rights movement brought changes to political access and especially to personal relationships and intergenerational interactions in the rural Black South. In crafting a narrative covering three generations, Walker also applied her feminist understanding of the harm an oppressed but rigid Black patriarchy with a misguided model of masculinity could inflict on families, especially Black women and girls in the family. In addition, she utilized the literary discoveries that she had made in preparing to become a writer-in-residence at Jackson State University and subsequently a lecturer at Tougaloo College. With an infusion of fresh models for work, she pressed on in writing her novel and garnered support from a National Endowment for the Arts award.

The birth of her daughter, Rebecca Grant Leventhal, three days after she finished writing her novel in 1969 compounded Walker's attention to women-centered themes. Although she considered her child an "incomparable gift" enabling her to view the world from a new perspective, Walker feared that motherhood would necessitate conforming to social definitions of women's roles and limiting her identity as a writer. She later affirmed in "One Child of One's Own" that being a mother and a writer, though difficult, were not incompatible roles, so that she did not have to choose one or the other social identity for herself: "It is not my child who tells me I have no femaleness white women must affirm; not my child who says I have no rights black men or women must respect."[37] Her daughter's birth initiated a period of feminist self-examination in Walker's development as a writer acutely conscious of her gender. One result is that her first novel and those thereafter acknowledge an inner struggle for control over the ideality and the reality of self as reflected in the actual physical world, and they privilege a transformative power necessary for a meaningful private and public life.

One of the several epigraphs *to The Third Life of Grange Copeland* is an acknowledgment of Richard Wright who in 1970 remained the premiere Black writer associated with the South. Walker selects from Constance Webb's biography a statement Wright made to Jean-Paul Sartre: "'The greatest danger . . . in the world today is that the very feeling and conception of what is a human being might well be lost.'" In quoting Wright, Walker emphasizes the relationship between her own life and first novel and Wright's. His sentiment would resonate throughout Walker's career: the dangerous threat of losing one's humanity or losing the affective and cognitive reality of being human. In this recognition, Walker provides one access route to her novel and a suggestion of how later her themes would circle around the ever-present danger of losing what constitutes a human being.

Walker's dedication suggests her perceived difference from Wright. Dedicated to her mother ("who made a way out of no way") and to her then husband, *The Third Life of Grange Copeland* draws upon two aspects of Walker's family life up to the end of the 1960s. In the first, she evokes her upbringing in the rural, patriarchal South where Black women, like her mother and foremothers, embodied hard work and familial contributions, yet were rarely respected as being equal. In the second, Walker encapsulates the personal and familial changes brought by young Black Southerners like herself, the civil rights movement, and their hope for the future.

The dedication to Minnie Lou Walker figures her presence as tenacious determination to accomplish the seeming impossible. It signals that Minnie Lou guided Walker to decipher positives in her Southern upbringing. It allows Walker to distinguish herself from Wright and to accept her evolution as a Black woman writer from the hardscrabble South who does not separate herself from her origins and who embraces the connection to her mother and Black familial relationships. Unlike Wright, whom she believed "found little in his childhood to like and admire . . . he often felt it was barren; I feel just the opposite": "When I go back to Eatonton, Georgia, I get these new reverberations of things, new enlightenment; I understand on a deeper level. That will probably always be there in the work."[38]

By including her husband in the dedication, Walker aligns herself with family but also with her significant difference from her mother's generation.

She acknowledges a sea-change that had taken place already by the end of the 1960s when an interracial married couple could live and work in Mississippi, even if their marital union was not sanctioned by state law. Her marriage and her residence in the South with a White husband mark a world already partly transformed politically and socially from any that her mother and foremothers had known.

The dedications introduce *The Third Life of Grange Copeland* as an intergenerational novel and one of the earliest fictional treatments referencing the modern civil rights movement. The text, however, is self-consciously historical and begins in 1920. Written at the end of the transformative 1960s, it does not turn to Ruth, a young girl raised by her grandfather to accomplish something great, until halfway into the narrative. Neither does it incorporate participants in the movement and the social and political changes they brought until late in the narrative and then only in a short chapter. Walker made a conscious decision to write a pre-history foundational to the necessary personal changes that would undergird the public civil rights movement in the South. Her historical construction attests to her belief that "nothing ever is" merely "a product of the immediate present."[39]

The novel opens with a focus on the boy Brownfield Copeland and his sad awareness of his "country" life in Georgia as his Philadelphia cousins and their parents depart in a new 1920 Buick. The contrast between his talkative city relatives and his silent parents, Grange and Margaret Copeland, magnifies the bareness of his life and stunted development. The descriptive strength of the section depends upon the depiction of Brownfield's lonely childhood while his parents are at work. Left unattended with only a "sugar-tit" to satisfy his hunger and thirst, he experiences neither love nor emotional attachment to his parents. The deprivations of his youth stunt his maturation and poison his psyche, so much so that he proceeds in the world as a destroyer of dreams, even the ones that he himself conjures up. Maria Lauret draws cogently upon myth from the story of Oepidus and psychoanalysis from Freud's essay "Family Romance" to analyzes Brownfield's recurring daydream of his grown-up self as the adored husband in a happy rich family with a White, powdery wife and a Black, glistening cook who seem to alternate or fuse places as a blurred enactment of his desire for a loving mother and his besting of a failed father.[40]

The strained, loveless, and ultimately broken relationship between Brownfield and his father Grange functions in the background of the first half of the novel. The absence of touch signifies the vacuum between father and son. In the foreground is Brownfield's experience after Grange abandons his family and precipitates the suicide of Margaret who kills her sickly baby. Their actions loosen Brownfield from all moorings in his sharecropping community and initiate a lonely search, ostensibly for his father, but actually for his own place in the world. His coming of age in a random town as he attempts to go North, his liaison with a rapacious older woman and her daughter, his marriage to a young schoolteacher, and his disintegration into debased, misogynistic cruelty toward his wife Mem and daughters, all occur rapidly.

The Third Life of Grange Copeland owes much to Hurston's folklore and her novel *Their Eyes Were Watching God* (1937). Walker refigures Hurston's representations of a husband's domineering treatment of a wife who comes into her own through the power of language in Brownfield's physical domination and verbal abuse of Mem, as well as in her rising to take physical and verbal control over her husband, though in her moral goodness she miscalculates the depth of his hatred and ruthlessness. Gentle, loving, and hardworking, Mem allows Brownfield to strip her of her educated speech, to beat her into submission, and to destroy her youthful beauty, all in fruitless acquiescence to his domination. Her desire for a better life with decent housing and indoor plumbing for her daughters determines her rebellion and not a hatred of her husband. Mem, who plants flower seeds at every rundown cabin they inhabit, is aligned with the natural world and seeks harmony and beauty, neither of which Brownfield can accept. He is so vindictively cruel that he sacrifices his own improved quality of life to bring Mem down into the most degraded circumstances of a sharecropper's existence. She signals a partial surrender to her fate and an acceptance of the impermanence of any residence when she becomes so dispirited that at their last decrepit dwelling "she threw a few flower seeds in the moist rich soil around the woodpile. Never again did she intend to plant flowers in boxes or beds."[41]

Brownfield's treatment of Mem anticipates Mister's abuse of Celie in Walker's major novel *The Color Purple* (1982), in which patriarchal abuse is central. When, for example, Mem searches for a livable house in town after Brownfield has lost yet another sharecropper's shack, she incites Brownfield's anger and jealousy because his one attempt at finding decent housing ended in failure and in refusal to try again. His verbal response is, "'I ought to make you call me Mister,' he said, slowly twisting the wrist he held and bringing her to her knees beside his feet. 'A woman as black and ugly as you ought to call a man Mister.'"[42] On releasing her, he "spitefully" flings another insult at her: "'Goddam rib-ridden *plowhorse*.'"[43] The incident previews the language Mister uses in *The Color Purple* to demean Celie as ugly and black while using her as his domestic workhorse.

Brownfield's own barbaric eating habits, gross sexual gestures, and vile speech mannerisms mark him as crude and animal-like. His wife and little girls watch in disgust as he eats like a hog, scooping up peas with his hands and sucking on meat. Shamelessly inhumane, he thrashes about believing in nothing and "knowing he could never renew or change himself for this changelessness was all he had, he could not clarify what was the duty of love."[44] He embodies the brutal Misfit's thinking, "No pleasure but meanness," from Flannery O'Connor's story "A Good Man Is Hard to Find." Brownfield's behavior erupts in an ultimate act of brutality when he uses a shotgun to blast Mem's face. While his devastated daughters rush to their dead mother, Brownfield turns emotionless into their shack to sleep. These disturbing events unfold in narrative flashbacks that neither penetrate Mem's interiority nor access her daughters' consciousness.

Mem's murder moves the narrative to its next stage. With a focus on Grange and his relationship with his granddaughter Ruth, the text develops the intergenerational bonding that places Grange at its center. He has married Josie and with her financial help from selling her juke joint, he has bought a farm; however, he remains a difficult, flawed man. He mistreats Josie, calls her names, and uses her sexually at will, all the while protecting and nurturing Ruth. His three distinct lives intersect in his raising her. His first life is the afterlife of slavery in which sharecropping controls his desperate economic condition, denigrates his manhood, and spills over to pollute his domestic space. His second life is an attempted escape from bondage in an emasculating system by migrating to the North where the anticipation of freedom dissolves into the bitter realities of urban racism, privation, aloneness, hunger, and hatred that result in an erosion his humanity. His third life back in the South is a reconciliation of his drive for emancipation, economic independence, and domestic security with his need for repairing his demoralized masculinity, reconnecting with his better self, and exercising control over his actions. In that life, Ruth plays the primary inspirational and motivational role. Grange recognizes something special about Ruth from her birth. Once he takes the virtually orphaned girl into his home, Grange realigns his emotional core and experiences love, which Ruth activates along with his physical protection.

Walker unfolds the relationship between Grange and Ruth in carefully paced vignettes that chart Ruth's development from a first grader to a sixteen-year-old. Grange raises her in the sheltering domesticity usually associated with women's work of child-rearing. That willingness to take on this typically gender-defined work signifies one aspect of his transformation out of traditional patriarchal attitudes. He raises Ruth to be strong-willed and self-sufficient. He teaches her to shoot, to make and drink moonshine wine, to speak for herself, to stand up for herself (even against authoritarian figures), to swim (so that she can save herself from baptism in the river), to build a fence to protect their property, and to drive a car.

A first glance, Grange seems to be turning her into a miniature version of his male self; however, his rearing practices acknowledge both the divide between men and women in their ability to exercise agency and the necessity of women assuming some of the prerogatives of men. He insists that tomboyish Ruth learn what he understands to be things that women want and what he perceives as feminine ways. He buys her a pink dress replete with ruffles and encourages the decorating of her room in frilly yellow and white and dotted swiss. Grange takes pride in confiding: "'I never in my life seen such a womanish gal,'" using a term that Walker would later deploy in defining her conception of "Womanism."[45] His child-rearing is at once revolutionary and conventional. Ruth's acquired skills and abilities place her on a spectrum of independence and freedom, despite her race and gender. Her education includes gaining financial freedom when Grange turns over his $900 bank account to her, along with his cash-filled cigar box, makes her the owner of his farm, puts his car in her name, and reveals that he has made his gambling buddies take out insurance policies naming her as beneficiary. Walker punctuates Grange's renunciation of traditional gender roles with a correction of racial economic instability; nevertheless, she demonstrates with unfailing clarity that while money and property can generate a measure of security for Black people, those assets will not eliminate racism or sexism.

Even while providing Ruth with the tools to succeed and become her fully human self, Grange still wonders whether the fight can be won, given the impossible odds against Black people. He extols Exodus and repeatedly reminds Ruth of the Hebrews' flight from bondage in Egypt: "'They done the right thing.' . . . 'Got out while they still had some sense and cared about what happened to they spirit.' . . . 'We can't live here free and easy and at home. We going crazy.' . . . 'I mean in this country, the U.S. I believe we got to leave this place if we 'spect to survive. All this struggle to keep human. . . . It's killing us. They's more ways to kill than with guns. We make good songs and asylum cases.'"[46] Ruth responds hopefully that everything might become "'better if something happened to change everything; made everything equal; made us feel *at home*.'"[47]

Through Ruth's eyes emerges a positive description of the tall, genial white-haired grandfather. In her accounts, Grange's loose-limbed dancing and singing, drinking, and gambling bear striking resemblance to Southern bluesmen, those mobile singers who voiced in their words and lives the suffering and pain of being Black as well as the joys and pleasures of living Black. Grange connects Ruth to her missing familial and ancestral ways, not all of which are positive, but some of which demonstrate the survival strategies of those who have gone before.

Walker telescopes Grange's appeal as an impressive presence in one remarkable chapter that evinces more of Hurston's influence on the novel. Grange appears there as an expert in crafting High John the Conqueror folktales that Hurston collected. Not only could he recite the Uncle Remus tales from memory, but he could also concoct much better stories about "a smart plantation man named John," who "became Ruth's hero because he could talk himself out of any situation and reminded her of Grange."[48] With Ruth and Josie as listeners, Grange entertains himself as much as his audience with his elaborate tales, including many from his past, such as his boyhood bargain with the Lord that if a fly entered his uncle's mouth during a church service, he would allow himself to be "saved" and baptized. In giving Ruth the experience of the folk mores of their racial heritage, he encourages a positive social consciousness and an awareness of value in their past in a society that generally denigrates Black culture and history.

In his animated storytelling, Grange reveals how he has fought against emasculation and emancipated himself from the strictures that would deny his manhood. Whereas his son repeatedly falls into accepting the logic and rhetoric of a victimized Black masculinity, Grange stumbles into beliefs that approximate Black nationalism of the 1960s. Marcellus Blount, Marlon B. Ross, GerShun Avilez, and other critics, who read discourses of Black masculinity and Black power in the Black Nationalist Movement, point to the refuting of subordination and the wresting control of racial and family images from White domination as an assertion of Black manhood.[49] Walker presents Grange in this vein of newer ideology, even though she also connects him to Ralph Ellison's earlier *Invisible Man* (1952) in his experience of invisibility in New York, which held him in a "solitary confinement," an unseeing "pretending he was not there," and his street corner retaliatory preaching of hate in Harlem in an effort to be seen and to see himself.[50] Ellison's text, like Grange's experience after migrating north, predates the emergence of the modern Black Nationalist and civil rights movements, but it lends the longer arc of racial and historical continuity to Grange as a Black man grappling with his place within America. In the 1960s and 1970s, that place with Black emancipation at stake posed ideological and procedural clashes between nationalism and feminism that Walker witnessed.[51]

With so much of the text trained on representing Grange and coming to terms with both a racist oppressive White culture and a destructive Black masculinist culture, *The Third Life of Grange Copeland* does not strike an immediate chord as a feminist text. Walker's feminist perspective, however, is legible in her discerning treatment of women, who though brutalized by the men in their lives are not merely victims. Mem works to earn enough to remove herself and her daughters from abysmal conditions right up to the day Brownfield shoots her. Josie suffers Grange's verbal assault about hating Whites, but she refuses to hate. When Brownfield tells her that he put his last child, an albino boy, outdoors to freeze to death, Josie is horrified and stares in shock, "seeing for the first time that he was, as a human being, completely destroyed."[52] Walker visualizes these women retaining their humanity yet struggling to attain agency.

Woven into their threadbare existence are many of Walker's conclusions about women and patriarchy articulated prior to her novel: how alone women are because of their bodies, how pregnancy and bearing children can betray a woman's dreams, how men in the family can fail to protect women and even become the source of their harm. Brownfield, for instance, knows he can wear Mem down and deplete her strength by impregnating her: "She was ill; the two pregnancies he forced on her . . . although they did not bear live fruit, almost completely destroyed what was left of her health."[53] He taunts her: "'Your trouble is you just never learned how not to git pregnant. How long did you think you could keep going with your belly full of childrens?'"[54] Even Ruth after she begins to menstruate "felt her woman's body made her defenseless. She felt it could now be had and made to conceive something she did not want, against her will and her mind could do nothing to stop . . . being . . . trapped in a condition that could only worsen."[55] These issues in the text reframe Walker's experiential reality of pregnancy as a college student which directed her attention to the gender-based adversities of reproduction and motherhood, as well as to metaphors of rebirth and imagery of transformation.

Despite gender adversity, Grange chooses to give his granddaughter a chance to survive whole: "Survival was not everything. *He* had survived. But to survive *whole* was what he wanted for Ruth."[56] Without hesitation, he kills his own son who had endangered Ruth's safety. Grange understands that he bears some responsibility for Brownfield's damaged personality; he knows that shooting Brownfield will not compensate for that wrong, but he accepts his limited agency. He believes that recompense lies in choosing to give Ruth a chance to survive free and whole. It is a bleak, naturalistic end to a father and son who have no meaningful way forward in a changing world.

The final paragraph accentuates the human at the moment Grange himself is dying: "'Oh, you poor thing, you poor thing,' he murmured finally, desolate, but also for the sound of a human voice, bending over to the ground and then rearing back, rocking himself in his own arms to a final sleep."[57] Comforting himself in his own humanity, Grange embraces death, one resulting from the dynamic transformation of his humanity. Without absolving systemic economic and racial oppression for the sins committed against him and other Black people, Grange admits culpability, acknowledges responsibility, and bows to the redeeming power of love.

The strong familial tie in Ruth's and Grange's attachment is a major aspect of Walker's thinking about intergenerational relationships. It recalls the girl narrator's relationship to Mr. Sweet who is resuscitated by children's love in her earliest published story, "To Hell with Dying." That story held special meaning for Walker because, after surviving her traumatic experience in college, a "feeling of gladness" of being alive spilled over into the story, in which she figured herself as both an old man being revived from dying and the children bringing him back to life.[58] Associated with the grace of living witnessed across generations, the story facilitated Walker's friendship with one of her acknowledged models for writing Langston Hughes who selected it for his *Best Short Stories by Negro Writers* (1967). "To Hell with Dying" traces a girl's familial-like love for an elderly neighbor, who was a drinker, not much of a farmer, but a guitar-playing blues man experiencing loss and love, pain and beauty in his singing and his games with children. As a grown-up studying for her doctorate, the girl still believes in the extraordinary power of love to claim kinship and bring a dying man back from the brink of death.

The cycle of resurgence and resurrection within the simplicity of a soul lovingly raised from the dead in a rite of rebirth and renewal is the subtext from "To Hell with Dying" that Walker reconstitutes figuratively in *The Third Life of Grange Copeland.* That subtext is apparent subsequently in the intergenerational attachment, complex family bond, and emotive core shared by a daughter, her father, and grandfather in "A Sudden Trip Home in the Spring," from Walker's second collection *You Can't Keep a Good Woman Down: Short Stories* (1981). There, the daughter, an art student at a primarily White women's college, resolves to learn to sculpt her grandfather's face in the permanence of clay as a loving racial remembrance. The story highlights Walker's discerning description of older Black men from the perspective of a Black girl and also recalls her first novel with its extended family-centered themes. Observant early critics identified the importance of family in Walker's writing. Peter Erickson, for example, recognized her "exploration of intra-family relationships" as a major concern and identified "family as an imaginative structure—a way of organizing experience" in Walker's fiction.[59] That assessment holds especially true for Walker's *In Love & Trouble*, stories written during the same period as *The Third Life of Grange Copeland.*

The double-edged aspect of upheavals and change depicted in her first novel characterized Walker's own life and career between 1971 and 1973, the years immediately following its receptive publication. She returned to the North in 1971 after receiving a Radcliffe Institute fellowship to work on short stories, and with institutional support for her writing, she began lecturing at Wellesley College and University of Massachusetts, Boston, in courses that replicated her classes at Tougaloo College and facilitated her composition of essays. In 1973, she continued her teaching with a course on Black women writers at Smith College and shared her research in a Radcliffe lecture on Black women that would become her signature essay, "In Search of Our Mothers' Gardens." These successes, however, were not without darker changes. Separation from her husband Mel Leventhal and the death of her father Willie Lee Walker shadowed the two books that would appear in 1973, *In Love & Trouble: Stories of Black Women* and *Revolutionary Petunias & Other Poems*. Both volumes continued the imaginative exploration of Walker's social and historical relationship to the region of her birth, but her father's dying prompted her reconsideration not only of his life, but also of her relationship to him and her Georgia family. At the same time, the breakup of her marriage motivated her reassessment of her individual needs as a woman and an artist. These events and their aftermath in this period of self, familial, and communal reflection and emancipation undergird much of her subsequent work.

In Love & Trouble: Stories of Black Women features women and men, who, oppressed because of their race, often suffer irreparable physical and psychological damage. In these characters, Walker refuses to idealize the cost of survival. Victimized by racial and sexual oppression or dehumanized by economic exploitation, they often fail to recognize the forces distorting their lives, and as a result, they can grotesquely perpetuate the violence done to them. In telling their stories, Walker deploys methods of literary modernism and reflects the influence of several masters of short fiction, including Flannery O'Connor, the Southern White woman writer who spent most of her life in rural Georgia, and Jean Toomer, who wrote the poetry-infused masterpiece *Cane* (1923) largely out of a Georgia sojourn. In linking her early fiction to writers of the South, Walker indicates her relational place among them. Alongside investment in the orality of Black Southern voices and Black expressive culture for modern audiences, her stories display aesthetic experimentation with chronology and linear plots and innovative adoption of modernist techniques (stream of consciousness, narrated monologues, intertextuality, diary insertions, and journal entries), all of which indicate her expert craftmanship in short fiction. Further, the dedication, "in loving memory of Zora Neale Hurston, Nella Larsen, and Jean Toomer, the three mysteries," signals a double-voiced text speaking back to other authors and texts that had significant roles in shaping her vision in the stories.

Two epigraphs reinforce the dual expressive movement. The first, signaling Walker's diasporic awareness, comes from Elechi Amadi's novel *The Concubine* and details an African girl's inconsolable crying and angry outbursts that her parents attribute to the excessive influence of her guiding personal spirit, but the actual underlying cause is social custom and parentally approved practice: "*Ahurole was engaged to Ekwueme when she was eight days old.*" The epigraph points to thematic clusters in the stories centered on marriage, as well as on traditional beliefs and social rituals that impact women's lives. Marriage as a restrictive institution, for example, appears in an ironical approach to religion in "The Diary of an African Nun," which represents an African woman as a wedded bride of Christ in the mountains of Uganda. Her vocation as a celibate and thus barren nun is in stark contrast to the drums and rituals of sexual couplings in marriages between Ugandan men and women that produce children. The nun understands all the implications of converting her people from African ideology to a European faith: "To assure life for my people in this world I must be among the lying ones and teach them how to die. I will turn their dances into prayers to an empty sky, and their lovers into dead men, and their babies into unsung chants that choke their throats each spring."[60] In the one-sentence final segment, the narrative voice shifts from the nun's first-person contemplations to an omniscient musing: "In this way will the wife of a loveless, barren, hopeless Western marriage broadcast the joys of an enlightened religion to an imitative people."[61] Marriage is the trope that encodes the colonizing aspects of a subjugating Christian religion.

The second epigraph is a pronouncement against accepting easy solutions contained in Rainer Maria Rilke's *Letters to a Young Poet*. Rilke warns that convention exacerbates the problem by leaning toward the easiest of solutions when "it is clear we must hold to what is difficult; everything in Nature grows and defends itself in its own way and is characteristically and spontaneously itself, seeks at all costs to be so and against all opposition." This selection forecasts issues in the stories related to cultural hegemony when shared beliefs and values function against the possibility of becoming one's true self or against the acceptance of an individual's difference. Themes of oppression and resignation abound, at times linked to pervasive racism that destabilizes the natural self. In "The Welcome Table," an elderly Black woman with singing and worshipping Jesus on her mind walks into a White church, but the congregation, comfortable in its racist beliefs, vehemently rejects her, and quickly throws her out. Undeterred and in an enactment of an old spiritual, she walks in faith with an embodiment of her picture of a White Jesus, sings and talks with him, telling him how she has been mistreated until she collapses in death on the highway.

Problems within the very structure of marriage and the family appear as often as the problematics of systemic racism in preventing individuals from surviving whole. "Roselily," for example, displays Walker's subtle interrogation of marriage within an innovative handling of form. Interspersed between the familiar words of a marriage ceremony are segments of prose from interior states that counter the marital vows and reflect on the meanings of marriage. Walker utilizes the contrasted tropes of hearing and seeing. The words of the minister structure the heard as the public, and almost superficial, component, while the seen in the visionary past, present, and future thoughts of Roselily comprise the more substantive private element. The formal aspects evoke double consciousness, but rather than an interracial awareness, it is an intraracial reckoning of the difference between Roselily, a single Black Mississippi mother of four children, and the Black Muslim man from Chicago who are the subjects in the ceremony. Desperate to leave her old life and its many disappointments, she accepts that his love "makes her completely conscious of how unloved she was before," but her fear of a new cultural and religious environment is inescapable: "Something strains upward behind her eyes. She thinks of the something as a rat trapped, cornered, scurrying to and fro in her head, peering through the windows of her eyes."[62] After the ceremony, the portend of her entrapment looms as her husband takes her hand "like the clasp of an iron gate," stands in front of Roselily, and does not once look back at her. The ominous notes of inflexibility and control threaded throughout the ritual end the story.

A similar grip of control ignites the conflict in "'Really, *Doesn't* Crime Pay?'" between a husband and wife, but it is much darker in its revelations. Pages from Myrna's diary in the present year of 1961 and then in a past year, 1958, provide access to consciousness in a raw state. Walker focuses on upending mind-body dualism, the philosophical supposition of Descartes that mind and body are distinct, with the mind being nonphysical and the body physical substance. Over time the mind and mental capacity became equated with men and the body and physicality with women. Walker alludes to Toomer's seeming adherence to that dualism in his stories and sketches in *Cane*, where women are trapped by their bodies and descend into frustration, madness, resignation, suicide, or murder due to the absence of a viable wholeness in their existences.

Myrna's initial diary entry pictures her beautifully manicured Helena Rubenstein hands that write but deny that she is a "serious" writer. Her indulged hands become a synecdoche for her sweet-smelling body perfectly but uneasily fitted into her new brick house surroundings, "like a jar of cold cream melting on a mirrored vanity shelf," and tightly controlled by her dominating husband Ruel (or "Rule Britannia," as she thinks of him) who returned "from Korea a hero, and a glutton for sweet smells."[63] Myrna's emphasis on body parts and useless hands performs the disjuncture between her body and mind.

Acutely self-aware, Myrna describes her external posturing as a pampered wife with a husband who wants her to forget the past. That past encompasses the ways a woman's creativity can be crushed and reduced to her bodily functions. On the one hand, Ruel declares his wife "peculiar" for writing stories, demands that she not embarrass him by writing "*a lot of foolish vulgar stuff*," and suggests instead that she should have a baby or go shopping.[64] His denigration pushes her into a self-destructive revenge for his masculinist non-comprehension of her as more than a beautiful vessel to bear his child. On the other hand, Mordecai Rich, an imposter who receives national attention for Myrna's "One-Legged Woman" and plans to follow the stolen story with "The Black Woman's Resistance to Creativity in the Arts," is cunning in his soul-crushing theft and betrayal. He flatters Myrna with feigned interest in her creative capacity, but absconds with her notebooks after deceiving her into believing that he will promote her writing because she "'could be another Zora Neale Hurston . . . another Simone de Beauvoir!'"[65] The representation of Mordecai as a slick outsider and the title of Myrna's story, however, directly evoke Flannery O'Connor's Southern grotesques: the one-legged Hulga Hopewell in "Good Country People" and the rapacious Bible salesman who steals her wooden leg and leaves her stranded.

Unlike Hulga, Myrna extracts revenge, but on her husband. She attempts to kill Ruel with her Helena Rubenstein hands, which, for over twenty years, have been writing enough to fill a small shed. Her descent into a mental breakdown, however, is neither penalty nor culmination. Once she recovers and discovers the extent of Mordecai's deception, especially his sardonic disclaimer of Black women's creativity, she retaliates by surreptitiously taking contraceptives while complying with her husband's efforts to impregnate her. Ruel will never have the child he desires; however, she consciously recognizes her self-sabotage: "*And all the while I was grieving over my last story. Outlined—which is as far as I take stories now—but dead in embryo. My hand stilled by cowardice, my heart the heart of a slave.*"[66] One of Walker's most powerful stories, it is a devastating statement about the defeat and death of a woman's creativity and production at the "hands" not only of men with two different modus operandi for stifling a Black woman artist but also of the woman herself.

Devastation of subjectivity and descent into madness of varying types and degrees are major themes recurring throughout *In Love & Trouble*. "Her Sweet Jerome" traces the lack of self-love that precipitates the decline into madness of a big-boned, thick-skinned, business-owning Black woman who loves her husband too much while ignoring her own self-worth and who burns his Black revolution books and her own body in a failed effort to kill the words taking him away from her. "Entertaining God" presents a woman whose mental breakdown after her son's strange death worshipping a gorilla leads her to emerge from a sanitorium as an Afro-centric poet and lecturer whose dress, ideology, scarifications, and worldview infuse her poetry but isolate her from all except the ghostly image of her son. The male protagonist of "The Child Who Favored Daughter," situated as brother, husband, and father overcome by sexual obsession in each relational role, suffers a mental collapse into an atrocious act of violent physical disfigurement and incestuous desire fueled by his guilt over the death of his sister called Daughter and his conflation of his own daughter's sexual rebellion with his sister's.[67] These stories shock with the intrusion of mental decline and incapacity into seemingly ordinary Black lives. In them, Walker peers beneath superficial veneers to expose the ways in which living Black in a racially charged world can distort reality and destroy lives.

Her primary literary model for the folk vernacular, colloquial wisdom, and evocative speech of her ordinary women and men is Hurston. In "The Revenge of Hannah Kemhuff" and "Strong Horse Tea," Walker utilizes Huston's work in anthropology and Southern folkways, and her practical approach to Black lives sustaining themselves. The efforts by officials in power to brutalize and diminish Black life in Walker's fiction are never completely successful despite the legal reaches of Jim Crow and their replicated social hierarchies. "The Revenge of Hannah Kemhuff" encodes dual spaces of memory—the collective one Walker's mother remembered from the Great Depression in Georgia and told to Alice during her childhood and the social one Hurston collected and represented as a curse from folk culture. In her mother's story, two Depression-era Black women counter the official denial of relief aid by reassessing their commodity holdings; the one with an excess of processed flour can exchange it for the other's abundant corn meal. Under the mutually beneficial arrangement, the women reassign the value of the denied goods and dissipate arbitrary racism by diminishing the authority of the White relief worker over their lives. In breaking the hierarchical racial bonds signified by dependency, the exchange also levels the force of restrictive constraints and substitutes a horizontal gendered bonding marked by equity. Segregation has not been dismantled by the women's cooperative action, but it has lost its ability to imprison the women within its economic structure.

That, however, is not the narrative Walker tells in "The Revenge of Hannah Kemhuff," the longest story in the collection. Just as the dedication, "In grateful memory of Zora Neale Hurston" indicates, the frame story utilizes folk practices and rootworking that Hurston documented. Told from the first-person perspective of an unnamed apprentice to the rootworker and spiritual healer Tante Rosie, it is a story within a story designed to showcase the power of traditional rootworking to correct or avenge wrongs. Frail old Hannah Kemhuff seeks revenge for her debilitated condition that she blames on a young blond, blue-eyed "moppet" who long ago denied her Depression-era welfare because she, her husband, and children, though desperately hungry, were wearing good secondhand clothes sent by her sister from Chicago. Laughed at and rebuked for being too "dressed up" to need food or help, she left with nothing, but her husband drove off with another woman and piles of food. Her starving children die one by one, and she deteriorates into prostitution and alcohol. Aged and withered from loss and humiliation, she tells Tante Rosie that the moppet broke her spirit: "'God cannot be let to make her happy all these years and me miserable. What kind of justice would that be? It would be monstrous.'"[68] The rootworker responds: "'If you can no longer bear the eyes of the enemy that you see in your dreams the Man-God, who speaks to me from the Great Mother of Us All, will see that those eyes are eaten away. If the hands of your enemy have struck you they can be made useless.'"[69] For ten dollars, Tante Rosie can stop the moppet's grinning mouth or her hands hiding it, but for twenty dollars, she can destroy both. Mrs. Kemhuff decides on the destruction of the mouth because it most haunts her dreams. Tante Rosie asks for nail and hair clippings, clothing pieces, along with urine and feces from the targeted woman to make a potion with goober dust so that the woman will die within six months of Mrs. Kemhuff.

The second section of the story is the comprehensive curse-prayer to the Man God that Tante Rosie recites in ritual performance twice a day for nine days, but that her inexperienced apprentice reads directly from Zora Neale Hurston's *Mules and Men* until she and Mrs. Kemhuff learn the words. The reference to Hurston lends authenticity to the rootworking, the curse, and the story itself. The prayer's specifics include the four directional winds freezing blood, blowing out life's breath and crumbling bones, darkening minds, and drying up seeds, so that extinction will occur but not before disease and death plague all. The natural world of sun and moon, lightning and thunder, rains and floods is conjured to destroy everything the targeted one might attempt. The prayer asks that language and words be forgotten and the tongue paralyzed so the result will be "desolation, pestilence and death."[70]

The horrific climax comes after the apprentice locates the moppet, now the fifty-three-year-old Mrs. Ben Jonathan Holley, who enjoys life in a large country house. She entertains her hobbies, "shopping for antiques, gossiping with colored women, discussing her husband's health, and her children's babies, and making spoon bread," but according to the apprentice, she has a cook who drank muscatel and hated her—perhaps because the cook has a tan Holley son whom the Holleys sent to Morehouse College.[71] The apprentice visits Mrs. Holley to announce the request for her nail parings, hair from a comb, urine, feces, and worn clothing. Soon afterward as expected, the worn-out Mrs. Kemhuff dies, and the apprentice reports the working of the curse. Mrs. Holley, outraged and fearful, took to her bedroom where she became a bizarre recluse eating her own fingernails, desperately collecting her stray hair, and keeping her waste in barrels and bags in her closets. Her end aligns with her offense against Hannah Kemhuff: "The mouth that grinned behind the hands grinned no more. The constant anxiety lest a stray strand of hair be lost and the foul odor of the house soon brought to the hands a constant seeking motion, to the eyes a glazed and vacant stare, and to the mouth, a tightly puckered frown, one which only death might smooth."[72]

The best-known story, "Everyday Use," also emphasizes traditional aspects of rural Black life and changing conceptions of value and worth during the civil rights movement. Told in the first-person voice of a mother with a second-grade education awaiting the return of her daughter while honestly assessing her own real life as opposed to the reunions she has seen on television, the narrator knows she is a large country woman, strong, "big-boned" with "tough, man-working hands." Without illusions but with pride in her body and its ability to survive, she realizes that her cosmopolitan daughter would rather she were "a hundred pounds lighter," and more akin to televisual images: "my skin like an uncooked barley pancake. My hair glistens in the hot bright lights. Johnny Carson has much to do to keep up with my quick and witty tongue."[73] The major contrast is not between real and fantasy images of the mother, but between the two daughters: the "homely" and shy Maggie, who bears scars on her legs and arms from a house fire; and the world "in the palm of her hands" Dee, who is lighter in color and "with nicer hair and a fuller figure," than her thin scarred sister.[74]

Dee arrives in full Afro-centric glory, brightly colored flowing dress, gold earrings and bracelets, and a high, thick head of natural hair crowned with braids. She and her companion are eager to share African greetings and her new name "Wangero Leewanika Kemanjo," which her mother does not understand because Dee is the name of her sister Dicie and her grandmother and her mother before her, and not as Wangero states the name of people who oppressed her. "Wangero," the African name Walker chose for the ambiguously figured "successful" daughter, is comparable to "Wangari," Walker's Kikuyu name.

The reunion goes badly. Obsessed with their quaint rituals of ordinary food and homemade vessels, Wangero sees her country relatives as artifacts. Her intent is to turn the family's utilitarian objects into art pieces to decorate her home. She latches on to two hand-stitched quilts in the Lone Star and the Walk Around the Mountain patterns hand-pieced by her grandmother from clothing worn by a grandfather and great-grandfather, but her mother has promised them to Maggie as a wedding gift. Undeterred, Wangero wants the "priceless" objects to hang on her wall as art because she believes that she alone understands their family "heritage." The retiring Maggie, who has learned to quilt from her Grandma Dee and her aunt Big Dee, offers to let her sister have the quilts because she can remember her maternal relatives without them. That offer jolts the mother into appreciating Maggie by snatching the quilts from Wangero and dumping them into Maggie's lap.

The quiet reversal of new "revolutionary" ethics mines the rural Southern Black past and its traditional methods of survival within the family. It also celebrates a mother's ability to recognize the meaning of care and to demonstrate love for the plain, unassuming daughter who seems the lesser of the two but who ultimately encompasses the life generations in her family have shared. Both women live within and value their heritage, including the immeasurably rich art of quilt making as part of the living memory of family and kin. "Everyday Use" is adamant in seeing and honoring the Black Southern past and its people who have lived through the fire of racism (symbolized by Maggie's bodily scars) and in refusing to commercialize their lived experience as objects of radical chic. That cautionary reminder to the revolutionary generation is unambiguously reiterated in Walker's dedication, "for your grandmama."

In 1994, Barbara T. Christian edited *Alice Walker, "Everyday Use"* for the Rutgers series "Women Writers: Texts and Contexts" and placed Walker alongside major short story writers: Charlotte Perkins Gilman, Flannery O'Connor, Katherine Anne Porter, and Leslie Marmon Silko. Christian maintained that in the twenty years since its publication, "Everyday Use" had become a classic, "a cornerstone in [Walker's] large and distinguished opus" and that along with "In Search of Our Mothers' Gardens," it had introduced "the metaphor of quilting to represent the creative legacy that African Americans have inherited from their maternal ancestors" and made "an abiding contribution to African American literature, as well as to American women's culture."[75] Christian insightfully observed: "Walker is drawn to the integral and economical process of quilt making as a model for her own craft . . . creat[ing] out of seemingly disparate everyday materials patterns of clarity, imagination, and beauty."[76] Her observation contextualizes Walker's "Everyday Use" within the aesthetics of quilting and the definition of heritage, which Maggie and her mother understand even if they cannot define the word for Dee/Wangero.

In Love & Trouble won the Rosenthal Award of the National Institute of Arts and Letters in 1974; two stories from the collection, "Everyday Use" and "The Revenge of Hannah Kemhuff," appeared in the 1973 and 1974 editions of *Best American Short Stories* and have become Walker's most frequently anthologized texts.

The unwavering attention to everyday Black life and its traumas paramount in *In Love & Trouble* continues in *Revolutionary Petunias & Other Poems* (1973), while also raising perplexing issues about the nature and cost of transformative revolution. Themes of vision and sight, perspective and insight, and spiritual and physical transformation abound in this second volume of poetry that develops an emotive thematic response to autobiographical incidents and chronicles an emotionally ciphered exploration of formative ideas. The atypical table of contents provides a roadmap to Walker's concerns with poetry as a psychological exploration of self, a mediating of the consciousness of one's very existence, and an attending to the emotional determinants of that existence. "In These Dissenting Times . . . Surrounding Ground and Autobiography," for example, reiterates the significance of spatial and factual ground for the poetry, whereas "Revolutionary Petunias . . . the Living Through" suggests the value of role models for how to live in dissenting revolutionary times. "Mysteries . . . the Living Beyond" emphasizes the spiritual and psychic reaches of the poems. "The Nature of This Flower Is to Bloom" comes directly from a letter June Jordan wrote in 1970, which Walker quotes to launch the final part of her collection: "*And for ourselves, the intrinsic / 'Purpose' is to reach and to remember, / and to declare our commitment to all / the living, without deceit, and without/ fear, and without reservation.*"[77]

Jordan goes unnamed in the initial dedication, yet her name, words, and ideology appear throughout, especially in the second section of the volume entitled "Revolutionary Petunias . . . the Living Through," which is dedicated to Jordan and to the writer Julius Lester. Walker's attention to Jordan underscores how the eventful early years of Walker's career also allied her with "The Sisterhood," a cadre of Black women writers that included Jordan, Toni Morrison, Verta Mae Grosvenor, and Ntozake Shange. This sisterhood emerged from a shared awareness not merely of the general revolutionary times, but especially of the revolutionary feminist potential of Black women to make a difference as writer-artists in their creative sociopolitical statements about issues of gender interlocked with race.

In that second section, Walker returns to Camus for an epigraph. Instead of recollections from his poverty-ridden childhood, Walker selects an excerpt from *The Rebel*: "Beauty, no doubt, does not make revolutions. But a day will come when revolutions will have need of beauty." The theme of beauty, as aesthetics or philosophy, intermingled with struggle appears throughout these poems. The influence of Walker's reading of Camus carries through her entire career, noticeably foremost in her writings from the 1960s through the 1980s, the latter now considered the period of her most important literary contributions.

The primary dedication of *Revolutionary Petunias* is to very different individuals, all of whom Walker considered "revolutionaries," including her colleagues from the Student Nonviolent Coordinating Committee (SNCC). Walker is explicit in celebrating the various modes of struggle for Black rights during the 1960s and 1970s: George Jackson, prisoner in California; Bob Moses, activist founder of the Algebra Project in the South; Winson Hudson and Fannie Lou Hamer, heroines of the Mississippi struggle for freedom; and Mel Leventhal, civil rights worker and Walker's husband and father of their daughter Rebecca. Walker states directly: "These poems are about Revolutionaries and Lovers; and about the loss of compassion, trust, and the ability to expand in love that marks the end of hopeful strategy. . . . They are also about (and are for) those few embattled souls who remain painfully committed to beauty and to love even while facing the firing squad." Her statement considers a cultural moment filled with almost unbearable tragedy in the face of a determined struggle for rights and for a world order that would accept the equality and humanity of African Americans as full citizens.

Throughout the volume, Walker places the questioning mind in search of answers on full display. In "Reassurance," she refers to Rilke who counseled loving the questions: "like locked rooms/ full of treasure / in which my blind / and groping key / does not yet fit."[78] She gropes her way in this collection toward an understanding, loving and enlightened, of the men and women in her Southern family and community whose harsh circumstanced did not freely divulge how they came to comprehend their own lives or their commitment to an altered future. In the title poem, "Sammy Lou of Rue / sent to his reward / the exact creature who / murdered her husband, / using a cultivator's hoe / with verve and skill; / and laughed fit to kill / in disbelief / at the angry, militant / pictures of herself."[79] On her way to the electric chair, Sammy Lou's last words are "'Always respect the word of God,'" and "'Don't yall forget to *water* / my purple petunias.'"[80] Defined as a militant avenger, Sammy Lou refuses the images projected onto her as an angry Black woman. Having taken the life of a destroyer, she goes to her own death preserving both beauty and life. Walker in elliptical brevity deftly portrays the contradiction between simplistic images of Black women and their complex reality.

In the poems of *Revolutionary Petunias*, the civil rights movement becomes an agent for freeing individuals from a spiritually deadening lethargy that functioned as an escape from the racism circumscribing their lives, particularly those of old men and "gold toothed women" in what she attributes as "these dissenting times." Freedom burdens with isolation, loneliness, and death; nevertheless, Walker insists on acknowledging these relatives and ancestors. She honors them in poems such as "The Old Men Used to Sing," "Women," and

"Uncles," which show the awareness of death and the necessity of shepherding the youth through the rituals of church going and funeral services. A mindfulness of lives lost and a respectfulness toward those surviving dominate the first section in which Walker's Georgia relatives appear prominently. Funerals at the family's church, Wards Chapel, spark intergenerational awareness that forces the speaker, closely identified with Walker herself, to contemplate traditions, even though she has long rejected the religion of her forebears. Speaking in the voice of the writer-artist-daughter educated away from familial beliefs, Walker reveals a reverence for the constructs of faith she ascribes to those others. In "Burial," for example, the long autobiographically grounded poem, Walker returns with her daughter for the funeral of her grandmother Rachel Walker and meditates on that life with love and empathy. Rachel is the epitome of the hard "serviceable" life of Black women of her generation, the caregivers, homemakers, fieldworkers, gardeners, and mother-women, even when the children were not biologically theirs. Rachel, "*Not pretty, but serviceable*," lived her life giving to all and in the end "*Came to death blank, forgetful of it all.*"[81]

Rachel Walker's life is the stuff that marks many of Walker's women characters, such as Mem and Margret in *The Third Life of Grange Copeland* and most notably Celie in *The Color Purple*. Second wife and stepmother to children, Rachel Walker is Alice's "Ma-Ma," her paternal grandmother whose life from family lore figures in the background of much of Walker's early fiction. That old time religion at Wards Chapel cannot comfort when this life is remembered, but it can foreground the reality of a faith beyond self, whether that faith be in a daughter's touch or voice, in feminism or womanism, in civil rights or activism, in artistic freedom or determination, all figured somehow on the edge of the eye, as Walker reflects at the end of "Burial": "Not for the dead, but for the memories. None of / them sad. But seen from the angle of her / death."[82] Seeing and insisting on that internality's right to external meaning and being is what Walker does best in her poetry.

Her critical and dissenting vision of the movement underlays such poems as "Expect Nothing," "Be Nobody's Darling," and "He Said Come," in which she casts a cynical eye on unrealistic political demands. Equally problematical are the social expectations placed on "correctness" especially on women by men in the movement, as in "The Girl Who Died #1" and "The Girl Who Died #2" "who would not lie /, was not born / to be 'correct,'" so that the end result in "Nothing Is Right" is the unanswered final question "What was it kept / the eyes alive?"[83] These poems are vivid in their representation of the changing tenor of young Blacks who faced opportunities and challenges, often without enough guidance to make them undogmatic and expansive in coming "correct." Walker incorporates her own awakened political vision, racial consciousness, and feminist values and beliefs to establish, as Jordan had intimated, a fearless commitment to the living abetted by a trusting, truthful eye on her own self and her words.

Thinking back through incidents in Alice Walker's early biography and her entry into a creative writing life in the 1960s and 1970s provides one route to her prolific, multifaceted career. From the beginning she engages multiple genres simultaneously, and she utilizes her autobiography fully in poetry and prose. She immerses her social history as a Southern child of poverty and segregation and her personal experiences as a Black woman in her insistent discourses on human survival. In her first decade of publishing, Walker emphasizes the survival of self in hostile, restrictive environments that impact and delimit Black life by consigning African Americans to stereotypical racial constructions. Her origin in the rural South combines with her childhood transformation and teenage emergence to set the stage for the woman writer that she would become. An observant seer, Walker mines her familial history and transforms wounding from her injury and restoration, both stemming from the actions of brothers and the inadequate protection of a father, into a way of understanding masculine privilege and male domination of women. She configures her mother's determined assistance in giving her the tools of vernacular history, community wisdom, and formal education as a means of propelling her into a life of possibilities, one cognizant of race and gender but refusing the limitations of either. Her experiences coming-of-age being Black and female in the era of racial struggle for equal rights and in a world of changing racial and gender dynamics endow her aesthetic vision with a historical, political, and philosophical lens and enable her artistic gift for seeing imaginative structures that develop a complex social vision and configure an essential human spirituality. These developmental experiences contribute to her unblinking representations of a shifting social and political realty in poems, essays, and fiction—both the short story and the novel. Without allowing her life or her writing to be overcome by the unavoidable recognition of pain, suffering, and sorrow in the ordinary act of living, Walker forged a way forward that encompasses truth, realities, and ideals of existence. Her personal knowledge of transformation, of the multiple ways of having sight and of the joy of living and loving, would mark not merely her early publications, but also all those that would come in the next decade.

CHAPTER 2

The Sight of the Familiar

"I Love Myself . . ."

We are a people. A people do not throw their geniuses away. And if they are thrown away, it is our duty as artists and as witnesses for the future to collect them again for the sake of our children, and, if necessary, bone by bone.

—Alice Walker, "Zora Neale Hurston: A Cautionary Tale and a Partisan View" (1979)

In the mid-1970s, Alice Walker expanded her gaze to encompass a broader sense of family, but she also began to use her vision as a way toward greater personal and artistic freedom. She looked deeply into the historical literary ancestors who shared her attention to Black people, especially those who like her immediate family lived in the South. She discovered in her independent reading specific literary ancestors, notably Langston Hughes, Jean Toomer, and Zora Neale Hurston, whose work resonated in different ways with her own social and racial heritage and validated and extended the maternal legacies of her mother and grandmothers. By peering through layers of the past, Walker reflected on Southern folk practices, social history, raced rights, and gendered work, all significant aspects that had informed her writing and infused the autobiographical issues in her earlier publications. Her works in this renewed exploratory sighting of the contextual familiar demonstrate her counter to abjection and exclusion and assert her identification of an aesthetic that reconstitutes race and gender in terms of an inherited consciousness of difference constituted in strength.

A Radcliffe Institute Fellowship in 1971 and a second stay at the MacDowell Colony in 1974 propelled Walker more firmly into a career as a writer and into sustained work on her second novel *Meridian* (1976), which inscribed much of Walker's autobiographical experiences in the 1960s and early 1970s. With this book, Walker looked more profoundly at the political culture that had emerged since the 1960s. In situating the title character within a rural family, a Southern women's college, and a civil rights movement, the text recombined the divergent dialogical and ideological strands of a contemporary African American woman's life. It presented a modern parable, a search for spiritual meaning and racial justice amid political turmoil. Walker centered her vision on the multifaceted and unavoidable but abstract and contradictory aspects of political and moral struggle for human rights in the broadest sense. The resulting text is Walker's first extensive foray into freeing the individual self from all institutional, organizational, and personal ties. With Meridian Hill, Walker depicts a journey to freedom that arrives at alternative ways of living free, both within one's own interior and in the exterior world.

The epigraph from *Black Elk Speaks* anticipates the retrospective, elegiac vision central to Meridian: "I did not know then how much was ended. When I look back now . . . I can still see the butchered women and children lying heaped and scattered. . . . A people's dream died there. It was a beautiful dream. . . . the nation's hoop is broken and scattered. There is no center any longer, and the sacred tree is dead." Black Elk's forewarning is of seeing the death, destruction, and loss of a people and their dream through the lens of history.

The epigraph follows a dedication that evokes attention to the civil rights movement especially in the last person named "John Lewis the unsung." The son of Alabama sharecroppers, Lewis was the director of the Atlanta-based Voter Education Project of the Southern Regional Council in 1976 when *Meridian* was published. Lewis had been at the forefront of civil rights activism since 1961, but his nonviolent political philosophy had cost him a leadership role when the Black Power movement emerged. He figures prominently in Walker's portrayal of the evolving civil rights movement, its conflicting approaches to liberation, and the philosophical questions raised by her characters. A young, rural, Black Southern activist, Lewis inspired Walker's insightful framing of her title character as a fictionalized "unsung" in changing times.

Meridian Hill is the seemingly unremarkable Black Southern girl who is pregnant in high school, marries her boyfriend, and has a child. Meridian's ordinary life begins to change, initially from the inside when she realizes that neither marriage nor motherhood satisfies her, and perceptibly from the outside when she takes notice of young voter registration workers living nearby. After a firebomb strikes their house, destroying it and neighboring houses and killing three children, Meridian marks that day in April 1960 as the birth of her awareness of the larger world. At seventeen, she begins an extraordinary journey when she volunteers with the civil rights workers. Soon she accepts the college scholarship that her pregnancy had interrupted, gives up her son, and leaves for Saxon College in Atlanta, where she connects with the Movement and Truman Held, one of the field workers she had first encountered.

In narrating Meridian's unlikely transformation, Walker relies on flashbacks and internal dialogues, interspersed with set pieces about Meridian's parents, a father who revered the earth and his Native American ancestors and a mother who could not bring herself to be maternal. Against that backdrop of frustrated parents, Walker threads Meridian's memories of her own innocent awakening to the dangers and entrapments young girls face in the familiar realm of their own neighborhoods from grown men seeking sexual gratification. Walker conveys a detailed developmental arc for Meridian that places her physical and emotional growth within the broad contexts of US history, recent and immediately past, explicitly for African Americans and tangentially for Native Americans. Her resulting narrative shapes Meridian's becoming an extraordinary self in the process of coming to terms not merely with her particular subjective experiences but also with the larger social injustices of Jim Crow racism, the debilitations of persistent sexism, and the destructive greed of uncompromising capitalism and economic exploitation.

Meridian lives through a circular journey, segregation in the South, migration to the North, and a return to the South, to emerge as a new singular leader in a movement for social equality and economic justice that both encompasses and post-dates the organized civil rights movement. In ever-widening spheres, she becomes conscious of her rights as a woman, a citizen, a Black, and with the evolution of her thought, she moves to positions of greater isolation within the available communities. Meridian's evolving consciousness dictates the progression of the narrative's unlocking the past, engaging the present or anticipating the future. Elliott Butler-Evans has accurately pointed out: "Form becomes a signifier of a new consciousness."[1] In isolation, Meridian reconnects to the geographies of right and moral power that have reconfigured the history of the nation and its people. Inherent in her life and consciousness is the hard struggle with internal and external forces to achieve change.

Whereas within the civil rights movement and traditional political organizations, politics has generally focused on men and a masculinist enterprise, Walker turns the struggle for rights and power into a political realm that contains the domestic, the private or personal, and the physical body of a woman. The space Walker creates with Meridian is in keeping with the new geographies of gender and of raced gender beginning to achieve prominence in the 1970s. With the convergence of Black Power and Black Nationalism, Black men presumed leadership that too frequently relegated Black women to subservient positions as helpmeets and mothers, yet with the rise of feminist activism, Black women understood their capacities and roles differently. Walker, a participant in movement struggles and an observer of gender inequities, launched Meridian into the spatial gap and philosophical divide created by the contrasting views of the work for racial equality. Meridian stands as a witness to incidents of misogyny, sexual exploitation, interracial rape, and predatory abuse that the narrative unfolds in sometimes shocking honesty.

In *Meridian*, the cost of the movement, of activity across class and race lines, is personal loss, including alienation from family and community, yet ultimately the potential for rejuvenation and gain plays out in the body of Meridian. Walker reads the interlocking structures of history in tracing the development of Meridian's associates in the movement, Truman Held, Ann-Marion, and Lynne. The missing, the erased, the absent, the lost all are written on Meridian's very body. As John Fiske has put it, "The body and its specific behavior is where the power system stops being abstract and becomes material. The body is where it succeeds or fails, where it is acceded to or struggled against."[2] The "material terrain" of Meridian's body with its undiagnosed debilitating illness and concomitant hair loss concretizes the struggle and conflict at stake in the text.

Implicitly arguing against Ralph Ellison's trope of invisibility in *Invisible Man*, Walker shows that visibility itself is the issue for Black people, particularly Black women. She signals that at issue is the always visible, highly magnified Black body itself, and focuses on the unmistakable visuality of race and gender together, or what Kimberlé Crenshaw would define in 1989 as "intersectionality," the interlocking and intersecting aspects of social and political identity, race, gender, class, sexuality, and more. Walker invests in laying out the connections between visibility and the core of her text with an elaborate set of dictionary definitions of "meridian" to introduce her novel. By placing the word within a place location ("the highest point," "midday," "the south") and then within attributes of power ("the highest apparent point reached by a heavenly body in its course" and "the highest point of power, prosperity, splendor"), Walker emphasizes the visible aspects of "meridian" that are also associated with the middle period of life deemed the height of health and vigor.

In these prefatory selections, Walker formulates the significance of visibility as a distinctive characteristic, especially through recognizable naming that can be read as body, place, or site specific. By including multiple, convergent definitions of "meridian," she makes it impossible to ignore the symbolic nature of her title character's name. With decipherable coordinates, she also references a geographical location that is identifiably Southern, Meridian, Mississippi, which associatively anchors her character in the South. These tactical signs enable Walker's exploration of the feminist aspects of visibility as an elevated way of reading the Black woman's body in relationship to racial, political, social, and philosophical experience while functioning against the naturalized White body or in opposition to a dominate Black male body.

Meridian is no simplistic participant in civil rights activism. Instead, she is a leader akin to Fannie Lou Hamer who came to terms with society's construction of gender roles, with the hegemony of social attitudes around race, with the deficiencies in the expectations for motherhood and maternity, and with the burden of sexuality and heterosexual relations. Moreover, Meridian is a recognition of the Black women of Walker's mother's generation in Georgia that Walker knew as "Headragged Generals" who fearlessly "lead / Armies / . . . Across mined / Fields / Booby-trapped / Ditches / To discover books / . . . A place for us / How they knew what we / *Must* know / Without knowing a page / Of it / Themselves."[3] Meridian is, as well, a nod to the older women Walker worked with during her stay in Mississippi. In *In Search of Our Mothers' Gardens*, she identifies what she, a young teacher, wife, and mother, learned from them and what they brought to her life and to the struggle for freedom. Like these women, Meridian creates a visionary passageway for others to follow in transforming society. Yet, with the representation of a depletion of personhood in motherhood, the text also challenges a mindless acceptance of a generic Black matriarchy that could be easily stereotyped.

Walker allows specifically for both the political context and the unusual appearance of Meridian, who at the very beginning of the novel stares down a tank purchased "during the sixties when the townspeople who were white felt under attack from 'outside agitators'—those members of the black community who thought that equal rights for all should extend to blacks."[4] Justice, conflated in this instance with Meridian's body and her action, is not an overarching, large and opaque illusory pursuit, but rather it is immediate, personal, attainable, and transparent. Justice nevertheless becomes performative, necessitating conspicuous acts of intervention in order to secure notice. Walker emphasizes that point in making the object of Meridian's standoff the admission of Black children to see the mummified body of a woman in a traveling show on a day that is not designated for Black spectators. In theory, the civil rights movement had brought about the abolishment of regulations allocating separate days and separate spaces for Blacks, but in fact, much of the residue of Jim Crow restrictions remained. Legal segregation may have been dismantled, but its practices and customs persist in a blatant afterlife. Meridian's performative act underscores both the negligible impact of the former movement and the lowered stakes of protest activism. The confrontation provides a window into apprehending how the spectacle, the mummified body of Marilene O'Shay, advertised as "Obedient Daughter," "Devoted Wife," and "Adoring Mother," but "Gone Wrong," anticipates Meridian's disassembling of the ossified categories assigned to women.[5]

In undoing an explicitly masculinist understanding of politics within the volatile context of the South and African American life, Walker equates women's rights with the rights of "the people," as she repeatedly uses the term within the text, but also with the suffering that occurs within existing social and political structures and educational and economic systems. "'They're grateful people,'" Meridian states about assuming her role as a woman leading the new struggle, "'They appreciate it when someone volunteers to suffer.'"[6] Political space gendered male then becomes as much her subject as racially segregated space. Meridian seeks a means of controlling space and of positioning herself bodily within a public sphere previously denied to people of color, even after the hard work of the movement. To achieve her ends, she exercises a radical physical and metaphorical control over her female body by rejecting a consignment to motherhood: first, by giving up her child; second, by aborting an unwanted pregnancy; and third, by having her tubes tied.

Meridian's spiritual rather than physical essence, however, is part of the transcendence referenced by images of loss, vision, sight, renewal, and return. The discourse of spirituality is cycled through Meridian's vision, her trances and spells in which she clarifies reality and imagines potential. She falls into stupors that leave her weak yet empowered to continue on, strengthened by her ability to penetrate the unseen sickness of self, others, and society that ordinarily can go undetected. Her loss of hair and her diminished bodily vigor are preludes to her return with stamina and conviction, and with her new growth of hair and renewed strength, she resumes the necessary struggle for freedom, equality, and justice. Her work goes far beyond the recognizable goals that had marked the civil rights movement in the 1960s. Meridian is intent upon teaching and demonstrating that a foundational premise for the success of revolution is acknowledging life as sacred. Barbara T. Christian extends that premise by reading the novel as being based on the idea of "the sacredness and continuity of life" and on the paradoxical dilemma "of death giving life," so that when Meridian refers to a sense of continuity between her life and all the lives around her as "One Life," she is evoking "the African concept of animism, 'that spirit inhabits all life,'" but also its corruption by "societal forces that inhibit the growth of the living toward their natural state of freedom."[7]

One facet of the tension surrounding the idea of the sacredness of life for revolutionaries becomes clear in Walker's dramatization of the question: Will you kill for the revolution? That question sparks both a debate and a spilt among those in Meridian's Northern cadre working for social change in the aftermath of the Southern nonviolent movement. Meridian, who so loved the eyes of cows that she became a vegetarian, could not bring herself to make an unpremeditated response as did her zealous revolutionary friends, including Ann-Marion who could do so without hesitation but perhaps without serious thought. The question of killing for the cause, even in self-defense, drives Meridian into the innermost recesses of her being to assess truthfully her valuation of life. It is not merely a split second of philosophical reckoning but primarily a moment of path-altering ethical clarity. Meridian remembers the South, her parents, the people, church services and hymn singing, and realizes that she does not belong in the New York cadre of revolutionaries. She returns to the South, "remaining close to the people—to see them, to be with them, to understand them and herself."[8] It is her conscious commitment to the oneness and the sacredness of all life that compels her to continue on a solitary spiritual, yet political, path.

Two interconnected histories of people and land are central to Meridian's consciousness of the path she must travel. She denounces the structural violence against Black people in capture, enslavement, and segregation and against indigenous people in genocide, removal, and land seizure within the United States, and specifically the South. The Indian burial mound linked to the decimation of Native people and the Sojourner Tree connected to the enslavement of Black people form the interpolated articulations of these two histories that Meridian contemplates in separate segments of the narrative. Their indelible impressions determine how she proceeds in the world.

An Indian burial mound on the farmland her father owned is the initial map to Meridian's understanding of history and the human imprint on land. Mr. Hill preserves yellowed maps of lands in North America that had once belonged to Native Americans, and he surrounds himself with his photography collection of famous Native Americans (Geronimo, Sitting Bull, Crazy Horse, etc.) and unnamed Native women and children, along with drawings of the fictional Hiawatha and Minnehaha. He keeps these images and books on Native Americans and their land rights and reservations, because he has discovered that his working farm is on land native people once owned. After years of contemplation, he reaches the momentous decision to return it to its rightful owners, because as he put it: "'I was just holding it. The rows of my cabbages and tomatoes run right up along the biggest coil of the Sacred Serpent. That mound is full of dead Indians. Our food is made healthy from the iron and calcium from their bones. Course, since it's a cemetery, we shouldn't own it anyhow.'"[9] Mr. Hill delivers the deed to his farm to a native man, "a wanderer, a mourner," much like him, but who subsequently returns ownership to Mr.

Hill. Meridian observes the transactions and recognizes her father's gesture as acknowledging the complicity of all Americans in the decimation of native people and taking their land. Mr. Hill teaches his daughter a form of retributive justice and reverence for the land and its previous inhabitants, but he and she soon learn another lesson. By eminent domain, the town seizes Mr. Hill's farm to turn it into a "public" amusement park, Sacred Serpent Park, that ironically is closed to "Colored People."

Walker's narrative construes other lessons about race and the land. It interjects the story of Meridian's ancestor, her father's grandmother, Feather Mae who discovers by stepping into the center of the Serpent's coiled tail what is hidden in the Indian mound. In a fainting spell, she accesses another world and the hidden within herself. Thereafter, Feather Mae worships the sun and believes only in religion based on physical ecstasy. Not only is that story passed down to Meridian, but its details also replicate themselves in Meridian's own experience within the Serpent's tail when surrounded by the dead: "the walls of earth that enclosed her rushed outward, leveling themselves at a dizzying rate, and then spinning wildly, lifting her out of her body and giving her the feeling of flying."[10] During her out-of-body experience, Meridian has an apocalyptic vison intermingling family, trees, birds, houses, grass, flowers and all swirling together with such power that when she returns to her body, her eyes look into the sun just as directly had Feather Mae's.

Meridian responds to the topology of the secret graves as part of herself. She remembers her father's account that Native Americans had constructed the coiled tail to provide a sensation of dying, of setting the spirit free from the entrapment of the body; however, she believes instead "that it was a way of living, sought to expand the unconsciousness of being alive."[11] This apotheosis in the Sacred Mound becomes integral to Meridian's abiding spirit of remaining consciously alive. Her replication of Feather Mae's story, like the digressive narratives flowing through the novel, may be read as a recursive text, layering, as Karla Holloway has suggested, "memory and discourse and mythic figures within language and culture until each is folded into the other."[12]

In such layering, Walker connects poverty, racism, and sexism with economics. She examines the destruction of the Indian burial mound for a commercial park as part of the continuing commodification of culture and destruction of the spiritual. Importantly, she constructs the female body and its female progeny as the sites through which politics and spirituality must be viewed. In the representation of the burial mound, Walker juxtaposes the social configurations of segregated life in the South and the hierarchies of power inherent in physical spaces. Thus, the spiritual and political work that Meridian undertakes is an outgrowth of nature, history, and gender; it is, too, a more activist approach to her father's ethical attempt at recompense.

The importance of the Indian burial mound and Native American heritage to Walker's ideology became much more apparent at the end of the 1990s. In naming her passions for a *Ms. Magazine* interview, Walker mentioned the sovereignty movement in Hawaii and poet-scholar Haunani-Kay Trask's *From A Native Daughter: Colonialism and Sovereignty in Hawai'i* (1993), along with her own plan to initiate healing circles and women's and elders' councils on the land for the purpose of connection and grounding. She states: "Each circle will eventually connect with other circles around the globe so that, over time, we'll get a stronger sense of who we are. . . . present as loving, compassionate earthlings. . . . It's important to comfort and be with each other during this time because so many people are alone."[13] Walker expands these ideas about healing loneliness even further in terms reminiscent of Meridian: "[L]ife is about growth, struggle, and trying to expand your love of self and of other people. Also . . . to not cause harm—to cultivate a way of life that is harmless."[14] The embracing of land with circles of life beginning with women and extending into a global interconnectedness with all people signifies Walker's continuation of the ideology of Feather Mae exemplified in Meridian. At the same time, it identifies a woman-centered heterotopia distinct from any utopian idealization. It is not surprising that going forward after *Meridian*, Walker has increasingly identified herself with her Cherokee Native American ancestry.

With the attention to Feather Mae, Native Americans, and sacred land, *Meridian* also forecasts Walker's later turn in her approach to fiction. She would increasingly integrate the response of human beings to the natural world and their efforts as aware humans to repair and address the harm done to the land, which Walker later calls Mother Earth. Both Meridian's father and Meridian herself anticipate Walker's turn to mythic aspects of wrongs done to the earth that are intricately prefigured in the lives of Black people and people of color, which, under exploitive, oppressive conditions, entailed sacrifice and suffering but also awareness of redemption, restitution, and deliverance, even if by an allegorical return to ancient models, guiding spirits, and primordial beliefs, as exemplified in the Hawaiian healing circle she creates in her novel *Now Is the Time to Open Your Heart* (2003).

The Indian mound, feminized in *Meridian*, foregrounds the visual work that connects it to the Sojourner Tree, the second of the interconnected histories of people and land central to Meridian's consciousness of her chosen path. The Sojourner Tree, located on the campus of Saxon College where Meridian matriculates, encompasses another story from the past regarding the human imprint on land. In this instance, it is related to slavery and African Americans. According to legend, the Sojourner, a giant magnolia standing at the center of the campus, grew from the severed tongue of Louvinie, a woman enslaved on the Saxon Plantation. Louvinie was much favored among the Saxon children for telling scary stories that she remembered from Africa or made up about America. The children demanded "more and more extravagant" stories from her, and Louvinie obliged. Unknown to her the youngest Saxon child and only son had a weak heart, and while she was telling her chilling "masterpiece of fright" story of an African man who caught and buried White children with their heads sticking out like cabbages and licked by snakes, the boy died of a heart attack. As punishment, Louvinie's tongue was cut out and ground into the dirt. She suffered even more severely because according to the custom of her African homeland, absent "one's tongue in one's mouth or in a special spot of one's own choosing, the singer in one's soul was lost forever to grunt and snort through eternity like a pig."[15] According to legend, Louvinie recovered her tongue and buried it under a magnolia tree on the plantation. That tree grew so magnificently that other enslaved people believed it had magic powers, especially that it talked, made music, and obscured vision (the latter allowing runaway slaves to hide from sight in it).

Ascribing inherited storytelling powers to Louvinie, Walker incorporated a brief diaspora narrative of West African origins. Renowned as diviners, Louvinie's parents used their remarkable ability to concoct intricate stories from the questions they posed to entrap people who tried to get away with committing murder. By incorporating Louvinie's heritage, Walker constructed an expansive legacy of oral creativity connecting Africa and America, which she deploys to expose the crimes human beings commit against one another that should not go undetected, but it is less forceful in condemning the atrocity of slavery and its violation of the natural world than in pointing out the removal of Native Americans and the desecration of sacred lands. The backstory of Louvinie and the Sojourner nonetheless adds dimension to the concepts of the sacredness of all life and the significance of the natural world and the African diaspora in the global revolutions for freedom and the revolutionary acts perpetrated to make a difference in societies everywhere struggling to bring about change.

The Sojourner figures prominently in Walker's representation of Meridian's becoming a change agent in contemporary times. She unites the fate of the tree during Meridian's final year of college with that of a girl, approximately thirteen years old, who had been living on her own since about the age of five or six in the poor neighborhood bordering Saxon College. Her origins were unknown, but she was often seen scavenging in the trash for furniture and in the garbage for food. She never communicated with people in the neighborhood and ran away if approached. Meridian learned about the girl and her apparent pregnancy from neighbors who wanted, but failed, to capture her and provide a home in which she could give birth. When Meridian spotted the girl whom she had named "The Wild Child," she returned to her honors dorm and collapsed into one of her spells. When she woke two days later, she successfully set out to coax the girl into capture with treats. She bathed the girl, washed her hair, and took her to the dining hall where Wild Child horrified Meridian's proper tablemates and genteel housemother with her uncouth behavior, so much so that they convinced Meridian that the girl was not her responsibility and could not stay in the dorm. While Meridian was unsuccessfully trying to find a placement in homes for unwed mothers or schools for children with special needs, the Wild Child escaped and ran the street where someone driving a speeding car hit and killed her.

The tragedy of the Wild Child motivated Meridian, her friend Ann-Marion, and six other Saxon students to purchase a casket and new clothes for the dead girl and to hold a funeral for the neighbors to mourn the lost "Wile Chile," as they called her. The sanctimonious Saxon College president refused to allow them to use the chapel for the funeral and posted guards outside its locked doors. The lowly neighbors, unaccustomed because of their class and economic position to being allowed on the campus, slink away, but the students who had bedecked their dormitories' windows with banners, flowers, and paper streamers in gestures of love for Wile Chile and prayers to God to welcome her, were both angry and ashamed of the denial to hold the funeral in their chapel. They carried the casket to the Sojourner Tree, "whose heavy, flower-lit leaves hovered over it like the inverted peaks of a mother's half-straightened kinky hair."[16] The Sojourner welcomed Wild Child in an empathetic, natural, and seemingly maternal embrace. In grief and anger, the young women made wreaths from the leaves and sang the freedom anthem "*We Shall Overcome*" in their impromptu funeralizing. After the burial in a local Black cemetery, the students returned to campus to riot for the first time in the school's distinguished history. Instead of destroying the pompous president's mansion, as Meridian urged, "in a fury of confusion and frustration they worked all night, and chopped and sawed down, level to the ground, that mighty, ancient, sheltering music tree."[17]

Walker focuses on arbitrary forms of isolation in an urban setting and associates naturalized behavior (the Wild Child) with the desire for nature's empathetic existence (the Sojourner). Neither can survive the stifling demands for conformity. The Wild Child is run down by a car, the modern machine of individual mobility, and the ancient tree is cut down by rampaging students rebelling against the repressive authority of Saxon College officials who had previously reprimanded them for being activists against segregation. With these two tropes, Walker points to a displacement, a missing interdependence and an erasure of women's lives and an absence of ideology encompassing racial, gender, and class difference. The narrative strategy gestures toward realignment with the past as a continuum and toward understanding how economic structures lead to the mistreatment and abuse of women and children, or those rendered helpless by the overexertion of patriarchal power. Segregating the women into civilized and "primitive" (Saxon students and Wild Child) cannot be justified or maintained. The categories of separation in public spaces, whether by race, gender, or class, all come under attack.

In the final section, Truman Held tells Meridian "your ambivalence will always be deplored by people who consider themselves revolutionists, and your unorthodox behavior will cause traditionalists to gnash their teeth.'"[18] Meridian's response is unequivocal: "'But that is my value. . . . Besides, all the people who are as alone as I am will one day gather at the river. We will watch the evening sun go down. And in the darkness maybe we will know the truth.'"[19] Collective action remains Meridian's best hope for sustained combating and resisting corrupt, false power. She writes and does not destroy those of her poems that insist on the coming together despite whatever conventional supports fail: "there is water in the world for us / brought by our friends / though the rock of mother and god / vanishes into sand."[20] Two aspects of corporeal materiality conjoin—the body and the land. The "we," comprised of those who like Meridian are not just women, Black, and Southern, but also men (like Truman), and White (like Lynne), and Northern (like Ann-Marion) constitute a new political entity engaged with the world as it is but charged to come together in a transformative process.

Meridian actualizes herself as an artist and writes herself formally into being as a poet. Her artistry with the written word had not been evident in the chapters leading up to the final section. In the splintering ideology that had hampered the art making of Truman as a painter and the would-be photography of Lynne's seeing Black Southerners as art, the prospect of Meridian as a verbal artist was not intrinsic to the narrative. When she does not destroy her poems and leaves them on the wall along with Ann-Marion's letters as trace elements of her philosophy and faith, she validates the part of her existence that was emerging in conscious acceptance of herself as artist. In counterdistinction to Ann-Marion the erstwhile revolutionary achieving fame by writing poems "about her two children, and the quality of the light that fell across the lake she owned," Meridian writes poetry as substantiation of her belief in the sanctity of life.[21] Her mournful yet hopeful poetry is the culmination of a voice that had been reticent throughout the text, speaking little, or in riddles that only intensified the prevailing sense of her being an enigma. Throughout those exchanges and in her own thinking, there was "something missing," so that Meridian was always seeking a way of expressing herself, her true self, her feelings, her sexuality, her love, or her despair. By the end with her poems extant and legible, she is transfigured into an artist-poet of life and souls. Whereas Truman was consistently presented as an artist, Meridian was not given a conventional medium through which to express her art, even though she had used her body as a medium for her performances. She had intimated as much in the opening sequence of the novel when she confessed: some helpful Chicokema men "always follow me after I *perform*, in case I need them."[22] Ultimately, her medium is not only her body but also her words.

Just as in the poems of *Revolutionary Petunias*, the civil rights movement and its ancillary movements become agents for progress toward freeing individuals from a spiritually deadening lethargy that functioned as an escape from the segregation and racism circumscribing their lives. They were, nonetheless, neither wholly successful nor fully inclusive. The long journey to freedom burdens with death, as is written large in the chapter whose only title is the run-on list of martyrs, Black and White, from Medgar Evers to Viola Liuzzo, and in all capital letters. It opens with the ominous words: "*It was a decade marked by death. Violent and inevitable.*"[23] Forward momentum, nevertheless, is inevitable. The aloneness inscribed in Meridian's existence is a paradigm of human isolation that can be overcome. She writes, "and we, cast out alone/to heal/ and recreate/ourselves," in her poem of "catharsis, redemption and hope," and individual transcendence over suffering and confusion that signifies the ultimate message conveyed in the text.[24] Following the many deaths, literal or figurative, there is resurrection of sorts. Personal transformation can occur and the "we" of society can evolve and foment social change. Martyr-like in her commitment to revolution of the culture and of the spirit, Meridian acts out of the belief that though "alone," "we" have the capacity to "re-create ourselves." And she leaves that message written down in her poetry.

With this mystic notion of transformation, Walker launches the concept of "the return" that would prove to be a mainstay of her subsequent fiction. The return initially in *The Third Life of Grange Copeland* would simply mark the return to the South after northern migration. *Meridian* also follows that literal pattern of return from the North to the point of origin in the South; however, an overarching metaphysical and philosophical idea of return becomes pronounced as the text proceeds, and it is that idea that reemerges in Walker's later fiction as a return to past lives or deeper historical consciousness, especially in *The Temple of My Familiar* (1989) and *Possessing the Secret of Joy* (1992). Truman physically returns to seek Meridian in the opening pages, and as their intertwined stories unfold in flashbacks and memories, his return is cast as a spiritual return to aspects of his own identity, beliefs, and creativity that had been lost. The last section of the novel deals openly with the symbolic nature of the necessary return for all those who like Truman had been somehow lost. Meridian herself is a configuration of the return to physical and spiritual health, and with it a return to the work of teaching, healing, and enlightening. Her vision is an open invitation for others to return and join her in a renewed, therapeutic way of living and approaching revolution.

Some part of Meridian is, according to Truman, "exactly the same as she had always been" but a "new part had grown out of the old. . . . new, sure and ready, even eager, for the world."[25] Her body, however, is not the same; it has not changed gender, but it has constructed a new, multiple gendered identity. Meridian's preparedness for leadership moves her into a new role of identity once associated with masculinity in the narrative, but her readiness for struggle and battle includes forgiveness and love, and with them an unwavering commitment to spiritual revolution as power within a material world. Decidedly utopic in its rendering of a Black woman's body as pangendered, *Meridian* ultimately locates itself not merely in analogy to the South but to all political spaces of society, and as seminal in Walker's reading of transfiguration. The result is that *Meridian* may be Walker's most brilliantly conceived and realized novel.

Walker's divorce in 1976 followed the success of *Meridian*, but her personal crisis did not hinder her developing career. In New York, she held an editorial position at *Ms. Magazine*, where she formed a lasting friendship with the editor Gloria Steinem. A Guggenheim Fellowship (1977–1978) provided additional financial support for another novel.

During this period, Walker was also at work on *I Love Myself When I Am Laughing and Then Again When I Am Looking Mean and Impressive* (1979), an anthology of writings by Zora Neale Hurston, whom she had discovered during her years in Mississippi. Hurston's life and professional career of anthropological research, folklore transcriptions, and fiction publications provided Walker with a literary forebear to augment her maternal legacy. Hurston, as a Southern Black woman writer who roamed free in pursuing her career, spoke directly to Walker's own intersectional identity and her emerging career. She reflected on Hurston: "Reading her I saw for the first time my own specific culture, and recognized it as such, with its humor always striving to be equal to its pain, and I felt . . . I had been given a map that led to the remains of my literary country."[26] Along with cultural and literary kinship, Hurston armed Walker with the knowledge that Black women could speak for themselves, that Southern Black women could articulate their own reality, and that a Black Southern woman writer could create art out of that speech and reality.

Walker's editing of *I Love Myself* forwarded a major revival of interest in Hurston and was one catalyst for Hurston's placement in the American literary canon. The edition contributed as well to a burgeoning feminist attention to Black women writers in classes and scholarship, and further inspired Walker's own writing which began to take an even more decidedly feminist turn than in her initial fiction. The book's front and back cover images with Hurston in contrasting poses reflecting the title are iconic photographs taken by Carl Van Vechten, the novelist who promoted the works of Harlem Renaissance writers in the 1920s and turned to photographing Black celebrities in the 1930s. The dual title comes from Hurston's 1934 letter to Van Vechten complimenting his photographs of her.

Walker reflected the diversity of Hurston's writing and her persistence as a creative force even under adverse circumstances in her dedication, entitled "On Refusing to be Humbled by Second Place in a Contest You Did Not Design: A Tradition by Now." It presented a list of reasons why contemporary audiences would *not* love Hurston, but then turned to the essentials of precisely why she is so loved: "for her work, first, and then again . . . we love her for herself. For the humor and courage with which she encountered a life she infrequently designed, for her absolute disinterest in becoming either white or bourgeois, and for her *devoted* appreciation of her own culture, which is an inspiration to us all."[27] As illustration, Walker selected autobiographical and folklore sections from *Dust Tracks on a Road* (1942, autobiography), *Mules and Men* (1935, Southern Black folklore), and *Tell My Horse* (1938, Jamaican and Haitian folk culture). In addition, she included some of Hurston's published essays, articles, stories, and sketches, as well as excerpts from her novels, *Jonah's Gourd Vine* (1934), *Moses Man of the Mountain* (1939), and *Their Eyes Were Watching God* (1937), her masterpiece. The selected texts provided a new generation of readers with access to a significant writer who deserved an audience and merited critical attention.

Walker concluded the edition with her moving afterword, "Looking for Zora," which recounted her 1973 experience with Charlotte Hunt searching for Hurston's burial site in Florida. After locating the sunken spot that was Hurston's final resting place, Walker had the Merritt Monument Company carve on an "Ebony Mist" headstone a quotation from Jean Toomer:

Zora Neale Hurston
"A Genius of the South"
Novelist Folklorist
Anthropologist
1901 1960.[28]

This tribute to Hurston's genius would stand not only as a marker of her once lost grave, but also as a remembrance of her valuable contributions.

Walker's search for Hurston's grave was a search to recover the literal remains of a Black woman writer. That search, moreover, was also a much larger one; with it, Walker sought to locate and reinstate the literary and cultural offerings Hurston had posited in the world but that had been lost to generations, especially women readers who at that time in the 1970s were excavating and discovering their female writer ancestors. The conflation of body with world is a trope Walker employs throughout her writing but increasingly so in her later poetry and meditative prose. The body most frequently occurring in texts from the first half of her career is Black and female, and often traumatized by some physically threatening presence, such as racism or sexism, that has the power to occupy and destroy.

With her attention to recovering Hurston's bodily remains, Walker also begins to emphasize the woman's physical body in its capacity to produce and express creativity, or in the counterpoint, the stifling of that capacity. She deploys reproduction and motherhood as functioning in opposition to the creative expression of self or to the tangible actualization of self. The Black woman's body as a reproductive site appears in the enactment of traumas associated with the inability to live fully, whether from socially prescribed constrictions on women or from a woman's own internalization of the impositions of motherhood. In *Meridian*, for example, Mrs. Hill "in her first pregnancy . . . became distracted from who she was. As divided to her mind as her body was divided, between what part was herself and what part was not. Her frail independence gave away to the pressures of motherhood and she learned—much to her horror and amazement—that she was not even allowed to be resentful that she was 'caught.' That her personal life was over. There was no one she could cry out to and say 'It's not fair!'"[29] Once she experiences motherhood, Mrs. Hill understands that she had misread other women's eyes, and believes that instead of a "mysterious inner life she had imagined that gave them a secret joy," there was only "simply a full knowledge of the fact that they were dead, living just enough for their children" but in actuality "being buried alive."[30] Walker represents Mrs. Hill as a woman "walled away from her own life" so that she retreats into "abstraction," a refusal to be creative in any part of her domestic life and maternal responsibilities: "Creativity was in her, but it was refused expression. It was all deliberate. A war against those to whom she could not express her anger."[31] These ideas about reproduction, creativity, women's bodies had already appeared in a variety of forms in Walker's earlier poetry and fiction, though not in such a deeply felt, deliberate articulation.

At this point in her career, Walker deployed Hurston allegorically as a tangible model of creativity despite familial, racial, gender, or social constructs. She seized upon a message of self-love and self-confidence for her unapologetic approach to writing about herself and her subject matter. Walker's insistence on the necessity of creativity and of truthfulness as part of an active social and aesthetic consciousness manifests itself in *Goodnight, Willie Lee, I'll See You in the Morning* (1979), her third poetry book that appeared in the same year as her Hurston anthology.

The collection chronicles the poet's coming to terms with an all-encompassing painful love by sublimating that passion to the act of creative writing. It is a recapitulation of the experience that Walker lived with while writing *Once*, but the difference is that rather than contemplating her own death, she reflects on her father's death and the deaths of so many public figures and personal friends who had fought for justice. In this book, death and the grave constitute the geography of "rememory," Toni Morrison's terminology from *Beloved* (1987).

Walker begins the meditation on mortality and the meaning of life with an encoded return to her experience with the civil rights movement. Her dedication is a self-referential parable akin to an extended African-like proverb. A young romantic girl believes that "her own people possessed the lion's share of beauty and goodness in the world," but she "perceived the end was coming for them." She sets out to collect the "drops of sweat—the price of her people's goodness and beauty—from their rapidly freezing faces." She searches for the man with the quiet revolutionary ways who let the people decide what they wanted and then participated with them in that activity without dictating or demanding. She carries a book to press into it the faces of those who recall him. He remains elusive, yet she chooses to believe he exists, holds on to his memory, and dedicates her book to him, "wherever in the world he is."

Walker dedicates *Good Night, Willie Lee* to her five brothers and in memory of her father's "shining eyes." This dedication abjures all the pain caused by her brothers for their part in the injury to her eye and acknowledges her connection to her father in vision. In abstaining from assigning blame, Walker revisions a reconciliation with her own self. In commemorating her dead father with the volume's title and title poem, Walker honors the parent whom she loved but to whom she was not always able to show her affection. Earlier in her 1974 essay "In Search of Our Mothers' Gardens," she had voiced a profound appreciation for her mother's unique contribution to Walker's understanding of the art that women create, but she had been unable to express then how her father had helped to shape her.

Later, in her acknowledgments to *In Search of Our Mothers' Gardens: Womanist Prose* (1983), she initiated an appreciative recognition of her father: "My father's gifts, for which I deeply thank him, are daily surprises: my love of naturalness, the tone of my voice, my very face, eyes, and hair."[32] Subsequently, late in the 1980s, she began the essay "Father," included in *Living by the Word: Selected Writings, 1973–1987* (1988), with the admission, "Though it is more difficult to write about my father than about my mother, since I spent less time with him and knew him less well, it is equally liberating."[33] Her reason for trying, nevertheless, was important, because writing about someone with whom she shared so many physical features and traits was a way of understanding him and of accepting him as a part of herself. Almost a decade later in *Anything We Love Can Be Saved: A Writer's Activism* (1997), she looked back on her father in gratitude by associating him with her admired literary ancestor. Like Zora Neale Hurston, Willie Lee Walker also "had a story for every occasion," she recalled, "and taught me it is possible for the word to become sharper than the sword": "I thank my father for his wonderful sense of humor, which effortlessly undermined the racist nonsense that passed for white supremacist wisdom while I was growing up. He would have shared a laugh with Zora Neale Hurston, who said, when stopped for going through a red light in the segregated South, 'Well, I saw all the white people going on the green, so I thought the red must be for me.'"[34]

"Confession," the first part of *Good Night, Willie Lee*, includes a sequence of poems in the voice of a woman recognizing the multiple ways in which love fails women. "Did It Happen to Your Mother? Did Your Sister Throw Up a Lot?" opens with a wry look at painful love that afflicts the physical body but the unworthy man never realizes his unworthiness of love because the afflicted woman defiantly resists confessing the truth: "I will never / unclench my teeth long enough / to tell him so."[35] The emotional and physical toll of love continues thematically throughout poems such as "Never Offer Your Love to Someone Who Eats Hearts" and "Threatened"; however, in "My Husband Says" and "Confession," the speaker reckons honestly with the situation: "Despising lies / I have told everyone / the truth: / Truth is killing me."[36] These are spare, passionate poems that evoke both hurt and hope, parting and leaving, suffering and silence, along with therapeutic unburdening and saving recognition from a friend: "Whose glance said 'Really, / you've got to be kidding. Other / women have already done this / sort of suffering for you, / or so I thought.'"[37]

That precise, imagined comment from a friend draws the passionate drama to closure and prepares for thematic renewal and freedom in the second part "On Stripping Bark from Myself. . . ." The section begins with a short womanist poem "Janie Crawford." It celebrates Hurston's heroine from *Their Eyes*

Were Watching God who freed herself from men who wanted to make her what they desired in a wife: "I love the way Janie Crawford / left her husbands. . . . / a woman unless she submits is neither a mule / nor a queen / though like a mule she may suffer / and like a queen pace / the floor."[38] A similar feminist declaration would appear in the Combahee River Statement, which was first published in 1978 but was part of the Combahee River Collective from 1974 and its founding in Boston: "We reject pedestals, queenhood, and walking ten paces behind. To be recognized as human, levelly human, is enough."[39]

Walker concludes "On Stripping Bark from Myself" with the stanza: "My struggle was always against / an inner darkness: I carry within myself / the only known keys / to my death—to unlock life, or close it shut / forever. A woman who loves woodgrains, the color / yellow / and the sun, I am happy to fight / all outside / murderers / as I see I must."[40] This celebration is a critical awareness of what remains after shedding the unessential. That process allows the speaker to access her own ability to choose to live fully and to fight against all that would impede that possibility.

In the section "Early Losses: A Requiem," Walker returns to the format of an early African tale in the long title poem and in the graphic "In Uganda an Early King" in order to strip the bark away from mythic figures by contemplating the intricate histories of abduction, loss, greed, and pride that contributed to the sad reality of the African diaspora and the resultant hurts still wounding Blacks in the United States. The poet forgoes those African voices to speak as a daughter of today's world in "Forgive Me If My Praise," a poem attempting to comprehend a father who, a peasant and grandson of a slave, was denied manhood and unable to protect his daughter. That daughter now empathizes and wishes she could curl up on his lap so he could "Sing me a blues. / Be B.B. King to my / Mean Woman."[41] She recognizes a need in her life for a fully satisfying love that nurtures, embraces, and even kisses with lips as purple as Janie Crawford's Tea Cake, yet stands ready "to fight with me against / my evil dreams."[42] The poem ends with acquiescence to need and love for combatting the ever-present knowledge of what debilitates and destroys from the outside and from within. It leans forward into "The Abduction of Saints," an allegorical comparison of Malcolm X and Martin Luther King with Christ, who rebelled in his time and place, was wrong in his appearance, was denounced for teaching, and had his very body stolen away. That expressive analogy presages "Malcolm," the poem ending the section with disclaimers to those who alleged knowing Malcolm X without actually knowing "the ironies of the Saint," who preferred to see "all women free / and enjoyed a joke / and loved to laugh."[43] From beginning to end, this section rejects mythologizing and debunks easy mythmaking whether in the distant past or near present.

These poems move the collection to the hard remembering of the dead, the necessity of revolutionary struggle, and the heroes lost to sacrifice. They reveal nevertheless a determination to go beyond what Meridian had recognized about her mother's sad life: "Her mother's life was sacrifice. A blind, enduring stumbling—though with dignity (as much as was possible under the circumstances)—through life."[44] In "facing the way," the poem ending the penultimate section of that name, Walker returns to the question of sacrifice, but in the context of that fundamental question raised by revolutionaries: Are you willing to give your life for the revolution? Here Walker evokes Lorraine Hansberry's rethinking about what she was prepared to give up and what it means to produce "art that transcends time / beauty that nourishes a ravenous spirit," while knowing that the sale of art provides for the needs of ordinary living, yet knowing too that "the poor shall always be with us" is not a comfort for the poor or the poet.[45] That sentiment about poverty surfaces in "talking to my grandmother who died poor (while hearing Richard Nixon declare 'I am not a crook.')" with its acknowledgment of what has not come from generations of hard work and honesty, but acceptance of what will keep the poet alive, fighting, working, "and recognizing beauty" in her grandmother's "so nearly / undefeated face."[46]

The final section "Forgiveness" brings together in a healing grace for the living and the dead all the themes circulating throughout. The title poem concludes the collection and argues for resurrection and reunion both in the here and now and in the hereafter where promised renewals, returns, and beginnings can occur. Her mother looks at her father in his coffin and "said without/ tears, without smiles / without regrets / but with *civility* / 'Good night, Willie Lee, I'll see you / in the morning.' / and it was then I knew / that the healing / of all our wounds / is forgiveness / that permits a promise / of our return / at the end."[47] This tone, the civility of the mother's voice and the compassion of the daughter's thought, anticipates the conclusion of *The Color Purple*, published four years later, with a reformulated celebratory premise that healing, forgiveness, and return, literally from the presumed dead in the novel, are the balm for familial misery and personal pain. Those themes had already emerged as a promise in the poignant sadness ending *Meridian*.

Drawing upon the strength and pain of women's lives, Walker began to write her third novel, but her residency in New York did not allow for the visitation of rural folk characters who were her subject and whose presence she found essential for telling their story. She could, however, complete a second collection of short stories, *You Can't Keep a Good Woman Down* (1981), which converged in women's experiences topical in the 1970s and second-wave feminist concerns central to her editorial work at *Ms. Magazine*, but also related exponentially to her expanding conception of the freedom and independence necessary to be a writer.

The thirteen stories in *You Can't Keep a Good Woman Down* coalesce around the power, possibility, and potential of Black women who are not defeated even when they lose or suffer. The tone is often ironic and the themes often combative. Walker takes on a wider range of topics: the appropriation of Black blues music and the problem of understanding lyrics outside of one's lived experience ("Nineteen Fifty-Five"); the underbelly of iconic racial celebrity ("Fame"); lust across race lines ("The Lover"); the sexual exploitation of a young Black girl by a powerful White man ("How Did I Get Away with Killing One of the Biggest Lawyers in the State? It Was Easy"); pornography and its detrimental effect on couples ("Coming Apart" and "Porn"); rape and misogyny within the Black Power movement ("Advancing Luna—and Ida B. Wells"); abortion ("The Abortion"); sexual passion and love ("Laurel"); and the persistent desire for solidarity in revolutionary action to counter racial debasement ("A Letter to the Times, or Should This Sado-Masochism Be Saved?"). This brief categorizing of themes does not adequately capture the breadth of topical concerns in the collection. The stories reflect Walker's grappling with contemporary social, ideological, and political matters that range beyond the woman-centered lessons Hurston and her foremothers had taught about the determination to live fully despite the odds against them. Although these women protagonists are vulnerable to a variety of modern social ills, they experience a measure of their own worth and power.

Walker dedicates the collection to her contemporaries; however, with greater individuation, she thanks her sister Ruth "for the stories she tells," and a selection of African writers (Bessie Head, Ama Ata Aidoo, Buchi Emecheta, Wa Thiong'o Ngugi, Okot p'Bitek, and Ousmane Sembene) "for the stories they write," and three women from *Ms. Magazine* (Gloria Steinem, Joanna Edgar, and Suzanne Braun Levine) for publishing her stories "with sisterly welcome and enthusiasm," and four blues singers (Ma Rainey, Bessie Smith, Mamie Smith, and Perry Bradford) "among others of their generation, for insisting on the value and beauty of the authentic." Walker's precise list of contributions is key to unlocking connective threads in the collection: the oral tradition of Southern Black folk; the written work of Africans in the time of African American solidarity with their African roots and counterparts; the rise of feminism and sisterhood in the United States; and the music and songs of blues artists who kept it real in valuing their culture and themselves and finding beauty in the authenticity of their traditions and voices.

As the dedication suggests, Walker's approach to representing race, interracial interactions, and storytelling is complex. She especially explores Black women's relationship to White men and White women as part of recognizing what it means to be a writer in a world with changing racial dynamics and interactions. The Black Southern world bounded by strictures and homogeneity is not the primary world that Walker envisions in this collection. It is nonetheless a world still subject to the eye and mind of a writer who is knowledgeable about literary, cultural, and historical ancestors as material for art and the creation of the artist, whether in words, songs, paintings, or sculptures.

One of the best-known stories, "Nineteen Fifty-five," opens *You Can't Keep a Good Woman Down* with a double-edged exploration into making and disseminating music and achieving success. The value, intangible yet real, of creating songs out of lived experience is one of the meaningful areas Walker addresses as a contrast between the old blues culture and the emergent rock and roll in popular music. She critiques the appropriation of Black music and art by Whites who, even when their intentions are good, deprive Blacks of their due, whether in money, acclaim, or respect. The fictional nod is to Elvis Presley and Big Mama Thornton, from whom he learned much about music, singing, and performance. Walker's Elvis-like character is Traynor, a naïve well-meaning White boy who covers a song of an older Black blues singer Gracie Mae Still. He becomes a phenomenal success yet keeps trying to figure out the meaning of her lyrics because he somehow associates them with knowledge and authentic living. Over the years as his fame and wealth increase, Traynor showers Gracie Mae with elaborate presents and expensive cars, but also with questions about her life and music. She accepts his generosity, calls him "Son," and knows something is missing in his life that she cannot fill. For her part, Gracie Mae is content with who she is and what she has done with her music. She owns her song and her life; characteristically, as a young, unknown singer, she was even ready to fight the great Bessie Smith to prevent her from stealing her song. In old age, Gracie Mae maintains contentment with her authentic, familiar ways of living, while becoming more aware of the inexplicable sadness in Traynor's. His life ends abruptly, and his many fans mourn in tearful public displays, but Gracie Mae knows that they have no idea who he really was. She knows, too, that despite his questioning her and studying her songs, Traynor had never known her or, tragically, himself. Her final words assess the travesty of societal ignorance in its largest terms: "They crying and crying and didn't even know what they was crying for. One day this is going to be a pitiful country."[48]

You Can't Keep a Good Woman Down functions as a deep dive into the Black woman artist and her determination to be free to create her art and to live without encumbrances and independent of whatever would hold her back from her work, whether that might be marriage, husband, children, parents, friends, lovers, or expectations from gender norms or cultural roles. "The

Lover" and "The Abortion" are the two stories that most directly encompasses the themes of the writing woman artist, freedom, and independence, but they do not address the issue of race in artistic expression as emblematically as "A Sudden Trip Home in the Spring" or as forthrightly as "Source," both of which also tackle similar themes along with the complicating factor of racial identity. Walker projects more in these short stories than in her first collection. As a result, even though *You Can't Keep a Good Woman Down* is more focused on her messages and themes, it is less firmly embedded in storytelling that reveals through characters and actions rather than through sermons or conversations that read like set pieces promoting and extolling ideology.

From the first story to the last, this collection is about the creative mind, the ability to create, especially about writing as a creative aspect of the construction of an authentic self. Two of the shortest stories, "Petunias" and "Elethia," assume the dangerous work of reclaiming the authentic, whole past of Black people and of rewriting it by exposing the remnants of a suppressed and denied Black self or destroying falsely created narratives of Black subjugation and servitude. These stories are comparable in recognizing that violence done to Black lives may be both physical and psychological.

"Elethia," for example, confronts the stuffing, taxidermy style, of a formerly enslaved man to turn him into Uncle Albert, a smiling waiter in perpetual service. Elethia discovers that Albert was nobody's fawning "uncle" and nothing like the ever-grinning dummy displayed in the window of a famous White restaurant. She and her friends, acting as revolutionaries, steal and burn the stuffed body, but preserve vials of the ashes as a more fitting memorial. Their act, "perverse" yet freeing, allows Elethia to recognize all stuffed human remains, particularly of Native Americans, that she encounters in museums, but there are too many to liberate. Even more frustrating, Elethia cannot determine whether they want to be saved. Her experience is similar to Meridian's visiting her state capitol's Museum of Indians and seeing the "shamelessly displayed" bones of a Native American warrior "in a crouched position . . . his front teeth missing, his arrows and clay pipes around him. At such sights she experienced nausea at being alive."[49] With "Elethia," Walker continues mining the need for productive revolution that recognizes historical connections between the fates of African Americans and Native Americans in a culture of preserving artifacts but disrespecting people.

"Source," the longest story in the collection, is also Walker's most ambitious in coalescing divergent, autobiographical threads of living creatively and fully as a woman in shifting, unprecedented times and unstable spatial settings. It is a rich, embellished, self-referential narrative about "sources"—beginnings that may be taken literally as genealogy or symbolically as birth. Irene, the protagonist, had taught writing and reading in a federally funded antipoverty program, which was summarily killed off as "superfluous." With its termination, Irene's idealism waned and her commitment to the small Southern town with its secondhand trailer for a classroom flagged, though her appreciation for her older women students and their extraordinary desire to learn remained in tack. Irene would return compulsively to the forced ending of that educational program and to an internal reassessment of her work and worth. The narrative traces Irene's psychological attempt to refocus and refuel her life by visiting Anastasia, a college friend. On a parallel track of refocusing, Anastasia had, during their college days in New York, tried out dramatic transformations to anchor herself. A veritable chameleon in adapting her appearance to successive, discordant stylish models (e.g., blackened hair, black makeup "New York SuperVamp" look and a Faye Dunaway lightened hair, bangs to her eyebrows "little English schoolboy look"), Anastasia was a girl from Pine Lake, Arkansas, whose racial identity is not immediately given.

That absence of a racial marker becomes integral to understanding the narrative's late-twentieth-century interpretation of identity and passing. The question of what constitutes race, its production and manifestation, is an undercurrent. Absence of a legible sign of racial identity infers from the outset references to the 1929 novel *Passing* by Nella Larsen, one of the "three mysteries," Walker acknowledged in her dedication to *In Love & Trouble*. Irene is the name of Larsen's striving, but suffocating, middle-class Black woman whose unreliable narrative consciousness dominates the descriptions of her Black childhood friend, Clare Kendry, who escaped poverty and neglect by crossing the color line and becoming White. Anastasia, like Clare, is indeed escaping her past, but that past turns out to be anchored in staunchly well-to-do Baptist-turned-Jehovah's-Witnesses parents who bequeathed heavy racial baggage along with wealth. Irene, like Larsen's character, has an overwhelmingly self-satisfied perspective of her importance: "Who would *not* love me? was her attitude. The trauma of having lost the educational project had not damaged an essential self-serving vanity."[50]

Irene's search for reconnection with purpose is internal, but her journey to visit Anastasia becomes the physical manifestation of her inner quest for direction and insight. Walker draws a mirroring parallel in Anastasia's visible, external search for meaning in her existence through her bold, unconventional choices of lifestyles. Whereas Irene is purposeful in her agonizing review of her role as a teacher, her impact on the lives of Black women, and her potential for moving forward, Anastasia in consciously acting out an engagement with a higher plane of being that would bring enlightenment and peace to her living. The two different strategies for finding a meaningful way of life collide in

San Francisco when Irene encounters Anastasia as a flower child in a hippie-like environment replete with the new name "Tranquility," a new family, and a spiritual guide.

Source, Anastasia's guru, describes her as first looking "exactly like Kathleen Cleaver, 'dressed all entirely completely in black' . . . Her hair like an angry, wild animal bush. And her skin pale pale pale. . . . Militant."[51] Anastasia's telling response is, "'I thought I was black.'"[52] Source's repeated statement that "Nobody's anything" allows Irene to take stock of the racist implications in his comments about Blacks he knew while living in Uganda, and the backwardness of Africans in saying they were "black black black" when compared to other races who do not identify themselves by color.[53] Irene cannot contain herself at his racism, which Source amplifies in a racist joke; she speaks out and interrupts Source's pontificating and his silent daughters' transcribing his every word. Intuiting his misogynistic control and overt sexism from his verbiage and the submissive acts of the daughters-scribes (including one obviously pregnant with his child), Irene rejects Source's explicit domination of others and raises her voice in opposition. In so doing, she violates the sanctity of his word and is asked to leave.

In reading "Source" through the lens of the two women and the male sage, Deborah E. McDowell perceptively calls attention to "origins, beginnings, questions of male subjectivity and its relations to language, and representation," while also astutely explicating the parallel plots that stage "competing words and conflicting discourses framed as a secular myth of origins" and that confront "the belief in the text as *reflection* rather than *production* of self and world."[54] There is no avoiding the prominence of the exchange with Source, because it initiates a clarifying discussion between Anastasia and Irene that signifies Walker's intricate textual aims in digging deep into conceptual origins and discursive formations.

Anastasia believes in Source's messages and his role in transforming her life: "'I understand I am nothing. That is what Source was testing you to see. You still think you are Somebody. That you matter. That Africans matter. . . . And if they are nothing—if nobody's anything—it is impossible to humiliate them.'"[55] Irene cannot accept her friend's logic because she believes Source is a racist misogynist who treats his daughters like slaves and manipulates his followers, but she is unprepared for Anastasia's lengthy explanation of her life, both her early life in Arkansas and her more recent one in which Kathleen Cleaver figured. According to Anastasia, when she first saw Cleaver, they looked alike with long, light-colored straight hair, but this Cleaver was a mute woman sitting silently in a corner while all the radical men talked. Soon with the deaths, jailing, or flight of the men, Cleaver reemerged talking, cursing, wearing boots, sunglasses, and black clothing while posing with a gun. That Cleaver inspired Anastasia to imitate her look, launch her own radical stance, and unite with a revolutionary man, only he turned out to beat her and forbid her to talk. Her parents rescued her, took her back to Arkansas, and to all the memories of her childhood as a light-skinned child of privilege in a segregated world.

Irene then grasps Anastasia's history of mental breakdown, restoration, and release by her parents to Source, whom the parents support financially. Those same details compel Irene to concede that she is in no position to criticize her friend's life choices. She acknowledges what she had not allowed herself to admit—that her own life is falling apart and that she is struggling to believe in who she is and what she does. She cannot, however, accept Anastasia's conclusion—"'If you suffer in a place, *leave*'"—because Irene by upbringing, training, and disposition apprehends suffering not as place-defined, but as a condition.[56]

The resolution to the interrupted visit comes years later in Alaska, where Irene is lecturing on teaching methods to Native and White women educators. The setting, in clear view of Mt. McKinley, prompts Irene's to reflect on hilly San Francisco, Source, and Anastasia in that masculinity-dominated landscape. She locates Anastasia, now living near Anchorage, but is astounded by Anastasia's greeting, "'When I heard you were coming, and that it would be a conference about Natives, I thought I'd be the only white chick around. But I see I am not,'" which she follows with: "'I *love* being white.'"[57] Irene finds that admission incredulous, as she assumes passing for White is "passé, even though Anastasia insists that was only the case in old popular culture venues that she names—the movies *Imitation of Life* and *Pinkie* and novels by Jessie Fauset and Nella Larsen. Her astonishing admission continues: "'There *were* shades of *Autobiography of an Ex-Colored Man* in the beginning—you know, could a potentially great black woman find happiness as a mediocre white one?—but that passed. . . . Anyway, I am not passing; I am just through trying to correct other people's opinions.'"[58] Based on that remark, Irene realizes that she is actually looking into the eyes of a White woman.

These revelations make apparent Walker's allusion to another of the writers included in her acknowledgment of the "mysteries" from the 1920s—Jean Toomer. Toomer was not only a light-skinned man of African American ancestry from a privileged family (his grandfather was lieutenant governor of Louisiana during Reconstruction), but he was also a spiritual seeker who for a time followed the teachings of George Gurdjieff, a mystic philosopher and founder of the Institute for the Harmonious Development of Man at Fontainebleau, France, where Toomer studied and became enlightened. On returning to the United States, he led workshops on Gurdjieff's philosophy that there is no unified consciousness but through disciplined work, self-observation, and self-study, humans can emerge from a walking sleep, awaken to inner experience, and achieve higher levels of consciousness. Anastasia, in her childhood difference from Blacks around her, in her exceptionally privileged background, her shifting locational attachments, her search for enlightenment, her masking in physical disguises, and her changes in racial identification, is symbolically associated with Toomer, his persistent quest for a meaningful identity in his life and his final embrace of Whiteness as a practicing Quaker in rural Pennsylvania.

Anastasia's and Irene's ensuing extended reminiscences about race, their different experiences of being Black, their reflections on education in race matters, all hinge on Anastasia's finally feeling free to express her side of long suppressed issues about colorism and racial assumptions. Anastasia's awareness of the import of the conversation extends well beyond race, even though she admits that her attraction to Irene stemmed from Irene's very destiny as a Black woman remaining so stable and fixed. For Anastasia, the outpouring was about gender that linked them in a more meaningful reunion: "They were simply two women, choosing to live as they liked in the world," an assessment that Irene comes to agree with in remembering that always Anastasia had been her "objective correlative."[59] Irene admits that, even in college, she had feared becoming an ordinary Black bourgeois success story yet had known that failure was not an option. She expresses what she could never before say: "'At the same time, that I condemned you for your lack of commitment to anything I considered *useful*, I used you as the objectification of my own internal dilemma.'"[60] Irene spills all that she had withheld from her friend and her own consciousness: Anastasia's confusion minimized her own; Anastasia's search for a multiracial community was a reflection of her own desire to create precisely that kind of community; Anastasia's acceptance of a guru replete with dope for answers was akin to her own looking to government for solutions.

In thinking back on Source, Anastasia demonstrates an unmistakable growth. Despite her incongruous racial identification as White, she reveals that the mantra that Source taught her for obliterating her consciousness became merely an unattached sound that instead freed her. It propelled her into a new "longing and then a direction" so that she emerged out of that experience with a remarkable acceptance of an undefeated sense of and love for herself: "'I knew I had to merge this self with something really elemental and stable, or it would shatter and fly away.'"[61] Her love for a Native man with whom she hopes to have children is a reflection of what is now her fundamental, anchored, happy, and free self.

From divergent paths, the searches of the two friends converge in the admission that each had been looking in wrong directions for navigating life and constructing identity, that "*any* direction that is away from ourselves is the wrong direction."[62] This unexpected, but perhaps necessary conclusion is largely symbolic. Anastasia has assumed an essential Whiteness and incipient "Nativeness" along with her woman's identity; Irene has not made a fundamental change in locating herself in a particular production of a Black woman's identity, but she has learned peace with who she is and what she has to offer in teaching. Anastasia has become the artist of herself; Irene has become the artist of others. The convergence ending their respective searches depends on their individual, rather than collective, freeing construction of identity. Each relinquishes repressive aspects of what she has experienced in various phases of growth and maturation to free herself to move toward an unobstructed view of the future.

You Can't Keep a Good Woman Down rounds out this period of nonstop productivity and announces the major challenges Walker would face in the next stellar phase of her extraordinary career. She selected a quotation from Hermann Hesse's *Siddhartha*, a 1922 German novel tracing the quest for enlightenment and the meaning of existence, as the epigraph for the collection: "*It is harder to kill something/ that is spiritually alive/ than it is to bring the dead/ back to life.*" It speaks to the necessity of being spiritually alive as an act of resistance to any forces that would kill. Siddhartha's popularity in translation during the transformative 1960s and 1970s in the United States coincides with the period that Walker reflects most upon during this phase of her career. Remaining alive spiritually underlays *Meridian*; *Good Night, Willie Lee, I'll See You in the Morning*; and *You Can't Keep a Good Woman Down* and much of Walker's future self-reflexive writing. The tendencies toward mysticism and philosophical musings in *Meridian* and toward embryonic displays of social messaging in the stories would increasingly come to be centermost in Walker's fiction and meditations.

This period is noticeably a turning point in how Walker would approach her materials, how she would infuse her subject with a revolutionary spirit of rebellion from any expected trajectory, and how she would value her freedom as a whole human being. She begins the process of shedding much of her old life, even that most recent post-college, and charting out an altered life strategy and artistic course that would take her far from her origins but only to realign her preexisting interiority with her transformed externality. With her conscious interpolations of artists and artist-figures, she announced how clearly she had sighted her familiar with love in abundance and in the spirit of renewed life.

CHAPTER 3

The Work of the Woman

Coloring Purple

> But it is a great time to be a woman. A wonderful time to be a black woman, for the world, I have found, is not simply rich because from day to day our lives are touched with new possibilities, but because the past is studded with sisters who, in their time, shone like gold.
>
> —Alice Walker, "A Talk: Convocation 1972" (1972)

Harcourt Brace Jovanovich published "The Alice Walker Calendar for 1986." The caption and the first photograph serve as a verbal and visual epigraph for the entire calendar. That Walker selected a statement from her 1972 talk at Sarah Lawrence reveling in "a great," "wonderful time" to be a woman and Black to open the 1986 calendar with its photographs documenting her life from 1950 with her schoolgirl photo through her Georgia family and her college years and friendships, on to her marriage and motherhood, her career and move to California, her relationships, her travels, and finally to 1984 with her house, her flowers, her daughter, and her partner at "Wild Trees," as she named the homeplace where she found joy and beauty. The beautiful, photogenic Alice Walker of these images erases the sad story of the scarred girl with the wounded eye. The calendar with its amazing assortment of photographs chronicling a writer's life with her accompanying words was possible because of the success of *The Color Purple* in 1982 and *In Search of Our Mothers' Gardens: Womanist Prose* the following year. With the publication of these books, Walker became one of the best-known writers in the United States and, at that time, the best-known Black woman writer. The particular passage excerpted from her talk at the Sarah Lawrence 1972 convocation extols with good reason the sisters from the past: "They gave us hope, they have proved the splendor of our past, which should free us to lay just claim to the fullness of the future."[1]

The high point in Walker's career in the early 1980s coincides with her developing a dual but not binary vision: inward toward spiritual liberation and outward toward overt feminist politics. This vision culminates in her important theoretical work in formulating "womanism," a concept that signifies her recognition of the intersectionality of her identity (race, gender, class, sexuality) and her feminist ideology. This concept has since become especially significant to feminists of color and to feminist theology. During this major period of her career, Walker also wrote a sequence of books integral to *The Color Purple*: *The Temple of My Familiar* (1989); *Possessing the Secret of Joy* (1992); and *The Same River Twice: Honoring the Difficult, A Meditation on Life, Spirit, Art, and the Making of the Film* The Color Purple *Ten Years Later* (1996). In these texts, she remained attuned to her Georgia family as foundational for her writing and acknowledged as much in the dedication to *The Same River Twice*: "For my beloved family ancestral and present to whom the persistent audaciousness of Art has kept me close." That art, produced in multiple genres during the 1980s and 1990s, mirrors the expanding scope of her insight and activism as evidenced in two poetry collections, *Horses Make a Landscape Look More Beautiful: Poems* (1984) and *Her Blue Body Everything We Know: Earthling Poems, 1965–1990* (1991); and two essay collections, *Living by the Word: Selected Writings, 1973–1987* (1988) and *Anything We Love Can Be Saved: A Writer's Activism* (1997).

This expansive outpouring of creative and critical work all flowed from the major turning point in Walker's career, the publication of *The Color Purple*. When writing the novel stalled in the urban East, Walker moved to California where she located a rural place she could afford and, more importantly, as she said, "that [her] characters liked": "And no wonder: it looked a lot like the town in Georgia most of them were from, only it was more beautiful and the local swimming hole was not segregated."[2] In Northern California, she found peace in nature and an expansive space that ushered in an even more productive literary career. Initially in this new environment, she recalled calculating that it would take her five years to complete her novel, but in less than a year, she finished what would become her bestselling and award-winning *The Color Purple*.[3]

Told in letters from Celie, a poor Black Southern girl who develops into an articulate woman, the novel takes the unusual strategy of addressing Celie's initial letters to God. Celie's existence is shrouded in secret misery. Raped by the man she thought was her father and deprived of her two children by him, she is married off to an abusive husband whom she can only call Mr.____

and whose children disrespect her. Her beloved sister Nettie barely escapes a similar fate but manages to join a family of Christian missionaries who travel to Africa. Berated as ugly, Celie pours out her lonely, violated life in letters to God, without knowing that her sister is alive and writing letters to her that her husband has concealed. The turning point in Celie's devalued life occurs when her husband's true love, the singer Shug Avery with whom he has had three children, reappears and, while recovering from an illness, teaches Celie to value and love herself. During a subsequent visit, Shug discovers and delivers the hidden cache of Nettie's letters to Celie. With these revelations, Celie begins addressing her letters to Nettie, but her primary transformation is in her different understanding of God which Shug inspired by her reading of the natural world. Celie grows freer both in her non-possessive love for Shug and in her own self-worth. The power of the narrative, however, lies in the expressive discourses of becoming and being in the letters.

An unattributed injunction standing alone opens the text: "*You better not never tell nobody but God. It'd kill your mammy.*" The voice of young Celie immediately follows with the first of her letters addressed to God that begins her writing herself into textual and corporeal existence. That letter reads in part: "Dear God, I am fourteen years old. I am [crossed out] I have always been a good girl. Maybe you can give me a sign letting me know what is happening to me."[4] Walker employs the epistolary form to give immediacy to her subject and to provide access to an immature young girl's interiority as she tries to comprehend bewildering experiences. The language of Celie's rape is graphic, and her pain palpable. Walker allows the letters to stand as an embodiment of Celie's physical being. "Letters become the surrogate body for Celie," as Wendy Wall points out in her perceptively titled essay, "Lettered Bodies and Corporeal Texts."[5] Throughout the novel, Celie's letters to God and eventually to Nettie hold the secrets of her body and mind in the process of shaping her experiential reality and unfolding her growing maturity.

Her letters produce a painfully exquisite American bildungsroman told in a timeless form. That form references the earliest novels in English that followed the trials and tribulations of a poor but good person who existed as an outcast in a classist society with hierarchical ranks clearly demarked and mainly unbreachable. Mae G. Henderson asserts that Walker "subverts the traditional Eurocentric male code which dominates the literary conventions of the epistolary novel," a genre "invented by men writing about women," and in effect embodying "male control over literary images of women."[6] Walker seizes control of the recognizable form, one that she had already experimented with in her short stories, and she takes it to an unprecedented place of liberation. Her vision of that place had been cycling through her previous novels, but with

The Color Purple, she actualized it to the most comprehensive conclusion. She holds up the life of a poor, Black dominated woman as a model for overcoming every social, familial, and cultural obstacle placed in her path, and she elevates that life to a level of wholeness, fulfillment, and happiness that she had not previously represented. Walker uses her creative platform to make visible the prototype of the unseen, obscured, and suppressed Black woman, and she allows that woman to occupy center stage not as a disembodied voice, but as a writer advancing and affirming her full presence on the page for God or all omnipotent powers, for her sister Nettie or all human kin, and ultimately for all the world to witness.

At the same time, the historical novel triumphs as Walker's quintessential oral narrative of transformation. The first-person perspective functions as voice in a told story rather than as transcribed writing. The quality Walker conveys is of listening to Celie's speaking voice even while following her written letters. Elliott Butler-Evans observed of Celie's letters, "The rhythm of the sentences and the spelling strongly suggest dialogue rather than narration," and concluded that both Celie's and Nettie's letters "constitute a monologue."[7] Only late in the text do they form a dialogue across time and space. Celie's letters remain within the realm of her curtailed education and limited experiences in a narrow, primarily rural, world; whereas Nettie's letters detail her expanded educational opportunities along with her far-reaching travels to New York, London, Senegal, Liberia, and the fictive land of the Olinkas. Nettie's epistolary travelogues place early-twentieth-century fictional African Americans into equivalence with the better-known cosmopolitanism of later Black international travelers and their writings.

Nettie's letters from Africa constitute one of Walker's most inventive, and controversial, feats. Their inclusion reaffirms Walker's commitment to representing Africa in her diasporic vision present from her first book. Her investment in portraying a wider world view by crossing geographical borders is one of the constant features of her work. From the 1960s through the 1980s, representation of Africa was a prominent cultural signal that African American writers had not lost sight of their origins at a historic moment when African nations were achieving independence and African Americans were journeying to the Motherland to reconnect with lost traditions and aspects of identity. Targeted for lacking faithful historical accuracy, Walker's fictional vision nonetheless took seriously the significance of Africa in the creative imagination of a major African American author. In creating Nettie's letters, Walker imagined an African people at the very beginning of the twentieth century looking back into an ancient way of life on the verge of being erased and into a present world losing autonomy and succumbing to colonization.

Nettie's vivid letters from Africa serve more than the purpose of reporting the daily affairs of the missionary couple, Samuel and Corrine, or of portraying their encounters with the imagined ancestral Olinkas. Without idealization, her letters perform the work of teaching separated African Americans about their African yet fictive counterparts; for example, Nettie's accounts disseminate information about gender issues—both the positive in terms of work through which women bond and form relationships of care and the negative in matters of limiting education for girls, practicing clitoridectomy and scarification, and devaluing unmarried women. All of these instructive issues are intricately connected to Walker's feminist concerns in the novel.

More importantly, Nettie's letters position her as the deus ex machina in the plot. The information she provides clarifies, reverses, and corrects much of the problematic and tragic elements that had propelled Celie's narrative. Nettie delivers the missing connections and hidden information that prove to be life changing for Celie. Nettie learns that Olivia and Adam, the adopted children of the missionaries, are the children taken from Celie as babies. Nettie also discovers that Pa was not her and Celie's father, but rather their stepfather; he had concealed that fact to inherit the house and property of their mother. His calculated chicanery in depriving Celie and Nettie of their rightful inheritance was an additional aspect of his deceitful, cruel nature. Ultimately, Nettie's written accounts, traversing Africa and America, signify a primary textual accomplishment: the collapsing of reading and writing into hearing voice. Her letters take the oral tradition into the realm of a conventional written form associated with the first person, and conjoined with Celie's, they stand in the interstices.

Verbal discourse patterned after the rhythmic talk and telling of Black folk culture is Walker's unique aesthetic achievement in *The Color Purple*. It is marked by her own autobiographical experience of suddenly losing innocence, becoming a wounded body, and believing she was an ugly outcast, and it commemorates metaphorically her own miraculous salvation through love and care. However, the text also encompasses the biographical accounts of her grandmothers who, because of the "other" women inserted into their marriages, had challenging lives with brutish husbands. In particular, Walker identified one prototype of Celie, Rachel Little, the woman her paternal grandfather married after the murder of his wife Kate Nelson, and she named Celie's beloved sister after her maternal grandmother, Nettie Lee Grant, who though a good woman was beaten by her husband.[8] These women and their family stories had been circulating orally before Walker transfigured them in her text. For all of its gestures toward actual people and events, however, *The Color Purple* is a brilliant, innovative feat of storytelling.

Celie's coming to voice and visibility through the power of storytelling is a defiant move to speak and function oppositionally in a society that would render her invisible and consign her to an unspeakable position within the cultural construct. Celie is an atypical instance of the subaltern speaking, and as such a signifier of a Black woman exerting authority over her body and her story so that she is an agent-player in determining the meanings and interpretations of both her story and body.

Initially, despite being raped and sexually abused, Celie is so innocent that she is unaware of the bodily signs of her first pregnancy, but by her second, she becomes resigned to her body's being used and its indication of her deprivation of the normalcy she craves as a schoolgirl. She marks her pregnancies in written terms that encompass her increasing isolation from community and the degree to which her swollen body removes her from access to schooling and from parity with her sister Nettie. Celie does not understand her changing body ("All us notice is I'm all the time sick and fat.").[9] Neither is she aware of the relationship between her physical transformation and Pa's pushing himself into her. His secret manipulation of her body results in his attempt to manipulate as well external perceptions of Celie's physical body by regulating the cultural construction and social meaning assigned to her. Pa makes it difficult for Celie's "bigness" to be detected or read accurately by the community.

The first pregnancy functions effectively to isolate her from her mother and the community: "The first time I got big Pa took me out of school. He never care that I love it."[10] Celie's punishment is her deprivation of school; inflicted by her presumed father, the perpetrator of the rape, the punishment is an act of concealment of Celie's body. It fixes her within the frame of illiteracy and secrecy. Her physical body alone becomes emblematic of the violation: Pa remains unmarked and therefore free to inflict upon his victim not merely the threat of physical violence but more importantly the actuation of physical containment, isolation, and communal erasure.

The primary external agent from within the community who has the potential for intervening is Miss Beasley, the teacher whom Nettie admires. While Nettie is persistent in her desire to reunite Celie with education, she is as ignorant as Celie of the implications of Celie's expanding body: "Nettie never give up. Next thing I know Miss Beasley at our house trying to talk to Pa. She say long as she been a teacher she never know nobody want to learn bad as Nettie and me. But when Pa call me out and she see how tight my dress is, she stop talking and go."[11] Nettie locates Miss Beasley within the culture of learning, but also within a woman-centered sensitivity of person, to body and mind. The holistic implications cannot be actuated because the sight of Celie's literal body, her pregnant belly swelling and tightening her dress, offends the sensibilities of this would-be champion of girls becoming women. Celie's body functions as a signification that Miss Beasley reads from the same script as the abuser, Pa. He has already correctly read the social response to Celie's body and knows that the sight will silence and deter Miss Beasley.

Walker reconfigures the desired savior-teacher Miss Beasley in Shug Avery, who becomes Celie's feisty and vocal teacher. That reconfiguration of Miss Beasley is a necessary redefinition of "teacher" and a correction of Miss Beasley's acquiescence to inaction and silence. Nettie's admiration for Miss Beasley is reconfigured in Celie's adoration of Shug Avery, whose role within folk culture and textual community is as a singer, who writes her own songs; her positionality registers Celie's letters within two different but interconnected traditions: oral/folk and written/textual. In critiquing both the ideologies and the rhetorical structures of patriarchal domination, Walker validates the power of Celie's dynamic, fluid, and individualistic construction of her social identities. Despite social and cultural norms functioning against Celie's coming into being, Shug enables a shifting of perspective.

Shug Avery is a blues figure, the familiar Black vernacular philosopher, incarnated as a woman. She functions like the legendary blues singers and popular early recording artists, for instance, Bessie Smith, Mamie Smith, Alberta Hunter, and Ethel Waters, who brought women's raced truth-telling, including their sexuality, into the public arena. Shug has loved Albert, the man who is now Celie's husband Mr. ____, but she is unwilling to ignore his mean-spirited treatment of Celie. Already enthralled by Shug's beauty and her Blackness, Celie notices that Shug sometimes talks like a man, and takes that as a sign of her power to function so freely in the world. To the contrary, Shug's power in the text comes from her ability to read the world around her, to understand human beings, and to recognize what she wants out of life, even when it puts her at odds with her community. Her no-nonsense approach to being is replicated in her response to the unloved Celie. She accepts Celie's infatuation and returns it with lessons about women's sexuality, body, and pleasure points that Celie had never imagined. Admittedly new to a lesbian relationship, she nevertheless shows Celie what it means to be loved physically.

Shug eventually teaches Celie a new way of understanding God, although Celie had been writing to God since she was fourteen. According to Shug's beliefs: "God is inside you and inside everybody else. You come into the world with God. But only them that search for it inside find it. And sometimes it just manifest[s] itself even if you not looking, or don't know what you looking for."[12] Shug explains that she came to her understanding God by contemplating trees, then air, then birds, and finally people, so that she could feel that she was not separate but part of everything, and that God loves everything including sex, which to her way of thinking was just another way to praise God. This set of revelatory insights leads to Shug's statement that provides the novel's title: "I believe it pisses God off if you walk by the color purple in a field somewhere and don't notice it."[13] Walker disseminates this philosophical conception of God as a way to recognize the spiritual being inside oneself and to formulate a conception of subjectivity that is full, neither derivative nor encumbered by artificial structures imposed externally, yet that is in harmony with all the natural world of living things, including humans.

Walker's text embraces feminist ideology about freeing and empowering women through a love of self as being just as important as loving others. Produced in the era of women's liberation and the sexual revolution, it acknowledges lesbian desire, along with bisexuality, not as a shameful aberration, but as a woman's right to fulfillment in the expression of her sexuality. *The Color Purple* is, in a sense, a protest against proscribed heteronormativity at a time when Black women were expressing the ways in which they were victimized for their sexual identities. In feminist groups and texts—such as the Combahee Collective, Gloria Naylor's *The Women of Brewster Place* (1982), and Ntozake Shange's *for colored girls who have considered suicide when the rainbow is enuf* (1976)—Black women were speaking their truths. This shift was from being ashamed to express sexuality, whether heterosexual, lesbian, or bisexual, to understanding that a Black woman's identity did not exclude her as a sexual being. For Walker, who would soon herself struggle with a more fluid sexual identity than she had previously recognized, it was a feminist period of recognition that a fulfilled sexuality was not exclusively heterosexual. Her novel may be read as an act of liberation in its discourse on Black women's expressive modes of sexuality.

The publication of *The Color Purple* brought an avalanche of attention. Though praised by many critics and feminists for unveiling the brutality of sexism within a racial community, the epistolary account of an abused, barely literate, Black Southern woman offended other critics who charged Walker with misrepresentation of African American men and promotion of negative racial images. Translated into twenty-two languages in the 1980s, the controversial book made the author a celebrity and became a Steven Spielberg film in 1985. Highly publicized, it also made ignoring the cultural map that Walker drew impossible. She focused attention not only on an individual Southern Black woman's journey to voice and visibility but also on a fresh way of representing subjectivity, agency, place, and power in fiction that was not flattering to African Americans struggling to achieve racial parity. There was no avoiding the overt feminist message in her text; neither was it possible to obscure the racial lens of her vision. Critical commentary was immediate and abundant.

Critics rewarded her creativity with a Pulitzer Prize for Fiction and an American Book Award.

At the same time, the novel unleashed a storm of outraged response to its representation of Black men and Black women. The main attacks emanated from the portrayal of abusive Black men, the representation of Black women in a lesbian relationship, the images of a rigid Black patriarchy, the depiction of Black women as "serviceable" for sex, childbearing, and house cleaning, and the exposure of beating a woman into submission as not only acceptable but "correct." The combination of the damaging role of masculinity and paternalism with the fulfilling role of homoerotic desire and lesbian sex intensified the vitriolic outrage. Overt homophobia drove some attacks; some were fueled by a righteous sense of racial betrayal, and some were ignited by a resentful misogynistic rage. Disgruntled readers magnified their perceived grievances against *The Color Purple* into personal attacks against its author, whose measurable success in prestigious prizes and publicity offended some and infuriated others.

The negative critical reception took a personal, gendered, and racial tone. Walker had laid bare sexual abuse within Black communities and particularly within Black families. That exposure, as Deborah McDowell maintains, of "family matters" seldom discussed at that time (physical and sexual abuse of Black women by close kin and patriarchal oppression and domination of Black women) enraged some male reviewers as direct attacks on men.[14] Michelle Wallace's 1979 *Black Macho and the Myth of the Superwoman* had already evoked a firestorm of criticism for its devastating conclusions that race and gender left Black women excluded from solidarity in common cause with Black men and White women. Wallace had taken a direct hit from Black men, such as Robert Staples's "The Myth of Black Macho" in *The Black Scholar*, who widely denounced her work as a misguided polemic only gaining a publisher and publicity because of support from White feminists at *Ms. Magazine*, where Wallace had appeared on the cover. When *The Color Purple* appeared a few years later, Walker, who already had been linked negatively to Wallace's book by virtue of her work at *Ms.*, faced lingering resentments from those already aggrieved by supposed stereotypes of Black men.

The disjunctive strands of attention to Walker converged in the most public of arenas with the book's adaptation for the screen by a major director. Although Steven Spielberg's 1985 film made $142 million at the box office and received eleven Academy Award nominations but no award, it solidified the mixed reception accorded to the book.[15] On the one hand, Spielberg was called out as a presumptuous White director making a film from an African American novel with a primarily Black cast in stereotypical roles. He was blamed too for not portraying the erotic and sexual relationship between Celie and Shug and for erasing the dark undertones of the novel. On the other hand, he was praised for his directing and the quality of the outstanding acting produced under his leadership. Critics, such as Roger Ebert, lauded Spielberg's film as the best of the year, while filmmaker Oliver Stone applauded Spielberg for taking on a project that no one else would have and turning it into a motion picture blockbuster. The reactions to the film kept Walker's name and book in the media.

The negative criticism often overlooked Walker's efforts to see, acknowledge, and represent the experiences of Black people in a specific time and place as truthfully as possible. Several of the major instances take into account the lived realities of a variety of Black women. These involve some correspondence to Celie's more conspicuous treatment: Shug Avery's rejection by her own family, and her would-be father-in-law's refusal to allow his son to marry her; and Sofia's efforts to avoid being beaten into submission by a husband who loves her but knows no other way to treat a wife. These inclusions clearly interrogate patriarchy. Walker had tapped into an emergent contemporary freedom to express the often-suppressed subjectivity of women, yet in so doing she had continued the trajectory already apparent in her fiction: a truthful reassessment of racial and gendered hierarchies of power.

In other instances, Walker takes on the larger racist oppression of Blacks by Whites. Her primary representations are: Celie's father's being lynched for being a successful Black businessman, and her mother's mental breakdown as a result of his gruesome death; Sofia's encounter with a racist penal system in her brutal beating and elongated jail sentence for offending a White woman, and the punitive continuation of her lengthy punishment in forcing her to work as a maid for a White woman; and Mary Agnes/Squeak, raised in the poverty-stricken second family of a well-off White father, being raped by her White uncle despite his recognition of her as kin when she attempts to get Sofia released from prison. These narratives add to the complex social texture of the early twentieth-century world that Walker portrays from the perspective of the multitude of dangers Black people faced in their ordinary, everyday lives.

Some of the negative criticism downplayed how Walker's brutalized heroine emerges whole in the end, and how she transforms her abuse into a renewed life of love and care that includes the transformation of men as well into better human beings. Celie inherits the house and land of her father, but she had already become successful in her own right as a seamstress, designer of pants for women, and owner of a store. She had early in narrative taught both Albert and Shug to piece a quilt, and later she continued to teach Albert to sew and change his aggressive masculinist behavior, which Harpo eventually recognizes as the way forward in his own life and relationship with Sofia. Celie emerges from near illiteracy and silence to intelligibility, subjectivity, and autonomy.

In the conclusion, which is perhaps like a fairytale in terms of its miraculous reunions, reversals, and transfigurations, Celie is surrounded by all those who love her and whom she loves. That shared love allows for a celebratory reunification of family, the long-separated sisters and children, and the coming together not merely of displaced people, but also of Africa and the American South, in the African spouse accompanying a Southern mate on their return home. That return reunites African Americans with their African relatives but not in the expected way on African soil but rather on the ever-fraught land of the termination of the Middle Passage and the resultant enslavement and racial subjugation.

The final letter is a testimony to how far Celie has come: "Dear God, Dear stars, dear trees, dear sky, dear peoples. Dear Everything. Dear God. Thank you for bringing my sister Nettie and our children home."[16] Despite the fairytale quality, Walker turns as she did in *Meridian* to the symbolism of the return, the full circle accommodating all. The expressive discourses of faith and love, especially of oneself, and of happiness as the right of human beings as much as is justice and equality pervade the ending and rewrite the abjection and suffering that had marked so much of the text.

By the time Rachael Lister published *Alice Walker,* The Color Purple*: A Reader's Guide to the Essential Criticism* in 2010, Walker's novel had long been considered a classic. Lister's comprehensive undertaking examines positive and negative readings, especially in the important chapters on "Reading Race" and "Gender and Sexuality," and ends by acknowledging the extensive existing scholarship and suggesting additional avenues of research and approaches.[17] Lister's work and Salamishah Tillet's *In Search of* The Color Purple*: The Story of An American Masterpiece* (2020) speak directly to the prominence of Walker's novel in contemporary literary criticism, feminist discourse, and critical theory. *The Color Purple* is undeniably a canonical text. The novel transmuted into a film three years after its publication and into a musical some twenty-two years after the novel first appeared. The musical premiered at Alliance Theatre in Atlanta in September 2004 and moved to Broadway in New York a year later in December 2005 and has since been revived. The novel lives on in the cinematic and stage adaptations, as well as in the musical cast recordings, that celebrate Celie's inspirational story. There has been a continuing reinvestment in the textual matters of gender, race, history, sociology, religion, and politics that Walker brought to the Black woman's contested body as a space of liberation in her remarkable text.

Taking full stock of the book's reception, however, there is also no avoiding the pain that Walker experienced when her novel first appeared. Just as several texts, such as Sapphire's *Push* (1996), inspired by her work and taking on difficult topics were coming into print, Walker had been revisiting *The Color Purple* during the same time frame. The result was her 1996 book, *The Same River Twice: Honoring the Difficult, A Meditation on Life, Spirit, Art, and the Making of the Film* The Color Purple *Ten Years Later*. In "Acknowledgments," she states: "A book like this, that takes a lingering look backward at a dangerous crossroad in one's life, requires the unequivocal support and love of many people."[18] Understanding her project as movement backward to a "dangerous" intersection, she incorporates her pain, frustrations, and disappointments at the time of the appearance of the novel and later the film. Much of her response to that period reveals that some of her hurt was still unresolved even though the text functions as an aspect of healing.

Walker has remained unequivocal in believing that *The Color Purple* is her gift to her own Black people. She arrived at this certainty after reflecting almost obsessively on the novel and its reception. "I belong to a people so wounded by betrayal, so hurt by misplacing their trust, that to offer a gift of love is often to risk one's life," she asserts in her preface.[19] In acknowledging a sense of having risked her life in presenting her novel, she underscores several painful realities about race in America and about the role of the artist, a role she had insisted upon from the very beginning of her career. She reiterates it throughout her reassessment: "Art is the mirror, perhaps the only one, in which we can see our true collective face. We must honor its sacred function. We must let art help us."[20] With that commitment to her art and her people, Walker recounts all the many wounds that she suffered in the years following the publication of her most celebrated work: her undiagnosed illness with Lyme disease, her mother's stroke and death, her break with partner Robert Allen, the negative letters and attacks on her novel, and her unused film script for Steven Spielberg and Quincy Jones, who scored the music. She charts her progress to recovery and her acceptance of therapy, which she would put to greater use in later novels.

The epigraph introducing the title chapter, "The River: Honoring the Difficult," is a return to Camus, who figured prominently in her earlier texts: "To create today is to create dangerously. Any publication is an act, and that act exposes one to the passions of an age that forgets nothing. Hence the question is not to find out if this is or is not prejudicial to art. The question, for all those who cannot live without art and what it signifies, is merely to find out how, among the police forces of so many ideologies . . . , the strange liberty of creation is possible." Taking from Camus the idea that liberty in creation is necessary for her as writer, Walker reflects on her own art and aesthetics in the context of the political and the personal. Just as *The Color Purple* encouraged women writers pushing the boundaries of subject matter and form, *The Same River Twice* with its bold conception of recognizing the danger of creation and of honoring the difficult within one's own era, inspired other Black creative writers to take stock of who they were and what they risked in speaking to the issues of their age. Camus's words that Walker pulled to the forefront sparked Edwidge Danticat to entitle her book *Create Dangerously: The Immigrant Artist at Work* (2010). Danticat's text began as her Toni Morrison lecture at Princeton University; there she explored what Walker had charted in revisiting *The Color Purple.* These inspirational aspects of Walker's writing and her approach to the political implications of creativity have been one of her major contributions to American letters.

In fact, among her published essays, letters, and journal entries supporting the achievements of other writers, politicians, public figures, mentors, or friends is a tribute offered to Danticat, "Edwidge, my younger sister, *couraj, ma chérie*," in which Walker praises Danticat's writing as "so pure and grounded and wise . . . the quiet stream flowing in the background of the present chaos and noise in Haiti," and celebrates her "exquisite, word-perfect" *Brother, I'm Dying* (2007). "A writer's heart, a poet's heart, an artist's heart, a musician's heart is always breaking," Walker knowingly observes, "It is through that broken window that we see the world, more mysterious, beloved, insane, and precious for the sparkling and jagged edges of the smaller enclosure we have escaped. . . . Know the sturdy structure of words you have constructed about and for Haitians no earthquake can destroy. Your words will be part of the mortar that rejoins the soul and self-confidence of your people."[21]

Throughout *The Same River Twice*, Walker similarly interjects the positive aspects of her experiences that emerged because of the novel, and with a poet's eye, she makes the ebb and flow of water and the symbol of the river her entrance into acceptance and forbearance. As she states in the end:

> Like my mother who seemed to switch over to another mode of coping after her body failed her, so that she remained radiant . . . I felt, after a time of dimness and exhaustion from what seemed like utter meanness of spirit, racism, sexism, homophobia, hypocrisy and craziness, lifted up by an inner spiritual reserve that I hadn't been sure I had: the assurance that life is grand. . . . That suffering has a use. . . . that I deeply love courage and creativity and the boldness to try something new, all of which I experienced among the collective who created our film. That even to attempt to respectfully encounter 'the other' is a sacred act, and leads to and through the labyrinth. To the river. Possibly to healing. A 'special effect' of the soul.[22]

With those words, Walker puts to rest as best she can the anguish she had experienced with the reception of *The Color Purple* and the debilitating onslaught that followed, and she embraces the joy in love, creativity, and healing after that anguish.

Given her attentive gaze on her mother and her inspiration even as she neared death, it is not surprising that Alice *Malsenior* Walker on her fiftieth birthday (February 9, 1994) changed her middle name from that of her mother's sister to "Tallulah-Kate" in honor of her mother, Minnie Tallulah Grant Walker, and her paternal grandmother, Kate Nelson Walker.[23] Her mother's death on September 10, 1993, had marked a closure and a beginning again for Walker. These momentous events all took place as she was recovering from the toll of *The Color Purple*.

The deep well of Walker's thinking on display in *The Same River Twice* had first captured attention in her essays in *In Search of Our Mothers' Gardens: Womanist Prose* (1983), which appeared shortly after *The Color Purple*. That collection earned her a reputation as a major feminist thinker and essayist, whose womanist prose reached across racial and regional divisions. The essays placed Walker among the significant American writers of social and political essays. Her profound and provocative attention to matters of art and aesthetics, politics and beliefs, women and gender, race and racism, came through in a fresh voice from a young Black woman, Southern by birth and upbringing. The role of the artist is especially prominent in essays such as "The Black Writer and the Southern Experience," "'But Yet and Still the Cotton Gin Kept on Working . . .'" and "The Unglamorous but Worthwhile Duties of the Black Revolutionary Artist, or of the Black Writer Who Simply Works and Writes." These essays make *In Search of Our Mothers' Gardens* a valuable handbook of Walker's conception of art and of herself as an artist, and stand out for the clarity of her unpacking and explaining her vision of art. In it, Walker's truth-telling and vulnerability in describing what constituted her own chosen work as a writer and, incidentally, the work of those within her purview or in proximity to her as models, separated her from the voices of major Black essayists during this period, including James Baldwin whose writings Walker admired without imitating.

A more conspicuous consideration of artistic and personal freedom followed Walker's extended definition of "womanist," as she identified her prose. Terming her essays "womanist" out of a sensitivity to an African American tradition of naming, Walker articulated a different way to embrace feminism and a freedom to define women's identity that was not ensnared in political conflicts associated with White women's domination of the feminist movement. It also referenced an individual element of freeing the self from social constraints. She defined womanist as "[a] black feminist or feminist of color," so specifically linking the term to feminism which often in the early 1980s applied to White women and not to Black women or other women of color. She gave the origins (from womanish, the opposite of girlish) and the applications (acting like a woman, courageous, willful, responsible, serious). At the same time, she provided the definition: "A woman who loves other women, sexually, and/or nonsexually," and with the added meaning of appreciating and preferring women's culture, including "women's emotional flexibility (values tears as natural counter of laughter), and women's strength." Walker's definitions did not exclude loving "individual men, sexually and/or nonsexually. Committed to survival and wholeness of entire people, male *and* female," and included being a "universalist," and capable as in Harriet Tubman's walking family and other slaves to freedom in Canada. Walker expanded her term in every possible direction without inhibiting its application or confining it within discursive limits.

Her claiming of "womanist" has had traction, and the term continues to be deployed by women, especially women of color, in critical analyses of race, class, and gender and in fields other than those associated with literary study. Over several generation of scholars, the word "womanism" in a variety of contexts appears in the titles or subtitles of numerous books, essays, and lectures, all acknowledging a debt to Walker even if interrogating her work. Much of the most sustained and impactful scholarship referencing "womanism" recurs among scholars and teachers of religious studies and Christian ethics. Katie G. Cannon, Renita Weems, Emilie M. Townes, Marcia Y. Riggs, and Traci C. West, for instance, are among the many religious scholars who adopted "womanist" as a way of approaching and theorizing their work.[24]

The landmark title essay "In Search of Our Mothers' Gardens," delivered as a talk nearly a decade before, had already become pivotal in Walker's thinking about the creative production of Black women, indeed women generally, whether in past or current generations. Walker accessed a way of seeing what women of any race, but especially Black women, have contributed to culture. She made the invisible, underappreciated, and unrecognized work of women in the domestic sphere and in the making of everyday beauty visible as art and creativity. She reformulated what Zora Neale Hurston identified in her essay "Characteristics of Negro Expression" as "the will to adorn," one of the important and identifiable aspects of African American expressive culture.

In writing about Black women's nontraditional arts, Walker simultaneously performed an act of recovery and a construction of meaning. She asked a searing question with far-reaching implications: "What did it mean for a black woman to be an artist in our grandmothers' and great-grandmothers' day?" Fully aware of the viciousness of racism and the omnipresence of sexism, Walker believed that the answer was "cruel enough to stop the blood," especially given the situational particulars of her query:

> Did you have a genius of a great-grandmother who died under some ignorant and depraved white overseer's lash? Or was she requested to bake biscuits for a lazy backwater tramp, when she cried out in her soul to paint watercolors of sunsets, or the rain falling on the green and peaceful pasture lands? Or was her body broken and forced to bear children (who were more often than not sold away from her) eight, ten, fifteen, twenty children—when her one joy was the thought of modeling figures of Rebellion in stone or clay?[25]

Walker's very questions function to reconstruct history as raced and gendered and to focus on the lives of Black, oppressed women with an indomitable drive to be creative.

Walker comprehended artistic production in relationship to the art of living fully. Recounting her own mother's "working day," laboring in the fields, tending the household, and raising children, she called attention to the unobserved that also constituted her mother's day: "feeding the creative spirit," her own and others. That aspect of her mother's life would go unseen by traditionalists looking for creativity only in high art, but for true discovery of creative artistic production, Walker maintained, one must look in places contrary to conventional assumptions about who produces art. That vision would result in redefining gendered and, by extension, racialized art in a contextualization of domestic geography that would demolish debilitating racist ideology and level hierarchies of creative significance. For Walker, creativity was directly manifest in vernacular landscapes, gardens, and especially quilts. She effectively visualized quilting, the sewing together of old pieces of fabric to form a new creation, as a symbol transmuted into experiences and representations of lives usually seen from the margins, if seen at all. In her utilization of the metaphor, the transmuted forms a whole new construction in which no center is complete without the edges and in which no marginalization of any of the pieces is possible.[26]

As illustration, Walker considered a priceless quilt depicting the Crucifixion and hanging in the Smithsonian Institution. She noticed that despite its unorthodox pattern and material, it stood out as the accomplishment "of a person of powerful imagination and deep spiritual feeling," who was unidentified but labeled as "an anonymous Black woman in Alabama, a hundred years ago." Walker recognized her hypothetically as a foremother artist, a grandmother "who left her mark in the only materials she could afford, and in the only medium her position in society allowed her to use."[27] She envisioned that relational inscription in the very art of the quilt as a signing of a creative racial self whose identity was not erased because her name is absent. Walker concludes,

"[O]ur mothers and grandmothers have, more often than not anonymously, handed on the creative spark, the seed of the flower they themselves never hoped to see: or like a sealed letter they could not plainly read."[28]

In reading the sealed letter as a message on gender, race, and art, Walker offered her essay as a metaphorical quilt whose pieced fragments are markers of individual and group creativity that cannot so easily be extricated or ignored. She suggested that social constructions of race not be used as a weapon against the anonymous Black woman artist or her progeny, and that no cultural ladder in a chain of creative human beings be used against the racial artist. In making legible the discursive expressiveness of creative wholeness in human life, she vocalized the necessity of understanding contributions made to art not only by Black women, who may not have followed or had access to the conventions of culture and art prevalent in majority culture, but also by women, people of color, immigrant and ethnic groups, working-class people, and all people traditionally marginalized in designations of art. She did, however, particularly valorize a matrilineal racial heritage in reading nontraditional arts as expressions of agency and empowerment.

The impulse to create art is what drives all the essays in *In Search of Our Mothers' Gardens*. Walker connects that impulse with the need to express oneself, to tell one's own story, to concretize one's own perception, and to create one's own order and meaning in a world often chaotic, random, and disorderly. Her striking, expressive grasp in the accessible essays solidifies her overarching conception of art and its place in lives, including her own, in a compelling and lasting discourse. Throughout the collection, Walker returns to the implications of her Georgia roots and Mississippi sojourn as a locus of meaning for her writing. Identification with a geographical space heatedly contested and divided racially in the 1960s and 1970s enables her assertion that revolutionary art can upend the domination of Black bodies by White supremacist regimes. She embraces her sense of belonging as a Black woman writer without ignoring the indignities and inequities of the segregated world. The identification she makes with everyday racial work is revolutionary: "*The real revolution is always concerned with the least glamorous stuff*. With raising the reading level from second grade to third. With simplifying history and writing it down (or reciting it) for the old folks. With helping illiterates fill out food-stamp forms. . . . The dull, frustrating work with our people is the work of the black revolutionary artist."[29]

Walker locates her revolutionary work in a variety of contexts but insists on her own status: "The artist . . . is the voice of the people, but she is also The People."[30] She includes essays that engage the work of prominent White Southern writers (Kate Chopin, Flannery O'Connor, William Faulkner), and she accesses their work in relation to her own. She compares her experience growing up poor in Georgia to what she encountered in a trip to Cuba. She uses her knowledge of the South as inspiration for her work, and she delves into the complexity of the region as a fertile site of memory, which for her meant engagement with the work of women, ordinary storytellers like her mother and published writers like Hurston, who from their various capacities and reservoirs exhibited their creativity. The kinship connection to Southern literature that Walker forged in these essays is one of her most enduring literary contributions. She comprehended how her writing, its models, and politics required a reassessment of an established way of designating a regional literature. Moreover, with her epigraph from the Southern Cherokee writer Marilou Awiakta's poem "Motheroot," she pushed the limits even further for diversity and racial inclusion in Southern literary studies.[31]

After the publication of *The Color Purple* and *In Search of Our Mothers' Gardens*, Walker remained a resident of California and acquired a house in Mexico, where she often works. Initially in the 1980s and early 1990s, she made frequent trips back to the South, but less so after her mother's death. In locating spatial contexts in Northern California and Mexico that complemented her sense of self and her art, Walker has continued to produce visionary prose and poetry but her relationship to the contemporary South has grown increasingly distant even when referential touchstones persist. She considers her move to the West one of the best decisions she ever made: "My spirit, which had felt so cramped on the East Coast, expanded fully, and I found as many presences to explore within my psyche as I was beginning to recognize in the world."[32]

Texts in the aftermath of *The Color Purple* explore issues of women's identity, sexuality, pleasure, freedom, and joy. Though African American men accused Walker of being a lesbian and anti-men in her explorations of intra-racial brutality and abuse of Black women and her treatment of a same-sex relationship between women, Walker was, for a long time following her divorce, in a heterosexual relationship with Robert Allen, whom she had first met when they were students in Atlanta. That partnership dissolved following his infidelity which she revealed in several of her commentaries and specifically in *The Same River Twice*. Since her personal revelations in that book, she has embraced a bisexual identity and has not shied away from acknowledging women partners.

Her second book of essays, *Living by the Word: Selected Essays, 1973–1987* (1988), confirmed Walker's evolving sense of personal freedom to be herself in the wider world. It also affirmed her visionary faith in the healing powers of the word and of human interconnection. In the "Preface," Walker reveals "a map" of her journey toward discoveries and reconnection with the planet she had known and loved, but that she feared no longer existed given the daily onslaught of death and despair in the news and the apparent human battering of the planet itself. Her conclusion, espoused in this book and others going forward, is one of resolution to respect and love the planet: "I spent many hours and days considering how it must be possible to exist, for the good of all, in what I believe is a new age of heightened global consciousness. . . . I found many people sitting still and thinking thoughts similar to my own. . . . I was taught by these people, by the art and the history of past cultures, by the elements, and by the trees flowers, and, most especially, by the animals."[33]

The materials in *Living by the Word* encompass journal entries and musings about family and friends interspersed with reflections on the natural world and its relationship to Walker's understanding of herself, human beings, and all of creation. One of the most revealing, from "In the Closet of the Soul," looks back to *The Color Purple* to reflect on that work, but the value of the essay lies in her attention to freedom as a concept for herself as artist and for every human being willing to grow and to heed the suffering emanating from the soul itself. She clarifies that a multitude of workers—Black, White, Native American, women, and men—have over time "provided in this culture the most inspiring directions for everyone's freedom," and that the world pays a price for closing off anyone or any part of self: "To cut anyone out of the psyche is to maim the personality, to suppress any part of the personality is to maim the soul."[34] Walker attempts to understand the factors at work in the attacks on her and to peel back the layers of her feelings to expose not only her wounds but also her healing and hope in "a generosity of heart and a tolerance of spirit" that she has witnessed in "our children, our next generation of rebels and poets."[35]

She moves to a formative experience of a peaceful sense of unity with the world in "Everything Is a Human Being." She recounts walking with a friend to try to hear what the earth was saying. Her vision, after lying down at the feet of old trees, revealed that the grove of conifers was suffering from the chemicals dumped into the earth, and that the trees were dying in great pain. Though she declares herself a lover of trees and innocent of inflicting pain on them, she realizes that she lives in a house made of wood, eats on a table made of wood, and sleeps in a bed made of wood, so that even her more modest uses of wood have implicated her in the suffering of the aging trees she encountered: "We are judged by our worst collective behavior . . . not by our singular best. The Earth holds us responsible for our crimes against it, not as individuals, but as a species."[36] That message imparts a sense of oneness to Walker's future writing.

The final essay in the collection, "The Universe Responds: Or, How I Learned We Can Have Peace on Earth," reiterates the message most prominent in her subsequent writings: "I know now [prayer] to be the active affirmation in the physical world of our inseparableness from the divine; and everything, *especially* the physical world is divine. War will stop when we no longer praise it. . . . Peace will come whenever it is sincerely invited. Love will overflow every sanctuary given it. Truth will grow where the fertilizer that nourishes it is also truth. Faith will be its own reward."[37] This fervent stance for achieving change in the physical world prioritizes prayer as a way to find peace, love, truth, and faith. "The Universe Responds" is a keystone for Walker's philosophical, spiritual, yet activist approach to the world in the decades since the 1980s, and it contextualizes her mission in those essays recording her travels to China, Bali, Jamaica, and other distant lands.

In stating the lessons she learned from animals, trees, and flowers and from her daughter Rebecca Walker and Robert Allen, Walker began to emphasize global peace and universal interconnection in *Horses Make a Landscape Look More Beautiful: Poems* (1984) and *Her Blue Body Everything We Know: Earthling Poems, 1965–1990* (1991). She meditates on her poetic oeuvre and rejuvenates her writing with a fresh awareness of the implications of the intersectionality her identity and subjectivity and its oneness with the earth. *Horses Make a Landscape Look More Beautiful* displays her commitment to poetic expression not only as "saving lives," as she had conceived of her poetry from the beginning, but now also as healing hearts. In "How Poems are Made/A Discredited View," for example, she concludes with the knowledge that poems are in fact made from places of fear, choice, loss, shame, laughter, gain, and "leftover love": "They are the tears / that season the smile."[38]

Walker follows that understanding of writing poetry with a series of poems on Mississippi, all entitled "Mississippi Winter" and numbered I through IV. These poems ruminate on Walker's experience of Mississippi as a changed place, so different from when she could have been killed for her movement work or her marriage. Written in a variation of the sonnet form, they are also brief missives to her estranged daughter, to remember her as she was, according to her own religious mother, "a sinner" questioning God, but wanting only to be happy: "a concept not understood before the age / of twenty-one. / She was not happy / with fences."[39] The sense of breaking with boundaries of religious dogma or familial dictates to find personal freedom and happiness is crucial to the poet's sense of herself as a writer who embraced much of the political as personal ideology of second-wave feminism in the 1960s and 1970s, and crucial as well to her explanatory messages to her daughter, a founder of third-wave feminism in the 1990s.

In the long poem "These Days," subtitled "*Some words for people I think of as friends*," Walker extols the basic goodness and love exhibited by a number of people for whom she believes the earth must be saved and saved ultimately for all from threats inner or outer, including ineffectual leaders and nuclear warfare. There are underlying life lessons that men and women must learn to save the earth for one another. She acknowledges a hard lesson that Gloria Steinem, one of the friends for whom the world must be saved, imparted: "Gloria made me aware of how much we lose by denying, / exiling or repressing parts of ourselves / So that other parts, / grotesque and finally lethal / may creep into that light / 'Women must seize the sources of reproduction,' she says, / knowing her Marx and her Sanger too."[40] Those words hit the dual note of holding on in hope while fighting against whatever fears, angers, institutions, or dogmas inhibit love and caring.

The poem-like dedication to the collection reaffirms the widening of Walker's markers of identity and of excepting an imagined positioning in a historical spectrum. The shift in emphasis is toward encompassing the mantra "Rest in Peace" as the still unfolding meaning of lives, her own and the "two who / slipped away / almost entirely": her maternal great-grandmother Tallulah (Grandmama Lula), who was part Cherokee and remembered for hair long enough to sit on; and her paternal great-great-grandfather who, though nameless but perhaps Anglo-Irish, was known for raping an eleven-year-old child who bore his son, her great-grandfather.[41] Walker embraces parts of herself and her familial heritage that are opaque and not easily traced. These aspects of difference in her background suggest her moving toward unforeseen ways of transgressing regulatory boundaries and countering racial exclusion that had been so much a part of existence in the segregated South. The process is related to her freeing herself from much of the expected and anticipated as she transitioned out of 1980s, but it would continue to ignite criticism.

Her dedicated mission involves identifying and decrying the ills in society. Hierarchies of power oppress the powerless until by miracle, action, or verbal design, the powerless transform by accessing and subverting the very resources that might otherwise be labeled liabilities. Walker particularly notices Southern segregation, American racism, family violence, macho expressionism, female reproduction, and more, while linking her evolving identity as a mature poet vigilant of social evils. In "Remember?," the invocation, she asks: "Remember me? / . . . . I am the dark / rotten-toothed girl / with the wounded eye / and the melted ear."[42] The inscription of self in the poem's autobiographical references conveys that the particles of a fully alive being are not merely aspects of health and happiness, but that sickness and despair also make up her litanies intoning worlds different from her archetypal South, worlds in which the dark, wounded girl becomes the woman, "Dark, / repaired, healed," the woman "with the healing eye / the ear that hears" and "offering two flowers / whose roots are twin / Justice and Hope."[43]

Walker's strongest poems may be those in which her history, heritage, and hope in the South collide, implode, and reverberate with pain, longing, and desire for changing the landscape of oppression delimiting her youth everywhere it may still linger in the wider world. "What is the point / of being artists / if we cannot save our life?" Walker asks in "Songless": "That is the cry / that wakes us / in our sleep. / Being happy is not the only / happiness."[44] Midway in the poem, she turns to an archetype that has, in fact, guided her own aesthetics and politics: that art saves lives. She locates it not in her homeplace South, but in the global South of revolutionary Nicaragua. She envisions "the whole government" in Nicaragua participating in writing, creating music and paintings that will save the government and, by means of making art, show its citizenry how to save their lives, because these creative acts "are not containers / void of food. / These are not decorations / on empty pots."[45]

In *Horses Make a Landscape Look More Beautiful*, Walker revisits one of the major ideological questions that first emerged in *Revolutionary Petunias* in the context of revolutionary struggle: "Would you kill for freedom?" That question preoccupying Walker reemerges in varying forms in much of her subsequent writing; for example, in *Meridian* it is posed both literally as "Would you kill for the revolution?" and metaphorically "Have you stolen anything?" (in terms of stealing away the life of Meridian's mother). Walker reformulates the question in the poem "Family Of": "Sometimes I feel so bad / I ask myself / Who in the world / Have I murdered?"[46] This question is the basis for an ongoing debate that Walker raises among individual characters and her own divergent humanistic ideals and revolutionary ideas. It is worth critical notice because as Walker moves toward her all-encompassing embrace of the earth and renunciation of all violence done to the earth and its inhabitants, she encounters the complex reality that revolutions have brought about change and that rejecting revolutionary ideas outright may imply the abandoning of the potential for change.

Her Blue Body Everything We Know: Earthling Poems, 1965–1990 Complete (1991) mainly contains poems from each of Walker's previously published poetry books. It demonstrates that, when collected, her poems work not merely individually but contextually together and progressively suggest that they work intertextually with her novels and essays. The short prose statement introducing "We Have a Beautiful Mother: Previously Uncollected Poems" is a major testimonial to the importance of poetry: "For most of the years, I have been writing poetry, I have envied musicians. Only musicians . . . were always at one with their creations. But lately I see that poetry, too is inseparable from the heart and soul from which it comes. . . . *Poetry, I have discovered, is always unexpected and always as faithful and honest as dreams.*"[47] This confession is tied to the section's dedication: "*In memory of my father / who, somber, / left me/ his smile. / (Proving magic survives/ even under patriarchy.).*"[48]

Remembering her father and a connection to "magic" is Walker's means of interrogating her writing life as she signals in two poems in the penultimate section extracted from *Horses Make a Landscape Look More Beautiful*: "Poem at Thirty-Nine" and "I Said to Poetry." "Poem at Thirty-Nine" revives a dead father with the refrain "How I miss my father"; the small lessons he taught consolidate into a grown daughter's admission: "Now I look and cook just like him: / . . . tossing this and that / into the pot / seasoning none of my life / the same way twice; happy to feed / whoever strays my way. / He would have grown / to admire / the woman I've become: cooking, writing, chopping wood, staring into the fire."[49] The reference to writing advances into a full dialogue with poetry in the poem that follows, "I Said to Poetry." "Poet" attests to being "finished" with poetry for many reasons, all of which "Poetry" demolishes, so that Poet and Poetry end with each declaring "Bullshit" to the other.[50] These two poems are directly connected to the dedication to Walker's father and to "My Heart Has Reopened to You," a brief essay that serves as the introduction to the poetry. Perhaps Walker's most important pronouncement about her work, the essay forecasts not only what she would attempt in the 1990s, but also what she would strive to achieve thereafter.

Subtitled "The Place Where I Was Born," the introduction begins with Walker's proclamation, "I am a displaced person."[51] The essay serves as seminal in Walker's ideology about writing in the latter part of her career. It follows the poet's looking out from her deck in Northern California to survey with awe and in peace the beauty of her surroundings, the valley and lake below, the mountains beyond, and the trees—redwoods, bays, and firs. From her high perch, she takes in this natural world and the outspread wings of turkey vultures and hawks that remind her of ancient Egyptian Africa. While this home place inspires her appreciation and love for "the beauty, the quiet, the cleanliness, the peace," it also makes her nostalgic for the land of her birth. She recites two relocations that resulted in her leaving her birthplace: first, when she moved at thirteen out of the country and into the town of Eatonton; and second, when at seventeen, she left for college in the city of Atlanta. With great emotion, she remembers a tree for having warmed her father on his walks to school and for becoming her childhood friend, whom she loved and grieved for when it was struck by lightning and reduced to firewood. She understands that her memory is not merely of gratitude for the tree's companionship, but also of regret for not having a similar emotional closeness with a family member. Walker relates her early love of nature and a particular tree, yet her account is more about loss than love: "As a child I assumed I would always have the middle Georgia landscape to live in. . . . It was not to be. The pain of racist oppression, and its consequence, economic impoverishment, drove me to the four corners of the earth in search of justice and peace, and work that affirmed my whole being. I have come to rest here, weary from travel, on a deck—not a southern front porch—overlooking another world."[52]

Walker's nostalgic looking back in such broad terms serves a purpose. By reflecting on her past and its present contours, she ventures into thinking about her work, the writing at hand, and what she may still be capable of producing as she ages and faces her own mortality. She admits: "I am content, and yet, I wonder what my life would have been if I had been able to stay at home?" She does not attempt to answer; instead, she bows to memories of early mornings in Georgia where the fogs were as magical as those in California primarily because: "the Southern fog of memory tramps my dark father, smiling and large, glowing with rootedness, and talking of hound dogs, biscuits and coons. And my equally rooted mother bustles around the corner of our house preparing to start a wash, the fire under the black wash pot extending a circle of warmth in which I, a grave-eyed child, stand."[53]

Immediately following as part of the essay is a long untitled poem that begins "O, landscape of my birth," a line that will repeat strategically unchanged throughout. It voices an unmistakable correspondence with Jean Toomer's Georgia in *Cane*. Walker's sentiment comes through in the line: "because you were so good to me as I grew / I could not bear to lose you." In expressing the great sorrow in her heart, she acknowledges that as she turns fifty, she wants to remember her childhood self "so lonely and so small," with a "crushed spirit and stricken heart" when she "ran in circles looking for a friend" after her dearest tree was cut down. In returning, she likens herself metaphorically to "the Aborigine or Bushperson or Cherokee / who braves everything / to stumble home to die / no matter what cowboys are herding cattle where the ancestors slept," so she will risk all in a determined return. "I return to you, my earliest love. / Weeping in recognition at the first trees / I ever saw, the first hills I ever climbed and rested my unbearable cares / upon, the first rivers I ever dreamed myself across." She ends with "O landscape of my birth / you have never been far from my heart. / It is *I* who have been far. / If you will take me back / know that I / Am yours."[54] This unabashed lament is a commitment to writing in remembrance of and return to the landscape of her birth that propels Walker toward the poems in "We Have a Beautiful Mother," which celebrate and interrogate her connections (true, tenuous, yet constant) to mother earth.

The poem evokes Jean Toomer's homage to his Southern roots in his Georgia song poem "Song of the Son." He writes in the first stanza "Pour O pour that parting soul in song, / O pour it in the sawdust glow of night, / Into the velvet pine-smoked air to-night. / And let the valley carry it along." Toomer then continues: "O land and soil, red soil, and sweet gum tree, / So scant of grass, so profligate of pines, / Now just before an epoch's sun declines / Thy son, in time, I have returned to thee."[55] His words, "O land and soil," reverberate in Walker's deliberate refrain "O landscape." In essence, Walker returns to what Toomer understood: that a world was passing but leaving him as its recipient. He sang his acceptance of the gift, a legacy from "O Negro slaves, dark purple ripened plums," who "before they striped the old tree bare" saved a single plum "for me, one seed becomes / An everlasting song, a singing tree, / Caroling softly souls of slavery, / What they were, and what they are to me." Figuratively, he anticipates what Walker also accepts in her ode song to the landscape of her youth: a gift from the past that is no longer an actuality but that can retain a viable presence and meaning in mind and memory and in the poet's vocation. Like Toomer, Walker cannot remain literally within that Georgia place, but she can commit to enfolding it symbolically within her writing, her poetry and her prose.

The fifteen poems vary in approach to the larger theme of the earth mother. "Some Thoughts I have on My Triple Blood," "Telling," and "Pagan," for example, think through autobiographical incidents that serve to produce intimate bodily connections, whereas "If There Was Any Justice" and "Beast" directly address what it means to create, to be an artist in paint or words in the world as it exists. Still other poems, such as "We Have a Map of the World," "Ndebelle," and "The Right to Life, What Can the White Man Say to the Black Woman?" confront political issues constantly besieging and lay wasting people of color globally, particularly in the African diaspora. In the final poems, "Armah October 12, 1990," "The Awakening," "A Woman Is not a Potted Plant," and "Winnie Mandela We Love You," Walker embraces love, peace, and freedom as the rights of all children of the earth mother whose wholistic natural body encompasses all in the fertile archetypal "We Have a Beautiful Mother." The last poem is a restatement of the commitment to poetry that introduced the uncollected poems; in "Once, Again," Walker references her very first poetry book and evokes Walt Whitman's "Song of Myself" from *Leaves of Grass*. In a four-line, compressed poem, she returns: "Once again simple / Once again childlike / The poem opening out/ into the grass."[56] *Her Blue Body Everything We Know* is at once a retrospective selection of all Walker's poems and an inventive announcement of what is to come.

The metaphysical concerns with remembering and retrospection as an impetus for creating texts with an acute awareness of the earth had already begun to surface in Walker's transformative fiction of the late 1980s and 1990s, especially *The Temple of My Familiar* (1989). Walker pursued a range of her creative concerns and historical parameters by making the African diaspora central to her representation of people of color and, in particular, Black women. While the South persists as a cultural backdrop for the international geography apparent in her representations of Africa, it is less influential in the relevant geographies she draws upon in California, Mexico, and Latin America. These accessible landscapes spring from memory and imagination, from reading and lived experience. *The Temple of My Familiar* is a major experimental fiction of the African diaspora and the identities produced in its dispersed locations over time. The long novel covers actual and invented ground in past and present journeys and affirms Walker's determination to push the limits of fictional forms beyond the expected or safe. She delves into different modes of creative expression dispatched in the service of storytelling, family formation, time travel, and shapeshifting.

The plot clusters around two parallel characters, Carlotta and Suwelo, whose lives have intersected in the past and will again late in the narrative present. The pair, both people of color, forward the thematic threads of history and feminism that expand outward to encompass Carlotta's and Suwelo's families and the knowledge necessary for healing and becoming whole. Racial history, political struggle, identity formation, and gender relations in their individual and larger familial stories all impact the narrative's approach to healing and well-being.

Healing emerges as a primary theme in the narrative progressions through multiple perspectives and characters who exhibit fractured states comparable to the form of the narrative. Talk or storytelling, associated with Jungian therapy, facilitates the discourse of healing. Walker incorporates two therapists in sessions with characters: Dr. Bernie Kesselbaum described as Suwelo's "shrink"—"a middle-aged Jewish man" who only listens; and Robin (or Alamo, the daughter of Esperanza or Hope) a Mexican analyst treating Fanny, Suwelo's ex-wife, through hypnosis. Although not extensive, these inclusions add to the larger, vast narrative of self-discovery, access to subconsciousness, and healing though revelatory, therapeutic talk and telling.

Talking through incidents, events, or entire past lives is a means of achieving healing and forwarding the narrative. Characters in need of healing acquire what they must have from stories. Time travelers Lissie and Hal share stories with Suwelo of the shaping of their identities into male and female on an island off the South Carolina coast where they were born. Their insights bear directly on Suwelo's struggle with his learned dominate masculinity, which has led to his separation from Fanny who questions his approach to sexuality and ways of being in the world. Carlotta's estranged husband Arveyda returns from traveling with her mother Zedé in South America to tell Carlotta the story of her mother's imprisonment and union with the Indian who was Carlott's father and whose love, beliefs, and indigenous culture sustained Zedé despite losing him. Fanny's African sister, Nzingha tells her about the life of Ola their rebel playwright father and her "Bush" mother a freedom fighter alongside Ola, who left her behind as he ascended in the postcolonial world but later reclaimed her in his plays.

Inextricably connected to discourses of healing in the text is the theme of fathers. Characters attempt with varying degrees of success to fill in the void or fissure left by a missing or unknown father. Olivia, Celie's biological daughter, who had never known her biological father, arrives for her reunion with family at the end of *The Color Purple*, pregnant with the child of an Olinka rebel whom she never expects to see again. Her daughter Fanny has little knowledge of even having a father until well into her adulthood when she is already suffering from fractures in personal beliefs that implode her marriage. Fanny's amazing history of communicating with human and animal spirits unfolds gradually but is central because her discovery that her father Ola is a celebrated Olinka rebel and playwright precipitates her travels to Africa and the plot engagement with an even larger cast of characters. She observes: "'I never dreamed I would so enjoy having a father. It is like having another interesting mind, somewhat similar to your own but strangely different, to rummage through.'"[57] Suwelo, her ex-husband, has little practical knowledge of his paternal heritage, but throughout the narrative receives history lessons about his father's family from Lissie and Hall, close associates of his great uncle Rafe. Only toward the end of the text does Suwelo picture his domineering father and fearful mother and can then visualize their deaths in a car wreck his father caused, and finally sees his resemblance to his father. His name from the Anglo-Saxon runes represents the "Sun" (Son, as Lissie calls him) and symbolizes cleansing, health, and wholeness among other attributes. Zedé has never revealed to her daughter Carlotta the harrowing story of her Indian father's horrific and brutal death in Central America. Arveyda knows he is somehow an Indian-descended Black person, but he knows nothing of his father's brief appearance in Indiana and unlikely union with a Black woman, Arveyda's mother, who perceived herself as racially different to the extent of changing her name and founding her own church, but who conveyed nothing of his father to Arveyda.

Walker establishes the necessity of accessing fathers and accepting stories of past lives, which artists make sentient, meaningful, cogent, and concrete in the production of art. Walker posits that the making of art, whether by weavers, painters, musicians, playwrights, photographer, filmmakers, or singers, emerges out of the suffering of people of color throughout the African diaspora, who seek ways to ameliorate the painful aspects of their existence and to create beauty in their worlds. She invents artists as the primary movers: Arveyda is a musician; Hal and Lissie are painters; and Ola is a playwright. She also returns to an artist character from *The Color Purple*, the singer Shug Avery who shares a home with Celie and often with an assortment of her musician friends visiting to participate in her church and partake of "The Gospel According to Shug," which she wrote with Celie's input. By the end of the novel, Ola's two daughters—Fanny the American and Nzingha the African—continue his legacy and unite as playwrights themselves. Fanny's calling shifts from college teacher and administrator to the less traditional art, massage therapy. Similarly, Suwelo turns from teaching American history to carpentry and woodworking, though he also plans to write the stories Lissie has shared of her many lives, and Carlotta has become a musician of bells and chimes after giving up teaching women's studies. All of these characters are connected to Africa and the African diaspora and find in art ways of repairing the wounds from the multiple assaults on bodies and minds as well as ways of coping with the residue of the shattered aspects of their relational and familial identities.

Categorizing himself as musician-artist, Arveyda articulates the concept of artist functioning in the text. While contemplating three ancient stones passed down from Carlotta's Indian father, Arveyda has an epiphany about artists that illuminates why he so easily falls in love: "Artists, he now understood, were simply messengers. On them fell the responsibility for uniting the world. An awesome task . . . His faith must be that the pain he brought to others and to himself—so poorly concealed in the information delivered—would lead not to destruction, but to transformation."[58] The ability of the artist to lead individuals out of pain and into transformation is the work Walker assigns to her artists as healers and to artmaking as therapeutic.

The Temple of My Familiar opens by framing Carlotta's family history in an unnamed old country of South America, where the artists are her mother and grandmother, skilled seamstresses named Zedé, who turn feathers into beautiful capes for musicians, dancers, and priests for traditional festivals. The magical quality of their lives and work of collecting colorful feathers from birds and sewing them into vestments changed abruptly with the outlawing of the festivals and the reduction of the priests to wanderers. The significance of their backstory unfolds piecemeal much later in one of the many myths of origins and goddesses that Walker weaves into her portrayal of the magical aspects of women who descend from the woman who made the earth and the women priests around her who adorned their bodies with beautiful found natural objects. A common denominator is remembering the personal and mythic past to navigate successfully the present and to mend the splintered parts of self.

That past, replete with mystic animals and goddesses, is relayed in multiple stories collected and told to cure the ills facing the listener.

Miss Lissie and Mr. Hal, the most important of the storytellers, function in relation to Suwelo, who changed his name from Louis Jr. to "the rune for wholeness," though he is in "fragments." Hal and Lissie connect him to his lost paternal past and to a larger racial family and human past as he settles his great uncle Rafe's estate in Baltimore and makes plans to use his inheritance to refocus his life after his marital breakup. His ex-wife Fanny has been shaped by the ideology of her grandmother Big Mama Celia and especially Mama Shug, who holds church in her own religion six times a year for an assortment of worshippers of trees, air, and God in many forms, so that Fanny was "a woman who periodically fell in love with spirits."[59] Suwelo's visit to Baltimore becomes an extensive stay with his uncle's friend Hal and his shape-shifting wife Miss Lissie as informants about his uncle's life and their shared background. Lissie is a magical Black woman who can recall her many past lives from thousands of years, as she discloses: "Lissie means 'the one who remembers everything.'"[60] In remembering, she also sees the previous lives of others, including Suwelo whom she recalls as a White man, which later sheds light on his problems with Fanny.

Lissie's elaborate memories form a major part of the many historical lessons imparted in the text. Her first precise and extended account of a prior life in an African village, her capture by slave traders enlisted by her father's brother, and her march to the sea with her mother, sisters, and brother precipitates a harrowing Middle Passage with explicit details of the physical violations, rapes, and deaths of the Africans onboard the ship, and her arrival on a plantation enslaved and pregnant. Lissie's graphic descriptions of this past life and many others fuel Walker's leitmotifs of history disclosures, especially the hidden aspects of evolution. Lissie remembers, for example, her harmonious existence as a little, hairless one (Pygmy) living peacefully with larger, furry gentle cousins (Gorillas) before aggressive humans decimate their way of life.

Lissie's letters in invisible ink to Suwelo after his departure for California and her tape-recorded memories continue the mysterious oneness communicated in remembered, conjoined animal and human lives. Lissie's and Hal's collaborative paintings provide furtive glimpses of the human and animal combined in conceptual oneness that Suwelo must decipher to unlock his future. The final image in the text is Lissie's painting of a lion. It requires close examination to detect the lion's red shoe and the climatic symbolism of Lissie's self-portrait as lion. Walker referenced those interconnections between the human and the animal in *The Temple of My Familiar* when she recalled a dream about "our collusion with the forces that suppress and colonize our spirituality," that gave her insight into the thematic core of women's subjectivity and relationship to animals that "in the outer world, symbolize women's inner spirit": "I saw that our essential 'familiar' is our own natural, untamed, 'wild' spirit and that its temple is the cosmos, that is, freedom."[61] She repeated that conception in a 1994 interview, but with a focus on herself: "What I was working with . . . was getting to the understanding for myself that your familiar is your own free spirit, and freedom is its temple."[62]

Textually freed in *The Temple of My Familiar*, Walker allows her imagination to roam over ever widening territories of creativity. She maintains that creative freedom in her next novel *Possessing the Secret of Joy* (1992), a modernist novel rendering the inventive reconstruction of a psyche severely divided and a body equally damaged. She focuses on African, African American, and European interconnections for her spatial and ideological framework which maintain an investment in storytelling and psychoanalytic healing. She structures the narrative around the incremental exposures of multiple narrators to aspects of one woman's life, that of Tashi Evelyn Johnson, who has splintered under the internal and external pressures of different cultures and conflicting expectations. The overarching narrative search is simultaneously for healing of wounds suffered culturally as much as individually and for understanding the burdens of tribal, clan, and nation-state affiliations as markers of identity. The halting, limited perspectives only allow the mental, spiritual, and physical manifestations of Tashi's pain to seep slowly into brief chapters that do not progress chronologically. Aspects of her pain emerge from the anguished consciousness of narrators who, though well intentioned, can neither alleviate her pain nor shelter themselves from it.

First portrayed in *The Color Purple* as a little African girl who becomes a playmate of Olivia and Adam, Celie's children adopted by the missionaries Samuel and Corinne, Tashi grows up to marry Adam and migrate to the United States for a new life. The specific elements comprising Tashi's life with the Olinka and friendship with Adam and Olivia were merely sketched in *The Color Purple*; neither Tashi nor Adam was fundamental to *The Temple of My Familiar*. Tashi becomes the central consciousness in *Possessing the Secret of Joy*, and Adam and Olivia serve as interlocutors whose interior monologues and letters advance information about Tashi's life and condition, as well as their relationship to her.

Walker extends the theme of healing and its connection to art in this novel, but she formalizes the role of art in healing by incorporating it directly into the Jungian analysis that Tashi, whose American name is Evelyn Johnson, experiences in moving through the stages of psychoanalysis: confession, elucidation, education, and transformation. In painting and drawing the sources of her trauma, Tashi recognizes and articulates the specific real-life configurations of her wounding. The novel proceeds from multiple viewpoints told in first-person monologues, reported dialogues, and written letters, but the primary narrator is Tashi, whose stream of consciousness, creates much of the power and tension. Her accounts of herself in process toward healing fracture into Tashi, Evelyn, Tashi-Evelyn, Evelyn-Tashi, Tashi-Evelyn-Mrs. Johnson, and finally Tashi Evelyn Johnson Soul. As chapter titles, the names signify the perspective from which she reveals her interiority, the dreams she has, and the stories she fashions while grappling with broken memories and raw wounds. She functions as Tashi, the Olinkan African, and as Evelyn, the American citizen, or as a fractured component of both. Tashi-Evelyn confesses to her psychoanalyst that her body left Africa, but her soul remained there. Her merging of the hyphenated identities in the final chapter signifies her unity and wholeness, but also her departure from the grounded physical body into the unconfined immaterial, which no longer is escapist but rather transcendent.

The depth of Tashi's pain unfolds in the opening words of the first monologue: "I did not realize for a long time that I was dead."[63] She speaks indirectly to her situation of being trapped in a deathlike vise through a parable of a beautiful panther who had a husband and a co-wife, but who, on the periphery of a love relationship between the other two, found herself lonely, unloved, and listening to her inner voice on how the sun, the moon, and the water loved her. In leaning over to kiss her reflection in the stream, she held "the kiss all the way to the bottom."[64] This fusion of the human and the animal is one of the signature moves that Walker makes in her work since the 1990s; snakes, fish, birds, lions, monkeys, and unusual hybrid creatures appear, for example, in *The Temple of My Familiar*. Tashi envisions animals as a way of accessing or talking about her experiences. From her early childhood she was able to invent stories and to imagine herself in relation to animals, including the leopard that attacked her mother and contributed to her premature birth. Oliva thinks that Tashi's way of expressing herself has been evasive, even as a child in talking to her mother through invented stories identifying herself with birds and flying creatures. This trait frustrates the therapists who had attempted in the past to help her unlock the trauma unsettling her and the individuals close to her who continue to help her in the present when she is jailed and facing execution in her African homeland. It leads to her confession at her trial for murder, as well as to the reader's difficulty in parsing the actual or truthful from her stories.

The primary story revealed in flashbacks to nonsequential points in Tashi's life is tragic. It presents her duality, madness, and malfunctioning in the world because of the trauma she experienced after seeking the Olinkan initiation rite as a young woman and observing her sister's death from that ritual as a young girl. Her beloved sister Dura bled to death when she was a child; however, Tashi did not understand that Dura died hemorrhaging from a female initiation until in her middle age. While undergoing psychotherapy with The Old Man Mzee (Carl Jung), she remembers witnessing her sister's screams and bleeding. Because Olivia had already revealed early on that Dura's death occurred on the same day the missionaries arrived and that Dura had undergone the rite of female circumcision, there is no element of surprise in Tashi's recovered memory. The point is the process by which she can remove the "rocks" from her throat and the "boulder" from her tongue so that she can acknowledge what she has suppressed throughout her life and especially in her American adulthood.

As a daughter of the ancient Olinkan people but associated closely with the children of the missionaries, Tashi evolves into a teenager who desires to be fully woman, African, and Olinkan, as she confesses to Raye, the African American psychoanalyst who takes over after Mzee's death. She wanted to heed the words of the one revered as "Our Leader" by adhering to the traditional practices of being bathed or cleaned in the initiation. That rite consisted of excising the clitoris and of infibulation in which the vagina is stitched almost completely closed. The removal of all or most of the external female genitalia, referred to as female circumcision or genital mutilation, was an accepted Olinkan cultural practice or rite of passage without which a woman was considered not socially integrated and unmarriageable, yet it left Tashi's physical body unable to perform easily normal functions such as urination, menstruation, or sexual intercourse. She also carried an odor from the buildup of fluids unable to escape her body, and she walked with a shuffle or slide from the inability to lift her feet. Moreover, her only child Benny suffered brain damage at birth due to her infibulation. Tashi's circumcision also precipitated mental harm that was as irreparable as the physical.

Her journey advances in a tight narrative that does not shy away from portraying the operation and its impact on her body and mind. Graphic and unflinching in short chapters, the descriptions make the enormity of Tashi's immediate ordeal and the extent of her subsequent suffering real. In the process, monologues, conversations, recollections, and letters fill in her biography and journey from a recurring group: Adam, her minister husband; Benny, her son; Olivia, her friend and sister-in-law; Lisette, Adam's French lover; Pierre, Lisette's and Adam's son; Mzee (Jung), her analyst and Lisette's uncle; and M'Lissa, her *tsunga* (circumciser). They join Tashi-Evelyn herself in casting the plot, along with additional characters who contribute revelations reported from dialogues, conversations, or testimonies: Raye, an African American woman psychoanalyst who introduces a race-gender element into her practice;

Amy Maxwell, a White woman from Louisiana who was circumcised as a child; Mbati, the young African woman who attended elderly M'Lissa and who accepts Tashi-Evelyn Johnson as a maternal figure; and extraneous characters who comment on the sociopolitical climate, such as Hartford, a young would-be medical student dying of AIDS.

When all the narrators and commentators are taken together, they contribute to Walker's most overtly political novel. Not only does she examine female genital mutilation, which is the controlling theme, but she also explores many other volatile political issues. She considers the negative results of African revolution in the aftermath of the overthrow of White colonial governing bodies. Using the fictional Olinkan country, she depicts hypocritical leaders who oppress and mislead their own people by keeping them ignorant and impoverished while taking full advantage of the country's wealth. She portrays the rampant corruption of newspaper journalists and court officials in an authoritarian state distributing great rewards and severe punishments. She considers how religion, whether tribal beliefs or Christian faiths, suppresses practitioners and deprives them of certain freedoms while elevating the necessity of suffering. She suggests that the inequitable, misogynistic treatment of women in contemporary societies is comparable to slavery, and that the ignoring of health crises affecting large populations of citizens who die in record numbers is as callous and intentional as overt genocide. These themes emerge, alongside mentions of rampant illiteracy, destructive consumerism, and more in the context of Tashi's journey toward healing.

Tashi's travel back to Africa in search of her circumciser occurs in flashbacks after she has already been placed on trial for the murder of M'Lissa, whom she considers a "madwoman," despite her own struggle with mental illness. Their encounters allow Tashi to hear a version of circumcision from a practitioner who has become revered as Mother M'Lissa, an Olinkan icon, but who calls Tashi a fool for not seeing the reality of the absence of women in the rebel Mbele camp where she was circumcised. M'Lissa is complicit in multiple deceptions involving traditional practices elevated by the government. From her own childhood experience, she is aware of the harm the circumcision ritual perpetrates. Her *tsunga* mother's futile attempt to protect her by administering only a partial excision resulted in others pushing to complete it and the severing of a tendon causing M'Lissa's permanent limp. She also reveals troubling details about Tashi's mother Nafa (Catherine) and Dura's death that may or may not be true, but that cause Tashi's reconsideration of her assumptions. Tashi comes to pronounce the "cruelty of truth" that her mother "had just sunk into her role of 'She Who Prepares the Lambs for Slaughter.'"[65] Tashi believes that being able to speak this truth might save Africans: "If we do not, Africa may well be depopulated of black people in our grandchildren's lifetime, and the worldwide suffering of our children will continue to be our curse."[66] Articulating this truth, however, does not alter her determination to avenge her sister's death and her own mutilation at the hands of M'Lissa. She remembers being admonished as a child not to cry for her sister. An underlying thematic message expressed by the African American missionaries observing Tashi's crying on the day of their arrival is that crying children must not be ignored but given attention to ease their suffering. That message is one that Pierre (Adam's son with the French feminist and educator Lisette) understands in the context of Tashi's remaining trapped in her crying childhood self.

By means of Pierre, Walker introduces several ideas about ancient civilizations, cultural practices, gender designations, and human sexuality that he connects to Tashi's condition. Pierre describes himself as bisexual and the only girl he ever loved as pansexual. He depicts the girl, a fellow Berkeley student from Hawaii, named Queen Anne for the wild flower and not for the African Queen Anne Nzingha, as experiencing an orgasm riding a horse or sitting on a rock. According to Pierre: "She could experience orgasm doing almost anything," and having been brought up by earth worshipping pagan parents, she did not believe it was necessary to be with a man, "unless she wanted to have children."[67] Pierre considers Queen Anne's ability to have organism easily a way to "understand something about the insistence, among people in mutilating cultures, that a woman's vagina be tight. By force if necessary. If you think about being wanton, being loose, as being able to achieve organism easily."[68]

Pierre's words about Queen Anne echo Walker's own about presenting in *Possessing the Secret of Joy* "a pansexual person, someone who is turned on by waterfalls, and elephant rides, and horseback riding, and all of that." She continues: "I think sexuality is something that, like spirit, has been colonized. . . . It's hard to believe that people would limit themselves to men, or even to people. It's a world that is full of great sensuous experiences and . . . the more we learn, the more mysterious the universe is. There is nothing that is solid, . . . there *is* no hard copy. The universe is full of space, and full of movement, and full of flux, and full of change. That's the nature of what reality there is."[69] Although Queen Anne only appears in Pierre's brief description, pansexuality is a concept Walker envisioned as central to the novel and its exploration of the inhibiting of female sexuality and sexual pleasure. The idea is also key to her emphasis on human sexuality and freedom in this and all her novels following *The Color Purple*.

Much like Queen Anne's pansexuality, Pierre's bisexuality does not play a role in the plot as a whole. His character is significant, however, in taking up his mother's attempt to unravel Tashi's frightening nightmare of being trapped in a dark tower. Pierre traces her recurring, haunting dream to a myth of origin, or a creation myth, having to do with anthills and termites and the creator's initial effort to have sexual intercourse in the clay earth. An anthropologist, Pierre achieves what Tashi's many therapists and psychoanalysts could not: a plausible explanation of her dream. He vows that after her death he will continue his work locating the various origins of male and female gender identity and sexual pleasure.

Pierre's influential place in Tashi's final years and his fraternal bonding with Benny mark the distance Tashi has traveled in her acceptance of Pierre, whom she had brutally stoned upon his initial arrival from Harvard to attend Berkeley and be near his father after his mother's death. Tashi's violent act was premeditated because she had been collecting rocks from the time of his birth and had checked herself into a mental hospital during Lisette's annual visits to California. Pierre's revelations ultimately help Tashi to understand her nightmarish dream and to reconcile with the dead Lisette whom she had rebuffed in life. Tashi-Evelyn-Mrs. Johnson offers her penultimate disclosure as a letter to Lisette: "But if heaven is like Olinka or even like America, there is much to be anxious about. . . . I will want a friend there . . . someone who has seriously thought about me."[70] She believes they will meet because through Pierre, "to whom my suffering became a mystery into which he submerged himself, we have already met on earth"; moreover, he is a "gift" who "continues to untangle the threads of the mystery that kept me enmeshed."[71] Tashi-Evelyn admits that she had not paid attention to Lisette before her death because she was unable "to comprehend death except as something that had already happened" to her, but now is no longer frightened of dying and signs the letter without the hyphens in the chapter title: "Tashi Evelyn Johnson / Reborn, soon to be Deceased."[72]

Tashi's journey ends in her execution, but it is a transformative, triumphant death in which she flies free of pain but leaves trace markers of her struggle against female genital mutilation in her country. Olinkan women holding their "red-beribboned" swaddled babies line the streets, and as she passes on her way to the firing squad, they lift up little girl babies, exposing their naked bottoms in a "protest and celebration the men threatening them do not even recognize." Even more of an affront to the oppressive regime and its illiterate soldiers policing the execution, Mbati, Adam, Olivia, Raye, Benny, and Pierre hold up a banner written in huge block letters: "RESISTANCE IS THE SECRET OF JOY!" Tashi witnesses it all: "There is a roar as if the world cracked open and I flew inside. I am no more. And satisfied."[73]

In "Looking for Jung: Writing *Possessing the Secret of Joy*," an essay in *Anything We Love Can Be Saved: A Writer's Activism* (1997) and comparable to the early search detailed in "Looking for Zora," Walker recounts her journey with Robert Allen from Amsterdam to Zurich to find Carl G. Jung's summer place on Lake Zurich. The brief trip in the spring of 1987 was remarkable not only for the flurry of Swiss people appearing almost magically to aid the travelers but also for the photograph that Allen took of Walker's hand fingering Jung's hand-carved alchemical stone once they arrived inside Jung's courtyard. That photograph of the stone, which "represents both transformation and transcendence," became the cover art for *Possessing the Secret of Joy* and for Walker's dawning realization that the novel she was to write would be "about the physical and especially the psychological devastation caused by female genital mutilation."[74] This journey with its whimsical serendipity concludes with Walker's somber admission: "[The] subject frankly frightened me. An unpopular story. Even a taboo one. An ancient story. A modern story. A story in which I would call on Jung's spirit to help me confront one of the most physically and psychologically destructive practices of our time . . . a practice that undermines the collective health and wholeness of great numbers of people."[75]

Her sense of mission in taking on the subject is apparent, but *Possessing the Secret of Joy* raised questions once again about Walker's representation of Africa. Nevertheless, her attention to what she considered detrimental practices impacting African women, including those who had migrated to other continents, would continue unabated. In *Warrior Marks: Female Genital Mutilation and the Sexual Blinding of Women* (1993), Walker and Pratibha Parmar exposed why female genital mutilation and female circumcision are unacceptable and harmful. They undertook a feminist political project despite being outsiders to the subject. Indeed, because they were not African and were condemning practices largely associated with Africa, they received harsh criticism as Western imperialists despite their inclusion of interviews with African women from Burkina Faso, Gambia, and Senegal, and African women living in the United States and England who had undergone clitoridectomy or female circumcision. The co-authors went against the strictures of cultural taboo and national identity to shed light on a practice that had been shrouded in secrecy and to empower women to resist and rethink all aspects of the operation and its cultural underpinnings. They focused attention on the dangers of the procedure, including harmful health repercussions. That publicity resulted in widespread acknowledgment of clitoridectomy as an unsafe practice and in the United Nations declaring female genital mutilation a violation of human rights.

The circulation of Pratibha Parmar's film, also entitled *Warrior Marks* (1993), which Walker produced, enabled more audiences to see women activists speaking out against female circumcision, women revealing the physical impact of the practice, and a woman who performed the operation. Widely distributed, their joint effort continues to ignite discussion. Although Walker has not persisted in the outright political activism of the film and the book, she has heralded that work as a major landmark in promoting feminist health and wellness care.

Walker continued conceptualizing an ethics of empathetic care and enacting a womanist socio-political consciousness possible for a writer in *Anything We Love Can Be Saved: A Writer's Activism* (1997), her volume recording her activism but also her joy in life and freedom. This collection of reflections on the first decades of her life and career formalized an aesthetics based on memory used in active engagement with the contemporary world. She substitutes a Muriel Rukeyser poem "The Place in the Ways" for an epigraph that honors her former teacher yet resonates with Walker's own intentions: "Having come to this place / I set out once again / on the dark and marvelous way / from where I began: / belief in the love of the world, / woman, spirit, and man."[76] The essays dwell on freely opening up for public purview some of the darker moments of Walker's life. "Sunniness and Shade: Twenty-five Years with the Woman who Made Me a Mother," for example, reflects back on the unrealized hurt she caused her daughter, which duplicated her own previously unacknowledged hurt by her busy mother. This realization is significant because Walker analyzes what being her free self has meant to those around her. She nevertheless declares that her anthem, sung to the tune of "Oh, Freedom," is "Joie de vivre, joie de vivre / Joie de vivre, over me / And before I'll be a slave / I'll be dancing on my grave / And go home / to my soul / and be free." This declaration of joy and freedom is one of the resounding aspects of Walker's writing throughout the 1990s. She accompanies it all with an acknowledgement of the personal costs that the work of resistance to cultural and gender norms requires.

The emphasis on health and wellness emerged with intensity in Alice Walker's work after *The Color Purple*. At once, the success of the novel freed her to pursue her own creative interests and hammered her with debilitating assaults. Success in delivering a remarkable literary text situated Walker for the freedom and independence she had articulated in her discourses during the middle phase of her career when she made plain the destiny of the true revolutionary writer: the artist free not only within her own self but within her environment and physical world. With two major texts, *The Color Purple* and *In Search of Our Mothers' Gardens*, she achieved precisely the platform for her work in the world. Yet, as her subsequent essays and poetry revealed, she suffered under the weight of the personal attacks. Her sustained efforts to heal, to achieve a healthy balance, and to overcome trauma moved her to find solutions in therapy and meditation. These evoked a closer association with nature and a greater reliance on her innermost self, including her capacity to dream and to identify spiritually with the wounds of the earth. *The Temple of My Familiar* and *Possessing the Secret of Joy*, her texts of healing, function in conjunction with Walker's recovery from personal pain and professional negativity. Neither disapproval nor rejection has dampened her womanist sense of mission as writer and artist. Each subsequent text in poetry and prose has forwarded her visionary construction of herself, her work, and the world; in turn, each places her within the realm of global awareness marking new geographic demarcations at the center of word and world.

CHAPTER 4

The World of the Word
Mediating Self

The world—the animals, including us humans—wants to be engaged in something entirely other, seeing and delighting in, the stark wonder of where we are: This place. This gift. This paradise.

—Alice Walker, *The World Will Follow Joy* (2015)

The elongated arc of Alice Walker's attention to justice, equality, and peace thickened as the twentieth century was coming to an end. With an increased sense of urgency in her messages, Walker moved to an elevated plane of spiritualism in her activism and her understanding of the force and potential of her writing. Fictional texts—such as *By the Light of My Father's Smile: A Story of Requited Love, Crossing Over, and the Sexual Healing of the Soul* (1998); *The Way Forward Is with a Broken Heart* (2000); and *Now Is the Time to Open Your Heart: A Novel* (2004)—turn toward introspection that casts again her autobiography and the concomitant biography of the contemporary world as coevals. Concurrently, she produced books of social and political essays and of topical and philosophical poetry. She acknowledged that this work has much to do with the state of the world and the condition of the earth, as well as with her fluid way of interconnecting all. The emphatic titles she has given her work tell the truth of her convictions and aesthetic vision. Her poetry book titles speak to multiple but convergent concerns: *Absolute Trust in the Goodness of the Earth: New Poems* (2003); *A Poem Traveled Down My Arm: Poems and Drawings* (2003); *Hard Times Require Furious Dancing: New Poems* (2010); *The World Will Follow Joy: Turning Madness into Flowers* (2015); and *Taking the Arrow Out of the Heart, Poems* (2018). Similarly, her titles for her essay collections leave little doubt about the urgency of her thematic messages: *Sent by the Earth: A Message from the Grandmother Spirit After the Bombing of the World Trade Center and the Pentagon* (2001); *We Are the Ones We Have Been Waiting For: Inner Light in a Time of Darkness* (2006); *Overcoming Speechlessness: A Poet Encounters the Horror in Rwanda, Eastern Congo, and Palestine/Israel* (2010); and *The Cushion in the Road: Meditation and Wandering as the Whole World Awakens to be in Harm's Way* (2013). These titles also reflect her mimetic conception of art and its place of honor within a matrix of nature and a matrilineal heritage. No matter the specific, convergent content, the essay and the poem appear more frequently to be her preferred genres, even though she has not abandoned fiction.

The spaces that Walker identifies are both natural and infused with spiritual values, and the eye of Walker herself as poet-witness is consistent across the formats for the message. Her texts become her responses to the degradation of a world distorted by the divisions of racial segregation, gender discrimination, economic exploitation, class suppression, and their visible inequities in material and human conservatorship, in horrific landscapes of war and brutality, and in the injustice of extraordinary oppression rendered ordinary. One result has been that she is now often perceived as an outspoken activist and prolific writer but with critical attention to her creative writing relegated largely to her work from the earlier decades of her career.

Walker, nonetheless, continues to transform subjectivity into a verbal art that is transcendent and multiple in terms of identity, race, gender, sexuality, politics, and location. Her deployment of the word as not merely creative but importantly as also sacred has become increasingly apparent in her advocacy of world peace along with inner, spiritual peace and of environmental conservancy stemming from a love of all humanity and the whole world in its twenty-first-century transnational and global contexts. Her unwavering ability to see, to observe herself and the world, and her determination to tell the truth about her vision combine in unique political and spiritual awareness. Although politics and spirituality manifested themselves as concerns early on, the two have intensified and become inextricable in the years since the publication of *The Color Purple* in which the idea of finding "God" in the natural world appeared.

In seeing the negative and destructive aspects of oppression, misogyny, racism, and sexism ravaging the external world and registering their seepage into interior regions, Walker formulated her own brand of resistance. She first espoused resistance as "the secret of joy," in her 1992 novel, but since then she has expanded her view to include a determination to avoid doing harm to the world or to herself as a way of adding peace to joy. As a result, introspection and reflection have become the staples of her visionary approach to her own writing and to the larger world. Increasingly, Walker writes to bear witness to the harm that humans do to one another and to the earth. She gives testimony to what she has seen and understood about the human condition and its impact on the earth and global environments. In each new text, however, she envisions the transformation possible and that she continually posits as probable.

By the Light of My Father's Smile: A Story of Requited Love, Crossing Over, and the Sexual Healing of the Soul (1998) is Walker's narrative of the repair that is possible for damaged human life, but it is also her excursion into an unabashed celebration of women's sexuality. It demonstrates her recent tendency to use allegory and parable to convey her messages. Given her expressed desire to tease out hidden or unobserved (and sometimes surprising) connections in the ordinary experience of living, it seems obvious that Walker would take on an explication of sexuality's place in spirituality. To illustrate, she focuses on the role fathers play in their daughters' sexual and spiritual development and their emotional and psychological maturation. She includes an epigraph of her own words to emphasize a dominate aspect of her text: "The reason people and angels hover around human sexuality is because it is a light source that has been kept in the dark."

The novel casts light and wonder on Walker's preoccupation with death and the dead. She has often veered toward embedded memories of older relatives and ancestors who have passed on, or "crossed over" as alluded to in the subtitle. At other times, as in her returns to the significance of the revolutionary 1960s and 1970s, she has emphasized those lost to death and martyrdom. Death and dying are frequent themes in her earliest poetry and prose, but in her work from the end of the 1980s onward, death stands out as a major component of her vision, particularly in *The Temple of My Familiar.* With *By the Light of My Father's Smile*, she no longer is content with having living characters remember their previous lives and deaths, rather she turns directly to meditations on mortality and to characters speaking from the dead. It is both a stark device suggesting inexorable truth telling and a blunt declaration of the dead's being always with the living. The unavoidable intermingling of the two concepts is recognizable in a father, an insider to a family's background and intimate history, and a would-be lover, an outsider from the family in race and tradition, who meet in death and interact with those they left behind.

The father's voice from the dead opens the narrative as he attempts to contact his daughter Susannah. He remembers that when she looked down on his face at his funeral, she did not cry or miss him but only felt that "something heavy and dark . . . had rolled away off her soul."[1] This view of his daughter's stoic passivity is quickly countered by his watching her and her Greek husband Petros make love that night. The daughter's sexual response to the father's death and the father's watching without shame establishes the two prongs of the storytelling. From this beginning, however, Walker complicates notions of the role of patriarchy and of heterosexuality with the father's voyeuristic presence constituting not a disciplining authoritative figure but a felt aspect, a third aura, in a husband and wife's sexual pleasure. The opening scenario is a conscious attempt to engage the reader in an unusual way of approaching the characters. This difference becomes clear after a barely perceptible yet lengthy time-lapse. Walker presents in stark, graphic detail the lovemaking of two women, not the heterosexual coupling the initial focus might imply, though the father is once again transmitting the scene. With the father's witnessing years later the passionate intercourse between Susannah and her lover Pauline, Walker launches another of the novel's major concerns: the freeing and liberating of the soul, which is also implied in the opening with "something heavy" rolling off Susannah's soul.

Although Walker has forgone representations of traditional African American families, she persists in relying on what she knows of those families for her fiction. Her black Robinsons in *By the Light of My Father's Smile* come across as placeless, despite place names from New York (Harlem and Sag Harbor) and North Carolina appearing as family background and referential spaces of their past. For a time, they live in Mexico, but thereafter their residential and workplaces seem vague, undifferentiated backdrops for a family unmoored even before the central splintering incident. That unmooring may be symbolized by the father's not having a given name or anything close to a personal, individualizing appellation throughout the novel, and by his description, articulated by his wife, as seeming not to have an identifiable center, and by his own assessment of his lack: "the *meness* of me was missing!"[2]

Walker transports the Black family to rural Mexico in the 1950s and to an invented territory occupied by the Mundo people. There she delves into history and culture using the dead father's voice to ventriloquize large segments of time and space. It is a delimited migration from the United States to the Sierra Madre and into a profound interaction with alternative cultures and people, which only one member of the family comprehends. It confirms that the world Walker sees in an unlimited sightedness is that same large encompassing one observable by Rebecca Grant Walker, who, as a toddler, stared into her mother's bluish scarred eye and saw a world there. In *By the Light of My Father's Smile*, the "I" consciousness, narrated voice is both opposed to the contradictory eye, the seeing and sightless orb or the sense and the senseless, and complemented by an omniscient, and other worldly, worldview, encompassing inner vision and visionary spirituality. The watchful eye of the dead father in "Angels," the opening chapter, looking at his daughter's life in Greece introduces the significance of sight as hindsight or looking back and limited inner or soul vision; at the same time, it establishes the connection between the relocation of the expected spatial markers obscuring affiliation and identity and the submerged ongoing searches for meaning in the external, physical world.

Sisters Susannah and Magdalena Robinson are the central characters. Children of anthropologists, they grow from the ages of four and six to their formative teenage years in an inaccessible area of Mexico where their parents located to study the Mundo, mixed-race descendants of Native people and Black people who had escaped slavery in North America and survived in their remote village as simply dark-skinned Mexicans. The Robinsons, though legitimately social scientists, but lacking the necessary research funding, pretended to be missionaries to receive an assignment to the Mundo before they die out. The mother Langley, an anthropologist with a suggestive convention-bending personality like Walker's literary ancestor Hurston, is oddly distinctive only in her penchant for sleeping in the nude and for enjoying sex with her husband. The family's uneventful existence among the Mundo turns dramatically when Magdalena (Maggie or Mac Doc to the family but Mad Dog to the Mundo), a high-spirited teenager who early on exhibited a fascination with zippers, worries her father with her rough, unfeminine ways. She listens to her father's complaint about her nickname and accepts his suggestion that at sixteen, she can choose her own name because they will be leaving the Sierra Madre and returning to New York. She decides on "June," and immediately her family accepts the name. What the father does not know is that June is an innately compatible spirit with the Mundo, and that since the age of fourteen, she been romantically involved with a Mundo boy Manuelito. When he discovers and confronts her, he beats her with a leather belt with silver discs that Manuelito had given her. Both her sister and her mother reject the father for taking a belt to his daughter and drawing blood.

This deterioration of family begins immediately, but it effects the daughters differently. Magdalena changes into a brooding figure who eats to compensate for her humiliation and lost love, but who still hums "Por la luz . . . por la luz," lines remembered from a Mundo song. Her extreme obesity hides the spirit that her father interrupted, but it does not mask a resentment even more bitter toward her sister. Susannah, who observed the beating through a keyhole, is seemingly implacable but suffers irrevocably from Magdalena's retreat from her and from her father's treatment of her sister, which manifests in Susannah's removing herself emotionally or physically from any relationship that insinuates dominance. Her unacknowledged loss is her unconditional love for her father which becomes evident in her ability to betray her own love, a betrayal the Mundo believe to be the greatest crime against oneself.

These early events unfold in short narratives much later in time from the perspectives of Susannah, Magdalena, and Langley, from the vantage point of the father and Manuelito after their deaths, and from the vision of Pauline, Susannah's lover. The voices from the dead observing the living give the text a surreal overlay, as the reunited father and Manuelito tell what they know from beyond the grave in response to crossing over. That process extends over many years and much of the text, but it intricately involves rituals and beliefs of the Mundo people and the lyrics from the Mundo song, "Por la luz . . . por la luz." These messages function as life lessons that can no longer assist the living but that can help them find peace in the afterlife. In a reversal of their earthbound life roles, Manuelito becomes the spirit guide–teacher and Mr. Robinson the reluctant but pliable spirit pupil.

The most illuminating of Manuelito's teaching reflects on the title of the novel and changes the meaning that has been implied throughout the narrative. The Mundo belief is that the crescent moon is a smile high in the night sky and that the moon, though "forever a woman," is not only connected to women and their menstrual cycles but also to men, "and for a little while becomes also a man," as a signal of good lovemaking to come when the moon is smiling down. Then the Mundo can practice complete lovemaking without interrupting ejaculation as a contraceptive measure. Manuelito informs Señor Robinson: "If you are in love, and going to meet your lover, to make love, you think of the moon as a father, happily looking down on you. For Mundo fathers are happy that their children, the girls as well as the boys, enjoy what your culture calls sex."[3] The concept is of the moon's smile lighting up the dark face is directed to men, or "the light of the smile" on the face of fathers. Rather than related only to the Robinson father, the title is instead correlated with a mythical conception of the unity and harmony between men, women, and nature, which allows for the blessing of sexuality as a natural part of the cycle of living. It is also a reflection on Mr. Robinson's repressive view of sex and his daughter's sexuality even while he himself enjoyed a sensual, passionate sex life with his wife. The information about the light of the moon arrives at the very moment when the spirit of the dead Magdalena riding Vado, Manuelito's horse, is approaching the men for her crossing over. The image carries the dual association of "sexual healing of the soul" and "requited love" from the novel's subtitle.

Manuelito and Magdalena have already reunited briefly before their deaths, but their meeting only emphasized the fracturing that had occurred in their youth. Magdalena, a successful college professor, ate her way into an extremely fat body with multiple piercings in her nose, chains on her nipples, a spike in her navel, and a cross on her vagina, all hiding her spiritual brokenness. Manuelito's whole body has been literally shattered in Vietnam and put back together with "baling wire," even his eyelids had been stitched together. Both bodies are maimed: one internally but with self-inflicted piercings as bodily manifestations of familial pain; the other externally, with visible signs of the damage war inflicted on his body. Yet, Magdalena and Manuelito recognized each other and attempted a physical reunion in love. In a perceptive reading of this poignant conjoining of two badly broken adults, Pamela B. June points out the correspondences between their two "punished and fragmented" physical bodies and the "parallel between the patriarchal, heteronormative violence" that Magdalena experiences and "the materialistic violence Manuelito encounters": "Magdalena's punishment and Manuelito's involvement in the war produce similar results, specifically a fragmented sexuality," so that their effort to find any remaining places where sexual feeling can be awakened becomes a "scene of fragmented sexuality brilliantly display[ing] the repercussions of embedded ideologies, which Magdalena's father and a militaristic American government perpetuate through violent actions."[4]

Manuelito functions as a pathway to spiritual transcendence, but there is simultaneously an emphasis on earthly clairvoyance to assist in the way forward. Walker introduces an elderly Greek dwarf Irene who has spent much of her life in isolation carrying for a church, tending its garden of lilies, and learning languages and tarot cards from her satellite television. Susannah, a novelist curious about everyone and everything, befriends Irene, who offers more than maternal friendship. An ancient spirit, Irene shares feminist allegories about Lilith, the first mother, who found Adam boring and set off on her own life. Her flower, the lily stems from the time when women could impregnate themselves without men. Irene traces the origin of the calla lily to the goddess Hathor, whose breast milk became the Milky Way and droplets the calla lilies. These mythical connections then reverberate in the given name of Susannah's lover, Lily Paul or Pauline.

Irene imparts the primordial wisdom gleaned from her inner resources, her adventurous mind, and her spiritual strength. Irene is an imaginative, queer, and magical creation rewarded in her old age with enormous wealth from a father, who raped and abandoned her mother. Despite having been shunned and confined for most of her life, Irene replaces her mental freedom with physical freedom. Embracing change, she embodies the freedom to roam the world, to be one with the Gypsies and the Pygmies in the best of their lifestyles and in the worst of their sufferings and that of all persecuted people. Irene's portrayal also contains a reminder that Walker from her earliest fiction has incorporated a queering of subjectivity that lends itself to queer studies analyses and a queers of color critique of nation-state ideology.

The text's cycle of recognitions and reconciliations is nearly complete with Magdalena's sudden death, a beer in one hand and a slice of chocolate cake in the other. It occurs before she can fully acknowledge what lies between her and her sister. Her insatiable hunger for fulfilment, acceptance, and love (from not merely her father but also her sister) follows her into death. A professor to the end, Magdalena leaves behind one final written, hectoring lecture to Susannah. For her part, Susannah realizes that she cannot remain trapped in the throes of "the rejecting power" she had discovered in herself as a child and that had permitted her manipulation by Magdalena, her "mangled psyche twin, stuck in her own pain."[5] This self-revelation allows Susannah to free herself from the "spiritual fracture" that had occurred when she witnessed her sister's beating and with it the rejection of her father. In an awakening to new implications of rejection, she refuses further reading of Magdalena's final letter. She reconciles her fractured self into a true adulthood, a grown up in charge of her whole life in her capacity as a novelist free to experience rather than observe life. This willing acceptance includes acknowledgement of the pain human beings suffer in the world and, on an identifiable level from interspersed textual mentions, the suffering of Black people from systemic racism and exploited labor, but especially the withdrawing of love from all marginalized human beings, such as the Gypsies and Pygmies in Irene's account or the meatpacking workers from Pauline's childhood. With that withholding of love comes the loss of access to one's humanity and the humanity of others. This understanding completes the cycle of life lessons on mortality that enables the living to cross over the river into the afterlife.

Susannah's own death occurs in old age at home in a dream-filled sleep after many years of success as a novelist. Hers is the kind of death that Walker described in "Longing to Die of Old Age": "One in which we will ripen and ripen further, as richly as fruit, and then fall slowly into the caring arms of our friends and other people we know. People who will remember the good days and the bad, the names of lovers and grandchildren, the time sorrow almost broke, the time loving friendships healed."[6] White-haired and very old, Susannah has lovers (Pauline and Anand, her brother-in-law), friends, and even little children present during "a final time, to touch her and to say good-bye" but also to pour oil on "Notebooks of all colors and sizes. Copies of her published books, videos, recordings of her reading."[7] Her long dead sister Magdalena arrives to join those watching Susannah die and to observe the ceremonial ritual surrounding Susannah's passing. That relational act forms the conclusion echoing the narrative's beginning, in which Susannah's father had observed her witnessing his death. The books and papers Susannah had written and all the contents of her house become part of her funeral pyre, which prompts Magdalena to wonder what will be left of her sister's legacy. That very question resonates with the concept of the death as not an ending but a continuum inherent in Manuelito's and Mr. Robinson's discussions. The answer from Susannah is that Magdalena's presence is her legacy. In a sense, Magdalena is witness to and purveyor of the crossing over. The flames from Susannah's burning body and house remind Magdalena of a poem: "When life descends into the pit / I must become my own candle / willingly burning myself / to light up the darkness around me."[8]

Those last words impart a poetic overlay reflecting on the entire text. Walker conveys her themes in an almost a fluid, rhythmic, incantation of a guiding light in the service of the symbolic, the ever-present flow of the mythical river to cross from life to death. Critics have not embraced *By the Light of My Father's Smile*, and the initial reviews were largely dismissive. The novel is challenging in its approach to detailing the destruction that an overarching patriarchy can cause in a family, and it specifically deconstructs how an assumption of cultural superiority leads Americans, in this case Black American anthropologists, to dismiss and devalue other cultures and their people. It imagines obviously fanciful sexual rituals that overreach any willing suspension of disbelief, yet it places some views of the afterlife in an approachable cultural context. It also is unflinching in its honest treatment of the difficult realities all couples face in attempting to shape a shared life. Walker is, for instance, equally unsparing in depicting ideological conflicts besetting both lesbian and heterosexual couples.

In a less developed thematic, Walker interrogates two distinct prongs of a writer's life in the two sisters both of whom are writers. It is tempting to read Susannah's words to Magdalena, her "mangled psychic twin," as a Walker self-reference after a long career of writing and before looking ahead to next stages. An analysis of the text in relation to Walker's own struggle with parts of herself and with the dynamics of her family and especially her father might well be fruitful. She has written, for example: "I'm positive my father never understood why I wrote. . . . what I regret most about my relationship with my father is that it did not improve until after his death. For a long time I felt so shut off from him that we were unable to talk. . . . These days I feel we are on good terms, spiritually (my dreams of him are deeply loving and comforting ones), and that we both understand our relationship was a casualty of exhaustion and circumstances."[9] This sense of father and daughter communicating after death is a main component of *By the Light of My Father's Smile*. In addition, Walker has marked succeeding birthdays from her forties on with an abundance of such self-reflexive ruminations that return to unresolved aspects of her childhood and family life as source material for her writing. In the final analysis, she delivers in *By the Light of My Father's Smile* a text worth further critical deconstruction.

Walker's insertion of a poem as a flame to enlighten darkness at the end of the novel suggests her methodology in her collection of poetry, *Absolute Trust in the Goodness of the Earth: New Poems* (2003). Written after the air attacks on the World Trade Center's twin towers and on the Pentagon, when so much of ordinary life seemed to have descended in darkness, the poems display Walker's becoming her own candle burning to light the dark. She makes the connection explicit in recalling a "feeling a deep sadness about the events and an incredible weariness that once again whatever questions had been raised were to be answered by war."[10] For her part, she rose each morning to write poems, despite having thought that she was finished writing poetry. Out of the darkness of September 11, 2001, poetry came: "Its requirements for existence remain mysterious. In its spontaneous, bare truthfulness, it bears a close relationship to song and prayer. . . . we might still learn to feel our way among and through shockingly unfamiliar and unexpected shadows. To discover and endure a time of sorrow, yes, but also of determination to survive and thrive, of inspiration and of poems."[11] This expression of the coming of poetry informs her work as poet, artist, and spiritual philosopher, committed to a twenty-first-century revival of a metaphysical health and wellbeing.

One of the dominant discourses in Walker's poetry is the idea of "the too full self," the spilling over into a reconciliation of self, the healing of the fractured physical body or mind, and beautifying it to reflect the reality of inner beauty or essence, the "soul" in both a Black linguistic sense and a philosophical sense. To release oneself from the physical prison that the body maimed by cultural conditional and social constructs can become requires self-examination, but also self-confrontation. Meditation is one path, but Walker turned in her fifties to another: "the study of plant allies, seeking to understand their wisdom and . . . aid to insightful living . . . the earth provides."[12] The experience of gathering with a shaman and a circle of women to drink "*ayuascha*," viewed by indigenous people as a holy, healing medicine and "the vine of the soul," enabled Walker to see "visions of how humans might live peacefully and more lovingly upon the earth."[13] For Walker, poetry is the experience of emotional purging, a release of emotion in expressions usually brief, but occasionally extended over several moods encapsulating one dominant idea. Her poems of the twenty-first century are a visionary discourse on the liberation of the writer and the woman from formal poetic expectations and societal constraints.

The concern in her poetry with saving the earth, identifying with the Earth Mother, and living harmoniously in peace with all living things surfaces in *Absolute Trust in the Goodness of the Earth*. Many of the issues raised in representing the crucial recognition of Mother Earth are spiritual as well as environmental; they emerge out of a Walker's experiences in Mexico, in the Amazon, and throughout the hemisphere interacting with indigenous people, learning about "Grandmother Ayuascha" and Maria Sabina, a healer and priestess of the sacred mushrooms, who "left a legacy of an amazing freedom, the foundation of which is absolute trust in the goodness of the earth; in its magic, in its love of us humans, in its ever present assistance the moment we give ourselves, unconditionally, into its wonder."[14] The result is a large collection of new poems that take the poet in multiple directions.

Walker writes explicitly of September 11 in "Falling Bodies," "Why The War You Have in Mind (Yours and Mine) Is Obsolete," and "I Was So Puzzled by the Attacks," and in the aftermath, she contemplates loss in personal terms in "Someone I Barely Knew," "Coming Back from Seeing Your People," and "The Same as Gold." She also rhapsodizes about the need for love (e.g., "I loved You So Much, "I Can Worship You," and "The Love of Bodies") and the tenderness of a loving sister in "Poem for Arneta Chapman on Her 33rd Birthday." She includes a long poem she wrote for an illustrated children's book, "Why War Is Never a Good Idea." War as a political and social ill infecting the world is a theme she interjects throughout, especially because war destroys the lives of innocent children. In "Projection," for instance, she imagines "That at the back / Of each human's eyeballs / Resides the image / Of a little child."[15] That child, she believes, is watching and trying to understand the destruction of whole groups of people by other people: Indians destroyed on their own land; Jews gassed in ovens; Arabs, Chinese, and on and on. Walker envisions the poem as a dialogue with her teaching the child to answer back to all rationales for destroying lives a simple refrain: "All children of the Earth are perfect," and in a concluding statement, she writes, "*This poem expands to hold almost all countries and nationalities: / When he says those Israelis & their / Concentration Camps / Those Americans & / Their Genocide / Those Africans & / Their holocausts / You still say: All the children / of the Earth / Are / Perfect.*"[16]

Even as she has moved into a wider social and diasporic identity, leaving behind in time but not memory the South of her youth, Walker invests her rich present with the poverty of that past. In "New House Moves," she writes: "I dreamed / Last night / That I had moved / Into a roomy new house. / How many new houses / Have I moved into? / . . . . When I was a child / We moved each year / My parents / Working hard / Making nothing / For themselves / Except decency / That went / To the bone." She dreams that she is always moving,

"Finding shacks / & rundown / Houses / Fixing them up / & then moving / On." But she realizes in a comparative insight: "Poverty never prepared me / For this wealth. / Or to live / In the houses / My parents / Stubbornly / Dreamed."[17] The dual focus on houses, domestic spaces connected to her own childhood in Georgia, and on mobility, movement to other spatial locations and movement into other class and wealth categories, mark much of the world poetry Walker has produced in recent years.

Repeatedly, there is a global focus emerging out of the specifics of her Southern roots and her regional acculturation as a Georgia sharecropper's daughter. In "My Ancestors' Earnings," for example, she writes: "For over a decade / My ancestors / Earned for me / Over a / Million dollars / A year." The irony, of course, is biting: "With our righteous loot / We bought / For me / Every house / We truly / Loved / Every car / & work / Of art in earlier times / (Laboring, laboring / Over uncleared fields / & kitchen floors / That had no end) / Drenched in / Sweat / We were / Denied."[18] These poems return full circle to her poverty-ridden youth, but their content now lies within a diasporic context of exploitation of laborers. Experiences that once remained locked inside the known and felt history of the rural South are now comparative and global in consciousness in these recent ruminations.

The natural world that Walker values and the ecological awareness she champions with spiritual ferocity emanate from her memory of a rural Georgia environment, yet flow from there through the many permeations of her experiences in Africa as a college student, in Mississippi as a young woman, in California as a mature author, and in all the places around the globe—Cuba, China, Palestine, Mexico, and more—that she has visited in her search for justice and equality on the common ground of Mother Earth and her sacred spaces. Casa Madre, her house in Mexico, is but one of the structural pieces of the built environment that she uses as a segue into the natural environment, the extension of the body itself, and into the places marked by the contradiction of oppositional action, polarity harking back to the segregated world of her youth and the lessons of survival earned there.

Toward the end of *Absolute Trust in the Goodness of the Earth* with its global vision and hemispheric architecture, Walker commingles Mississippi, where she spent part of her early adulthood under fire, and Bolivia, where Che Guevara was murdered, in an elegant long poem: "If they come to shoot you / and because you lived in / Mississippi / where so many / died / you know / they might: / Ask them first / to let you find / your hidden / picture / of / Che Guevara."[19] The poem memorializes the brave Che standing on a wounded leg to face the ignorant youth paid to execute him and erase his promise to return to build a school, but it also reflects on why it is not merely forgiveness

Che's illiterate assassin deserves, but prayers because he has been sent by those equally ignorant of the true needs of the people.

Mississippi fuses politically, intellectually, and emotionally with the death of the revolutionary in Bolivia, but also with the life of the Mexican mystic, Maria Sabina, to whom the section is dedicated. Before the concluding poem "Bring Me the Heart of Maria Sabina," Walker inserts a photograph of a shrine to Maria Sabina with a prose meditation on Maria Sabina's reliance on her "own intense intimacy with the divine" to speak to "all people, all workers, all healers, all lovers of earth, of this time."[20] The divine enshrined in the ethereal, spiritual Maria Sabina melds into advocacy for tangible human bravery in the final poem. Heart imagery elevates love, generosity, and kindness as the exemplary traits of the visionary Maria, but it also beats out a political call for "Americans of all / The Americas" to claim this kind of bold encompassing heart if only they dare to do so and thus follow the true guiding spirit of the hemisphere.[21]

A similar attention to understanding the complex relationship between human beings and their spatial and situational reality results in Walker's experimental fusions of fiction and autobiography in *The Way Forward Is with A Broken Heart* (2000). There she creates a self-referential context for her short stories by introducing them with a preface recalling personal details of her early life in "a magical marriage," but insisting that the stories that follow merge fiction and fact in a blending of her version of the past, as she put it, "in an era marked by deep sea-changes and transitions. Stories that are mostly fiction, but with a definite thread of having come out of a singular life."[22] Inhabiting a space of reflection and introspection, she evokes much of the character of the 1960s and her young womanhood, as well as of the tenor of her early years in Georgia.

The Way Forward Is with A Broken Heart is divided into six parts and an epilogue, "The Way Forward Is with a Broken Heart" with the dedication "To the Husband of my Youth" which echoes in greater length the short preface, "To My Young Husband," framing the first part. The text begins with "Memoir of a Marriage," written in epistolary form, addressed to "Beloved," and signed by Tatala. It moves progressively through "Beginning," "Finding Langston," "Burned Bridges," "Passion," "Handling It," and "The Ruin." It attempts to put back all the autobiographical pieces of a loving union, a shared life, and a breaking-apart into separate paths that remain entangled in memories and explanations. Walker reflects on her marriage and life in Mississippi during the Sixties with a White husband and eventually a baby, who is simply called "Our Child" throughout the vignettes. The memories take into account the novelty of their union, but also the shared joys, secrets, and pursuits that others in their sphere also experienced. "Memoir of a Marriage" performs the emotional work of returning and reassessing, and although a mixture of fact and fiction, it carries the burden of truth and, with it, acceptance of responsibility for all the endeavors, whether good or bad, and all the missteps, whether big or small.

Underlining the entire remembrance is the description of love and of being in love in a time of war yet holding on to a passion for life and each other. The last paragraphs of "The Ruin," for example, is a reckoning in which the death of Martin Luther King, Jr., reasserts both the love the couple felt for him, but also their disillusionment at being left without his promised land, only "this poor country, like the orphan of the universe. . . . only the moment we are in is promised, and that it, whatever it is, should always be 'the future' we want."[23] Walker conveys why she is remembering and reminding herself and her former husband of how they, an "unlikely us," shared love in vision and reality: "One day there will be, created out of all of us lovers, an American race—remember how Jean Toomer, whom we sometimes read to each other in Mississippi, was already talking about this American race, even in the Thirties?"[24] Recalling Toomer in the last reflection also reiterates Walker's dedication of the book "To the American race" and addresses the hope that has not died with King after all, because, as she asserts: "We will simply not let the writers of history claim we did not exist. Why should the killers of the world be 'the future' and not us?"[25]

Although it occurs within the initial section "To My Young Husband," "Kindred Spirits" is a recognizable short story. The characters bear some resembles to discernable outlines of Walker's own life, but they veer away from members of Walker's family. As fiction, the story makes peace with the past by accepting personal flaws without assigning blame. Its added significance, however, comes near the conclusion of the book in "The Brotherhood of the Saved," when a father and his artist daughter are at peace with her lesbianism that has divided the family.

In "Kindred spirits," the less deferential ways of the writer Rosa have offended the family. She chose, for example, travel to Cyprus over attending her grandfather's funeral and she is divorced from her husband. On the trip to Miami with her sister Barbara to visit the aunt who cared for her grandfather until his death, Rosa remembers aspects of her childhood but little about her own father. Looking at her grandfather's belongings that her aunt has saved for the sisters, she queries her aunt about her father. The response is swift: "'I don't want to find myself in anything you write. And you can just leave your daddy alone too.'"[26] Rosa recognizes two things: one, that she is helpless to stop recording all she saw ("This was her curse, never to be able to forget, but only to appear to forget. And then to record what she could not forget."); and two, that her grandfather "was a recorder with his eyes."[27] The shared identification continues with her wearing one of his fedora hats on the plane trip home. She makes peace with a masculine side of herself that had refused submission to the family's expectations of roles for women and unsettled her relatives. Her sister, who previously always stood up for her, had remained silent at her aunt's reprimand, but her look agreed that Rosa was "always snooping about the family's business and turning things about in her writing that made the family shudder."[28] Barbara, sitting next to her on the plane, places the grandfather's other fedora on her own head, takes Rosa's hand, and acknowledges her right to be the artist that she is.

The sequences of stories that follow all have the quality of a back-looking glance ("Orelia and John," "There Was A River," "Growing Out," and "This Is How It Happened") or a historical incursion ("Big Sister, Little Sister") in order to draw attention to the present, either to question it or to make sense of it, but all within the context of love, sexuality, and bonds, most often marital and familial. They also tend to return to the issue of the woman who is an artist, whether a writer, architect, or some other instantiation of the creative female.

Love is a conceptual framework for creative living, but it is not a reflexive thematic nod to love as a guiding principle. The fragility or strength of love and the variety or toll of expressions of love link the stories in a complex mesh of ideas that lead repeatedly and independently toward forgiveness or acceptance, and especially toward the loosening of prescribed gender roles for women and men. "Orelia and John" portrays a relationship in which a wife leads a husband to discover the simple pleasures of oiling each other's ashy bodies and cuddling without assigning masculine or feminine roles, and he heals her pain of being attracted to another man by taking her away to an island sanctuary, where "he tended her as carefully as though it were her back breaking instead of her heart."[29] Some of the stories deal with shifting sexual identities and the movement between heterosexual and bisexual attractions or between various types of partnerships and conjugal unions. Much of the overall atmosphere seems more wishful and dreamlike rather than reality based, as in "There Was A River." At times a fragmentary and loosely portrayed history of the sexual abuse enslaved women and girls suffered, as in "Uncle Loaf and Auntie Putt-Putt" and the section "Big Sister, Little Sister," seems calculated to reveal the personalities and choices of contemporary Black women whose families issue from that legacy. The multiple threads in the lives of the sisters in the present and the relatives in the past fall short of making a pattern, even though they do come together on a level of compatible acceptance or coexistence in emotional bonding in the second story in the section "Blaze." There, the primary focus ostensibly starts out as the separation of a Black girl from her White friend when they turned twelve. In "Blaze" and elsewhere remnants of the segregated South crop up but quickly disappear. The overall thematic impact of the stories is mutual affection, acceptance, and caring in gestures of handholding, sharing intimacies, or even eating watermelon together, as the Black father and his lesbian daughter do in defying stereotypes at the end of "The Brotherhood of the Saved."

The ironic gaze Walker casts on the questionable practices of a new religious institution in "The Brotherhood of the Saved" is quite different from her genuine embrace of ancient religious beliefs and their contemporary practitioners in *Now Is the Time to Open Your Heart* (2004). There she combines the wisdom of the Earth Mother with the philosophical search of her earlier character Meridian Hill. Just as Hurston reappears through the decades in Walker's voice and stylistics, Meridian reverberates in Walker's thinking and in her subsequent writing, especially her poetry and fiction after the turn into the twenty-first century. The core philosophy in *Meridian* (ascetic spiritualism, redemptive political consciousness, transcendence over suffering, and belief in catharsis) finds its way emphatically into *Now Is the Time to Open Your Heart*, which continues a hybrid form of fiction fused with autobiography. The year before the novel appeared, Walker said of herself: "I would like to become a wandering inspiration. . . . I had an image of myself showing up wherever people gathered to express their determination to have a future or to celebrate the present, speaking, reading, playing one of my very simple musical instruments, and just being around."[30] Those words in the 2003 "Preface" to *Absolute Trust in the Goodness of the Earth* also serve to introduce the spiritual journeying that Walker undertook for a year and that found its way into *Now Is the Time to Open Your Heart*. In her commentary, she replaces the fictional Meridian with her own wandering body and like Meridian commits to being a wanderer.

Walker even connects the meaning of her given name "Alice" and her surname "Walker" to the idea of the wanderer. She decodes her name based on Sojourner Truth, her "spirit helper," with whom she shares a "mystical" bent and concern with the rights of women and men: "Sojourner ('Walker'—in the sense of traveler, journeyer, wanderer) Truth (which 'Alice' means in Old Greek)."[31] In *Now Is the Time to Open Your Heart*, she further explores the connection between her own wandering and that of a wandering woman character by giving the protagonist her grandmother's name, Kate Nelson, and investing her with facets of Walker's own autobiography. Kate, like Walker herself and her fictional precursor Meridian, travels through physical places and spiritual realms in search of meaning and unity in her life. She ultimately arrives and exists in a space where love and peace abide.

Now Is the Time to Open Your Heart is another of Walker's fictional texts rethinking her familiar South and transfiguring her Southern family into characters on a broad global scale. Walker initiates this line of assessment by including an epigraph from Winnie Mandela, "So far, there is no law against dreaming," and then following it with a separate paragraph that is neither dedication nor epigraph that reads: "My father's mother was murdered when he was a boy. Before she married my grandfather, Henry Clay Walker, her name was Kate Nelson. This novel is a memorial to the psychic explorer she might have become. It also made clear to me in the writing how much I miss her. And have always missed her." Walker omits one autobiographical aspect: her 1994 renaming herself "Alice Tallulah-Kate Walker" after her mother and her grandmother Kate Nelson. The novel imagines a Kate Nelson set free as protagonist "Kate Talkingtree," whose original last name had been Nelson, in the manner suggested in the first of the epigraphs from Marlo Morgan's *Mutant Message Down Under*: "Everything in the universe has a purpose, There are no misfits, there are no freaks, there are no accident. There are only things we don't understand."

One of the things hard to understand is the ordinary occurrence of aging. Walker's underlying discourse is how to comprehend growing old. She had broached the idea in several poems in *Absolute Trust in the Goodness of the Earth*, for example, "Loss of Vitality" and "Until I Was Nearly Fifty," as well as in an entire section entitled "Aging," in which "Lying Quietly" conjures both aging aching bones and death, as standing on failing legs is a reminder that "upright / was / an idea / an interlude / an illusion / that we are / as always / on our way / to dust."[32] In her meditative exploration in her novel, the aging process is physical in its first noticeable incremental imprints on the body, but less discernable is its small interstices impacting the emotional security and mental wellbeing of whatever has been familiar and comfortable. The narrative follows Kate, a writer, and her lover Yolo, a painter, on separate journeys at a crucial point in their lives. Kate is on a spiritual quest after realizing that her meditation group is all White and she is at an impasse in Buddhism. Yearning for a better understanding of her whole self, particularly as she recognizes she is changing and growing older, Kate takes stock: "She had felt [her life] begin to shift beneath her feet. Or above her feet, because the change had started in her knees. In her fifty-seventh year they had . . . mysteriously, out of the blue begun to creak."[33] Such seemingly ordinary observations of aging precipitate Kate's search, especially after realizing that the younger Yolo, unlike the woman lover closer to her own age who preceded him, cannot empathize with her aging body. For Kate, the problem intensifies itself in her inability to write and her writing pens going dry. Burning her journals and even hundred-dollar bills to free herself does not offset her sensation of things coming to an end as in the dry riverbed of her dreams.

This crisis of personal and professional life sends her seeking answers and leaving Yolo behind. She sets out first to the Colorado River where she joins with other women in working through their experiences of aging while trying to look young. The conversations take Kate back through her many marriages to her first marriage and to an assessment of what she suffered from an abusive husband, but also to remembering why she had sworn off marrying again when she had agreed to live with Yolo. She returns home having emptied herself of her past and with a commitment to celibacy. Her spiritual quest remains incomplete, however, and she leaves for South America with a group of seekers who travel to a rain forest with Armando, a shaman practicing the "Grandmother's Medicine." Her journey duplicates one that Walker undertook to the Amazon, where she experienced the medicine of Grandmother Yagé, a medicine of sortings and endings, in a variety of rituals leading to finding peace and love.

The narrative shifts between Kate and Yolo who knows that he wants a life with Kate but is more laid back and less determined to initiate a quest for answers to their stalemate. Opting for a vacation to Hawaii, he stumbles onto answers to questions he had not anticipated posing. The unanticipated melds into fate when Yolo watches over the body of a boy who turns out to be the son of a former girlfriend, Alma, from his youth. Yolo remembers meeting her years before in New England when she danced Hula and he thought her name was Leilani because, as she said, no one expects a Hawaiian to be named Alma. Back then, he had confessed to her that his given name was Henry, but he had renamed himself Yolo, from the "Poewin Indian word . . . mean[ing] a place in the river where wild rushes grow."[34] Walker gives him the name of her grandfather (Henry Clay Walker who married her grandmother Kate Nelson), and associates him with the river of Kate's dreams. Yolo's providential reunion with Alma begins an extended tutorial in the history of the Hawaiian people.

Although he is Black, Yolo participates by invitation in a Hawaiian circle meeting where he learns about the Mahus. Descendants of an ancient people, the Mahus believed that their ancestors gave them the charge to live as women though they were born male, and that they are fortunate to be in Hawaii, part of the Polynesian world, because elsewhere Mahus have lost the knowledge of their identity and purpose on the planet. Their leader, Aunty Pearlua, fascinates Yolo who imagines filling canvases with paintings of her colorful circle meetings. Aunty recounts the time thousands of years ago when women ruled and when, long before the time of the fabled Queen Lil'uokanlai, "Mother rule was the dominant way of life . . . everywhere."[35] Aunty Pearlua preserves the mythical past and origins of the Mahus, but moreover carries on their traditions by teaching that until they can overthrow the enslavement of woman, they must live openly as women in the feminine part of their nature, which Mahus believe is the dominate one at birth for women and men, and in that role they must protect and care for children. Yolo accepts the idea of the loss of intimacy with Mother land and reignites aspect of himself he too has lost. Determined to follow Aunty Pearlua's teachings and those of her sister Aunty Alma about food and cleansing the body, he acknowledges the human body as the earth's temple, and resolves to give up any violations of it. Yolo returns home with a renewed link to nature and paints Kate's house sky blue, because as he announces to an enchanted Kate: "It's the color you felt at home in, in my canvases."[36] Yolo's search is indirect compared to Kate's, but his answers also emanate from becoming part of a place with ancient roots. With his search, Walker again turns to an ancient people and to beliefs that provide fictive myths of origin to deconstruct patriarchy, elevate matriarchy, and seek balance and realignment between the powers of men and women.

In Kate's parallel journey, there is much more vision work with other seekers and with Ayahuasca, the Grandmother medicine that causes hallucinations. Though Ayahuasca only initially induces visions for Kate, she can assist others and their guide Armando in their visions. Several are excursions into purging guilt for crimes men feel responsible for, including stealing land from Native Americans and flooding Black communities with crack cocaine. The women in the group, however, are trying to overcome personal traumas from rapes and sexual abuse. Working together, the group experiences expiation, forgiveness, and acceptance in a common close, loving bond with one another.

In sharing what happened during their separate travels, Kate and Yolo accept that "*Being of one mind.* That is peace. The material and the spiritual come together in smoke, and the connection becomes invisible again almost immediately. Peace is as fragile as that."[37] They also decide that they will marry, thereby ending some of their fears about their relationship. They invite all from their journeys to the wedding. Kate has already begun writing again with renewed energy about her experiences during the retreat and the impact of Grandmother's medicine and teachings. With her professional, spiritual, and emotional life restored, she begins the physical restoration of her prayer altar and offerings to Buddha. Issues of aging and marriage dissolve in these final preparations that end the novel tranquilly with the impending wedding, an earned peace, a mutual farewell to the past, and an accession to growing old together in a balanced enlightenment.

Walker often seeks balance and harmony in the world. She begins the meditations comprising *We Are the Ones We Have Been Waiting For: Inner Light in a Time of Darkness* (2006), for example, by calling up the counterweights of the present moment in her introduction: "*It is the worst of times. It is the best of times.*"[38] She repeats the actual lines from Charles Dickens's *A Tale of Two Cities* as one of her two epigraphs: "*It was the best of times, it was the worst of times. It was the age of wisdom, it was the age of foolishness. It was the epoch of belief, it was the epoch of incredulity. It was the season of light, it was the season of darkness.*"[39] Walker sees these conditions, contradictions, oppositions, and dualisms in the world today, but she champions light to disrupt darkness, save lives, and make lives whole.

Not coincidentally, then, the first of the book's epigraphs is from June Jordan, Walker's sister poet from her early years who modeled a way of being a Black woman writer in the contemporary world. Walker also uses a line from Jordan's "Poem for South African Women" as the title of her book, "*We are the ones we have been waiting for.*" Jordan appears by name repeatedly in Walker's comments about her work, beginning with the landmark *In Search of Our Mothers' Gardens* acknowledging her as a friend, reader, and listener.[40] Walker evokes Jordan for the revolutionary consciousness she exhibited when they cofounded their Black women writers' group. Linked as poets, social critics, political activists, and friends in the 1960s, the two were part of a growing cohort of African American women writers who produced a remarkable body of work in poetry and prose. Poets such as Jordan, Lucille Clifton, Sonia Sanchez, Jayne Cortez, and Audre Lorde engendered a feminist vision while empowering a distinctly African American view of life throughout the 1970s and 1980s when Walker herself emerged as a leading creative voice. The women of this generation were multitalented and several, like Walker, gained critical recognition in more than one genre. Sherley Anne Williams, for instance, received National Book Award nominations for both *The Peacock Poems* (1975) and *Dessa Rose* (1982), a feminist historical novel. Williams also produced the pathbreaking *Give Birth to Brightness: A Thematic Study of Neo-Black Literature* in 1972 that helped prepare the way for the groundswell of published Black critical thought in the next decade. Toni Morrison, who belonged to the Black women writers group Jordan and Walker founded, published a steady stream of major novels throughout the 1970s, including *The Bluest Eye* (1970), *Sula* (1973), and *Song of Solomon* (1977), but with the appearance of *Beloved* (1987), she quickly overshadowed her sister novelists in critical recognition. Awarded the Nobel Prize in Literature in 1993, Morrison would herself become beloved as the most revered Black writer to emerge from the generation of the 1960s and 1970s; though, like Walker, she would elicit some pushback from Black men writers who believed their work was being overlooked in favor of feminist and women's texts. Walker's place in a late twentieth-century genealogy of Black women writers is significant, because it reemphasizes her centrality to the recognized flowering of Black women writers, especially now in the twenty-first century when her political activism frequently overshadows her creative work.

Walker's recall of her friendship with June Jordan is crucial to understanding the power of the nascent Black feminism of the first decades of her career. According to Walker, Jordan "was a brilliant, fierce, radical, and frequently furious poet. We were friends for thirty years. Not once in that time did she step back from what was transpiring politically and morally in the world. . . . We were the kind of friends . . . who understood that we were forever on the side of the poor, the economically, the spiritually and politically oppressed, 'the wretched of the earth.' And on the side, too, of the revolutionaries, teachers and spiritual leaders who seek transformation of the world."[41] She links Jordan and herself as rebels, kindred spirits, who could find the humor in the absurd events happening around them and could share sisterly laughter as support against misguided assumptions about Black women writing and expressing their truths.[42] Cheryl A. Wall, who treats Walker and Jordan's friendship and mutual support throughout their careers in several essays, concludes that their writing "recorded their aspiration to live and write honorably" and verified their "twinned commitment to a redemptive art and politics."[43] Equally significant, Walker deploys her friendship with Jordan as "a model," she states, "of what can help us rebalance the world"; her "us" includes all those seeking to transform the world.[44]

The meditations comprising *We Are the Ones We Have Been Waiting For* are indeed redemptive aesthetics and adhere to the hybrid form that Walker has favored in more recent books. The difference here is in response to her reflections on Jordan as poet and her acknowledgment of Jordan's never backing away from the moral and political realities of the world. Rather than a melding of factual or autobiographical accounts with fictional stories, Walker delivers a rich infusion of poetry into her prose reckonings of today's difficult times. She includes graduation and commencement addresses and occasional talks that are infused with poems. In "All Praise to the Pause: The Universal Moment of Reflection," a 2002 commencement address for the California Institute of Integral Studies, she delivers a discourse on the various private and public calamities that can force an unexpected stoppage. She folds into her encouraging conception of reflection and pause a generous mix of her own previously published poems: "Until I was Nearly Fifty," "Loss of Vitality," "My Friend Yeshi," and "The Writer's Life"; each poem, she suggests, came after a pause that enabled an enlightenment not possible before.

In a 2000 graduation address at Agnes Scott College, she uses a similar pattern but includes only one long poem to illustrate her creative talk about witnessing several childbirths and coming to terms with the inequities some children will face because of the material circumstances into which they were born. Given devastating disparities, Walker concludes, "*I believe there should be a moratorium on the birth of children*"; her startling statement to a group of young women graduates, however, comes with the explanation: "That not one more child should be born on the planet until certain conditions are met. Perhaps the most important of these is that the several missing pounds of plutonium—the most deadly substance ever concocted by man; the inhalation of a single particle causes cancer—must be found."[45]

Understanding the shock value of her bold statement too well, she guides her address into a loving poem about the birth of the three children she had imagined in her remarks. She names them Hope, Joy, and Song, and in her long poem entitled "The Day You Are Born," she incorporates "beautiful beings" who love the newborns but tremble in fear of what might befall them and yet who come to know that the infants have arrived as a "force" to "Rearrange our world / To make it better / . . . . "to help heal the confusion / You left behind / So many lifetimes / Ago."[46] This fierceness of thought and poetic expression Jordan would well have understood. Walker's meditations filled with poetry render her political messages in truthful straight talk that can be easily comprehended.

In *Overcoming Speechlessness* (2010), subtitled "A Poet Encounters the Horror in Rwanda, Eastern Congo, and Palestine/Israel," Walker explicitly places herself and her poetic voice in the service of conveying controversial political messages. She deploys an epigraph from Buddha: "Three things cannot be hidden: The sun, the moon, and the truth." By citing Buddha, she establishes the interconnection between the natural world and truth, the physical and the abstract, that are not invisible. In the context of revealing truth, she recounts her 2006 trip to Rwanda and the eastern Congo after the genocide had finally come to light and shocked the world. She remembered writing a college thesis on the "Belgian" Congo, and discovering then the practice introduced by King Leopold of Belgium of cutting off the hands of enslaved Africans who did not satisfy their quota in collecting latex for the manufacture of tires.[47] Years later during the filming of her novel *The Color Purple*, Walker met a former doctor from the Congo working as an extra; he spoke of the tragedy of losing his home country and his people, all lost to the practices of the Firestone Corporation taking "millions of acres of land, 'leasing' it for pennies an acre, in perpetuity."[48]

The uncovering of truth did not end with his revelation. Instead, Walker revealed herself as witness to the intricate linkages of practices that initially seem unrelated to a politically aware and empathetic individual. She recalled "every car [she had] owned and all the tires that ran under them."[49] Her calculated move from the atrocities of the past in a global setting a continent away to the cars with rubber tires she had owned is a conscious evoking of her heightened sense of belonging in a changed space of history, one that linked her back not only to the Firestone rubber plantation with trees tended by Africans deprived of their land while tending that very land, but also to the horrific practices earlier of King Leopold and the Belgians and Germans who followed him in maiming and brutalizing Africans.

This configuration, the collapsing of space between herself and the abuses to human beings for the wellbeing of other human beings, is Walker at work in honoring culpability and overcoming speechlessness without exoneration. The space she sees herself occupying in interconnected chains of horrific events or inhumane practices deliberately marks her present state as complicated by and implicated in all that has gone before.

Near the end of her travels to Rwanda, Eastern Congo, and Palestine/Israel, for example, Walker reaches Gaza where she attends a celebration for International Women's Day and makes unexpected connections. The women talk about the reason for wearing a headscarf wrapped around the neck in the hot desert to prevent the loss of hydration from the back of the neck that leads to heatstroke, and a scarf on top of the head to shelter from the blazing sun, which can cause dizziness, nausea, or stroke. Walker feels she is learning about the origins of customs that to an outsider seem punitive. She listens to an account of a Palestinian woman whose building was being hit by Israeli rockets; as she was existing to safety she was singled out for the offence of not wearing a headscarf. Although the woman relates the incident only "with appropriate shrugs and grimaces of exasperation," Walker muses on the unthinking, rigid adherence and attributes it to "backwardness," that she suspects "explains [the] lack of progressive movement in afflicted societies, whether under siege or not."[50]

That experience leads to Walker's empathetic chapter, "It Feels Familiar," in which she remarks the similarity to her experience in the American South: "One of the triumphs of the civil rights movement is that when you travel through the South today you do not feel overwhelmed by a residue of grievance and hatred."[51] She attribute that to the lessons learned about "Gandhian nonviolence" and about creating "the beloved community," both of which she believes prevented the country from falling into "violent hatred between black and white," or "continuous spectacle, and suffering, of communities going up in flames," and for which she confesses she will always love Black and White Southerners.[52] She reaches this most generous estimation even while speaking to the Palestinian women about the reality of America's apartheid: the control, torment, and intimidation of Black people "in the most barbaric and merciless ways" by Whites who "owned and controlled all the resources and the land, in addition to the political, legal, and military apparatus," and whom she compared to the "Israelis who have cut down millions of trees planted by Arab Palestinians, stolen Palestinian water, even topsoil" and "bulldozed villages, houses and mosques," and attacked women and children. After the litany, Walker concludes: "What is happening here feels very familiar. . . . When something similar was happening to us in Mississippi, Georgia, Alabama, and Louisiana, . . . our parents taught us to think of the racists as we thought of any other disaster: to deal with that disaster as best we could, but not to attach to it by allowing ourselves to hate."[53] The response from one of the women is immediate: "We don't hate Israelis. . . . What we hate is being bombed, watching our little ones live in fear, burying them, being starved to death, and being driven from our land. We have this eternal crying out to the world to open its eyes and ears to the truth of what is happening, and being ignored. . . . If they stopped taking everything we have, including our lives we would hardly think about them at all."[54] Because she knows there is no answer, Walker offers none: "There is really nothing to say. Nothing to say to those who, back home in America, don't want to hear the news."[55] Yet, she can also evoke Audre Lorde's warning: "Our silence will not protect us."[56] It is her way of acknowledging complicity even while recognizing the enormity of issues she cannot resolve.

This is the burden Walker carries with her. She accepts responsibility for her complicity in the trauma, just as she had for driving her cars on rubber tires, but in the end, she can do nothing to alleviate the suffering or end the conflict. She understands only too well that her very exposition of the issues as she now envisages them will place her in jeopardy or mark her as naïve. In keeping with the essence of the spiritual aspect of her journeying and truth-telling, Walker includes the transcendent, apolitical lesson she has learned: "That to willfully harm anyone of us is to damage us all. That hatred of ourselves is the root cause of any harm done to others, others so like us! And that we are lucky to live at a time when all lies will be exposed, along with the relief of not having to serve them any longer."[57] She asserts her unshakable belief that the whole world is awakening to the global dangers to all posed by disasters, horrors, and genocides and that a collective humanity will find a voice to speak and ears to hear. The assertion she makes, no matter its ethical embrace of the best in all humanity, continues to place her in opposition to many entrenched political views of what constitutes the right side of history.

Part of what makes Walker's political meditations in prose or poetry so accessible is her willingness to display how ordinary experiences of being human have impacted her life and to translate what she has learned into relatable messages. In *Hard Times Require Furious Dancing: New Poems* (2010), she sets out what might seem an unlikely solution to dealing with a plethora of serious problems besetting the world and disturbing her. She lists them as: "losses, health concerns, and other challenges common to the human condition . . . in these times of war, poverty, environmental devastation, and greed that are quite beyond the most creative imagination."[58]

Within the losses are two that are deeply personal. She shares one, her daughter Rebecca's decision to remove herself and her son from Walker's life to protect herself from pain, in the poem "Lost": "My daughter / is lost / to me / but I am not / lost: / She says / freedom to her / means / having a loving / mother." But in her newfound optimism, Walker does not allow her loss to become debilitating, and asserts that she has always been a loving mother, and the Earth is her witness: "However: / Liberation / is in / the heart. . . . Freedom / to me / means / love itself/ may not / be / chained / & / that / I / at the very least / may own myself. "[59] Walker is reconciled to her daughter's accusation that she put her own freedom and career ahead of all else, including her child. She admits nevertheless the steep price she has paid in "Meeting You," a poem in which she imagines meeting her grandson: "Kept from / your birth / still I realize / we / will someday / meet. / Hello, you might/ begin the conversation. / Are you / my grandmother?" Or alternately, she thinks she might start with "Yo, cute boy / are you / my grandchild?" These tentative possibilities give way to the waves of positive thought permeating the entire collection: "Life / keeps us apart / now / for a reason / only it / knows: / Understanding / this / we have only / to endure / a separation / that / instantly / disappears / whenever you / or I / smell / a / flower."[60]

The second loss, the death of her sister Ruth (Annie Ruth Walker on December 27, 2008) is a major cause for the way forward she proposes: "I have matured into someone I never dreamed I would become: an unbridled optimist. . . . I have learned to dance. . . . It struck me one day that the marvelous moves African Americans are famous for on the dance floor came about because the dancers . . . were contorting away various knots of stress."[61] In honoring the role of dance in healing families including her own, Walker hired a hall and a band, and hosted a Thanksgiving for relatives and friends, basically to dance away grief and sorrow in, she said: "a spirited dance line that assured me that, though we have all encountered our share of grief and troubles, we can still hold the line of beauty, form, and beat—no small accomplishment in a world as challenging as this one."[62]

With its graceful, flowing drawings by Shiloh McCloud, *Hard Times Require Furious Dancing* is infectious with the human spirit of movement and witnessing from the very first poem, "Yes, I Know" with its emphatic assertion:

"I was born to grow / alongside my garden of plants, / poems / like this one."[63] It announces the short, often one-word lines, and the pared down language evoking Buddha-like emblematic, translucent thought. With simplicity and clarity like the Taoist poetics she admires, Walker moves through expressing ideas about dictators, grudges, rejection, teachers, death, duty, prayer, love, and much more, all in a changed world of possibility, as she entitles one of the memorable poems, "The World Has Changed," which is also the title of her book of conversations edited by Rudolph P. Byrd. Walker sustains her minimalist stylistic aesthetic through to the final poem, "Morning *for Kaleo*" (G. Kaleo Larson who has become her partner sharing her life, journey, and commitments): "& / so / we / lie / entwined / sun / on / our / eyes / knowing / our / heaven / & / sleeping / the / cat / between / us."[64]

Within the often-heady seriousness of Walker's writing, she has come to dance and exhibit a playful side, a sense of humor when reflecting on her life and work. Prior to *Hard Times Require Furious Dancing*, she had produced *A Poem Traveled Down My Arm: Poems and Drawings* (2003), a short poetry collection with her own free-hand, fanciful sketches of plants and animals that grew out of her humorous recognition of signing five hundred tip-in autograph sheets for *Absolute Trust in the Goodness of the Earth*. She admits that she had felt she had written all she could, but in autographing she was inspired to draw and have fun with the process. The result she reveals in the introduction "This is a Strange Book": "It is like a plant in one's garden whose seed was blown in by the wind."[65] It is a playful book in its whimsical combination of free verse and free spirit.

Walker conjures up her own guiding spirits in *The Chicken Chronicles: Sitting with the Angels Who Have Returned with My Memories: Glorious, Rufus, Gertrude Stein, Splendor, Hortensia, Agnes of God, the Gladyses, & Babe: A Memoir* (2011). The extended title makes Walker's playfulness transparent alongside her determination to live fully a different kind of life and practice. The epigraph accordingly is from Buddha: "Drink deeply. Live in serenity and joy." The emphasis on joy is her tribute to her angels and her better self. This memoir begins with Walker's first full cognition of chickens as she watched a hen and her brood cross a road in Bali. Though she knew chickens for eggs and Sunday dinner from her upbringing in the South, she had not ever before really thought about chickens. Years after sighting that hen, she began raising chickens, observing them, and naming them. These chickens with their names, including the first she named Gertrude Stein, inspired her reflections on her past and her present in the memoir fueled by her "girls" and what their antics have called up.

In raising chickens, Walker told Rudolph Byrd, she experienced a link with Proust for whom a Madeleine brought Paris back to him in *Remembrance of Things Past*: "With me, with my rural background in Georgia, it's chickens. As I write about my chickens . . . I find myself being led into a part of my memory that was suppressed when I was a child. I was injured. Like most children with injuries, I was so intensely involved with the change I had experienced—and continued to experience in the way other people now responded to me—that my mind couldn't pay attention to anything else. Years of my memory were erased or rather, submerged."[66] Recalling being transfixed by a hen and her chicks in Bali, she understood they represented a message: "I realized they were grace-launched messengers with ties to the unconscious sent to awaken me to the possibility of regaining some of what I had lost: my memory of many, many years of my childhood that I had completely forgotten."[67] The final sentence of this exchange with Byrd concludes *The World Has Changed: Conversations with Alice Walker* and is another revelation: "What is fascinating is that now I see that writing fiction has been a way for me to have a memory, though it is largely, well, fictional."[68]

Having memory is perhaps an accurate way to categorize Walker's body of fiction, but it seems an especially appropriate way to describe her work in the twenty-first century. Her writing insists on remembering past lives and histories of human beings in a multitude of scenarios that depend on Walker's lived experiences, her educational training, her literary preferences, her spiritual convictions, her political beliefs, and so forth, but also on her imagination, her ability to create fictional realms and dreamed realities. The list is long and amazingly varied for what her memory encompasses. *The Temple of My Familiar* may be the outstanding example of the capacious memory that Walker unleashes, but she dispatches an amazing storehouse of memory in her prose, particularly in the recent voices of "Mommy" reflecting in *The Chicken Chronicles* and "Alice" meditating in *The Cushion in the Road*, but obviously also in her poetry. Memory is doubly a gift Walker shares generously.

In *The World Will Follow Joy: Turning Madness into Flowers*, a 2015 volume of new poems, Walker deploys an added dimension possible for modern memory—photography. She does not explicitly engage Susan Sontag's conception of the political implication of the photography, that the photograph became a means of leveling all events and making them equal, but she does display an acceptance of the photograph as a seeing, voyeuristic relation to the world and to the word.[69] Walker uses photographs, small in reproduced size, to accompany the words. The size of the photos forces the reader to stop and focus on the tiny images, to attempt to discern not only what they are, but what they represent and how they relate to the poetry. The technique is an insistence on vision and on the magnification of ways of seeing. In the "Foreword," Walker lays out her claims: "We will turn our madness into flowers as a way of moving completely beyond all previous and current programming of how we must use the familiar line of submission and fear, following orders given us by miserable souls who . . . have managed to almost completely control us. We will discover something wonderful: that the world really does not enjoy following the dictates of sociopaths and psychopaths, those who treat the earth, our mother as if she is wrong, and must be constantly corrected, in as sadistic and domineering a way as that of a drunken husband who kills his wife."[70] Abuse of the earth, abuse by dictators, and abuse by husbands, all become visual evidence of equated madnesses that can be overcome by intentional sight and refocused seeing, as in looking at the tiny photographs throughout *The World Will Follow Joy*.

Walker begins the book with "What Makes the Dalai Lama Lovable?" and moves to ponder the question in short lines and terse stanzas reminiscent of the poetics of *Once*, her first book. In *The World Will Follow Joy*, however, she does not leave the answer open to a reader's thinking. Instead, she arrives at an answer through her ruminations on the "Cool" that is visible in the Dalai Lama's practices and beliefs. This "Cool," she asserts, is "A modern word / For / 'Divine.'"[71] The reality of his being lovable ultimately resides in his "holiness," his desire for everyone's health, happiness, and collective well-being.

From that playful beginning through various divine and physical journeys, *The World Will Follow Joy* is a visionary and spiritual travelogue of meditations that she dedicates, "*In loving memory of Rudolph Byrd so deeply missed and of the miracle that was our trust. And for G. Kaleo Larson / My working-class hero.*" Byrd, the editor of the conversations and interviews covering Walker's career from 1973 to 2009, and Larson, the compatriot sharing her political work and journeys, hold a special, inspirational place in her recent work. Her poems cover a multitude of occasional subjects: revisiting the idea of ordinary heroes ("Don't be like those who ask for everything, *For Queen Miriam (Makeba) who stood on swollen feet and sang her people to freedom*" and "Word reaches us, *For Congresswoman Gabrielle Giffords*"); prisoners ("Occupying Mumia's Cell") and plain folk ("Working Class Hero" and "Listening to Bedouins, Thinking of Bob [Marley]"); ruminating on writing ("Every Revolution Needs Fresh Poems"), flowers ("Turning Madness into Flowers #1" and "Peonies, *For Oprah Winfrey*"), the natural world of places ("Coming to Worship the 1,000-Year-Old Cherry Tree"), friends ("She, *For Gloria Steinem*" and "We Pay A Visit to those Who Play at Being Dead, *For Rudolph, Beverly, Henri, Alice, Garrett, Angel, Pratibha, Kiietti, Arbie*"), and animals, including her chickens ("Worms Won't Need a Menu, *For my 'girls'*"); encountering tyranny ("Sailing the Hot Streets of Athens, Greece" on heading to Gaza, "The tree of life has fallen, *For the departing dictator, in perpetuity*," and "The Foolishness of Captivity, *An Open Poem for Who the Shoe Fit*"); and reflecting on resilience ("Despair Is the Ground Bounced Back From" and "The answer is: Live Happily!, *To all my relations who have known this suffering / And for Miles Davis, just because, Happy New Year*"), aging ("What do I get for getting old? A Picture Story for the Curious! *(You supply the pictures!)*"), love ("The Ways of Water" and "Knowing You Might Someday Come, *For Kaleo*"), and womanism ("Democratic Womanism, *For Wangari Maathai*" and "Democratic Motherism").

All the poems take on either troublesome matters or devastating things that in Walker's mind's eye can be turned into flowers, offerings of peace, love, recognition, and importantly happiness. The volume ends with "Going Out to the Garden," a poem of planting seeds and seeing a gecko that the narrator sprays with cool water and imagines she is washing them both clean so the two are joined in pleasure and joy, "as I with so much happiness / played Goddess / to Gecko."[72] The elevation of the ordinary human woman into goddess comes from the simple act of kindness and affiliation. The divinity that the poet cited in the Dalai Lama, thus resides in every human being, especially in those who are willing to recognize their connection with the smallest of living creatures. A tiny photographic image of a gecko ends the poem and the volume.

Walker has become expert and incisive, yet inspirational in writing her own experiences, wanderings, travels, and inquiries into a global correspondence and hemispheric awareness that would change not merely racial boundaries and old paradigms, but also the very nature of her work itself. Her longest book of meditations, *The Cushion in the Road: Meditations and Wanderings as the Whole World Awakens to Being in Harm's Way* (2013), is a compilation that displays Walker's renewed commitment to creating ways to communicate her urgent messages in ever more uplifting and speculative ways. In keeping with the hemispheric awareness that has characterized her writing in the twenty-first century, she dedicates this work "*In honor of the lives of Celia Sánchez Manduley and Fidel Castro Ruz—revolutionaries, teachers, and spiritual guides who were, as well one of the most inspiring power couples of the twentieth century.*" From her first visit to Cuba in the 1970s when she met Fidel and throughout her career, Walker has appreciated Fidel and Che for the hope, learning, and light they brought to the Cuban people, but more recently she has written about Celia's contributions with gratitude and respect.

This book embodies memory but of a less distant life that reactivates the present one of meditative quiet. Walker recalls in the introduction: "[T]he years following my sixtieth birthday seemed to be about teaching me . . . that, yes, I could become like a child again and enjoy all the pleasures of wonder a child experiences, but I would have to attempt to maintain this joy in the vicissitudes of the actual world, as opposed to the meditative Universe I had created, with its calming, ever flowing fountain."[73] The result was her reawakening to her "wanderings," her travels to attend to and help heal the harmful troubles besetting humans and the world; however, Walker also acknowledged the dualism that also characterizes her understanding of herself: she is also a homebody whose life of meditation suits her. Her memory of sitting on a Georgia porch with her grandfather counting cars going by provided a solution that emerged in a dream: "There, in the middle of the long, perfectly straight highway with its slightly faded yellow centerline . . . sat my rose-colored meditation cushion. Directly on the yellow line, right in the middle of the road." That solution prompts her to declare: "I was born to wander and I was born to sit. To love home with a sometimes almost unbearable affection, but to be lured out into the world to see how it is doing, as my beloved larger home and paradise."[74] *The Cushion in the Road*, then, is the metaphoric declaration of Walker's beliefs about her place at home in a world close by and abroad.

To encompass the balance in her beliefs, she divides the book into "Witness," "Meditation," "Wandering," and "Solidarity." Within these four large sections, she includes a variety of expressions, including letters, journal entries, poems, and photographs. "Witness," the engaging section on Barack Obama, and the beginning of her renewed acceptance of travel, follows his nomination and election with hope and anticipation, and celebrates his work for health care and his Nobel Peace Prize, while questioning the use of torture under his watch and expressing disappointment about the war in Angola. These essays and letters, along with those in "Meditation," demonstrate Walker's full engagement with her home country and the political and cultural realities of a nation under its first Black president. "Wandering" and "Solidarity" best display Walker's commitment to the wider world and the plight of people around the globe, including women in Korea, children in African orphanages, Aung San Sui Kyi, Nawal El Saadawi, the officials of the Knesset in Israel, and the freedom riders of Palestine. With these writings, she addresses the necessity of peace, empathy, love, and friendship to counter aggression, hate, war, and oppression. Her messages remain consistent with the values and beliefs she has set forth with remarkable clarity for so many years.

Nagueyalti Warren has called Walker "a literary theologian," based on her published and unpublished writings and the directions, themes, and concerns recurring throughout her career.[75] The term is especially fitting considering the life-shaping meditations comprising *The Cushion in the Road*, in which Walker provides a practical faith in perceiving the relationship of divinity—God and Earth Mother—to the universe as she moves creatively between wanting to retreat into the inner sanctum of meditation or spiritual isolation from the ravages she witnesses in the world and needing to remain in that world as a seeing witness alert to the necessity of testifying and seeking remediation for what is occurring.

Walker's final message in *The Cushion in the Road* is forgiveness, which, writ large, is the healing idea in much of her work. Forgiveness, however, is a concept that Walker now applies to her own life's experiences and utterances. In "Encountering the Unknown Brazil," the meditative entry concluding *The Cushion in the Road*, dated April 25, 2012, Walker admits she knows little about Brazil, but despite that lack, she was able see there "something of the spirit and soul of the people considered 'lowest down,'" which, in turn, enabled her to recognize that she loved and admired them.[76] Part of her admission results from her review of her first three novels for her lecture to illuminate the similarity between the lives of Black Southerners and the people she encountered in Brazil: "We are intrinsically a hopeful people . . . we earned this attitude the same way many Brazilians did: we survived hundreds of years of brutal enslavement, exploitation, apartheid, and general soul and body assault."[77] This insightful connection is striking because Walker never delivered it or the lecture intended for the Brasilia Festival of the Book. Brasilia was, she discovered, a man-made and recent government center in the middle of a desert and not the "real" Brazil she had imagined in solidarity with its people.

In choosing to end her collection with this particular non-lecture demonstrates Walker's ability to meditate meaningfully on her ordinary experiences and life lessons. It is a methodology she engaged earlier with essays that were never delivered; for example, "Getting as Black as My Daddy: Thoughts on the Unhelpful Aspects of Destructive Criticism" dissects the ways some critics miss the spirit of the discoveries creative writers offer them. Walker ends on a combative note: "I realize as I write this that mentioning this unwritten essay is sneaky way of 'writing' it. And since I am aware of this, I might as well tell you. . . . I end the essay here, not telling you the particulars, as a demonstration of what, because of battering rather than constructive criticism, is sometimes lost."[78]

This lesson was that she and all human beings must forgive themselves for mistakes or missteps of judgment and learn to accept with grace what is offered rather than what is desired. The lesson of forgiving for lapses of vision is especially important to Walker in the meditations she shares. She instructs that gracefulness is another form of gratefulness for whatever comes to any individual, no matter what one has prepared for, desired, or expected. Her conclusion signifies her continuity in offering in word and thought an ethical, honest vision of how to live in the world, a global world that needs fearless, truthful voices, even when a different more ameliorating vision might be desired.

Walker's 2018 *Taking the Arrow Out of the Heart* reaches further into the internationalist aspects of her thinking and practice. All of the poems included have facing translations into Spanish by the Cuban writer and poet Manuel Garcia Verdecia, whom she met in 1985 at the Havana Book Fair. She calls him "the brother I am always expecting to find, no matter how foreign the land."[79] Despite having only seen him once after their initial meeting, Walker states, "We work together as if we share the same mother. Which of course we do."[80] With that nod to the Earth Mother and to the connections she sees among humans, Walker launches her most ambitious book of poetry as a dual language work extending her message to the broad readership she already has in the global world.

This book articulates her commitment to a transnational audience. The epigraph clarifies her intention: "If we want a better world, we have to make it ourselves." She reiterates in the introduction: "Here, as a poet, I intervene."[81] Declaring herself "a poet" while acknowledging her work as an activist, who understands that if something is to be done about the state of the world, she must take it upon herself to do it, in effect, intervening to make a better world. The poems do what Walker said so many years ago as she set out on her career as a writer, to make the world better, and she asserts that it is incumbent upon her as poet-activist to do precisely that. Her message begins with a dedication that recalls the arrow that pierces and the insistent removal: "*Remembering Coretta Scott King / generous and kind / brightly smiling; / happy. / Before the arrow struck*," and continues "*for all of us who have ever fallen: / who have removed the arrow / sometimes many times / and stood up / again.*" While these poems continue the trajectory begun long ago, they originate primarily out of 2015–2016, "a time of sadness and feelings of loss and despair": "Worse to face, as now, are the brutal murders of children, the deliberate starving and abusing of them. The callous trampling on their rights as human beings, however small, and the brutal indifference . . . of the grown-up world. Entwined with this is the abuse of the planet, the literal draining of her blood, the carving up for profit of her very flesh and bone."[82]

Walker's recognition of the interconnection between the abuse of human children and the abuse of the earth herself gives rise to her willingness to stand up just as individuals throughout history have done: "there are those of us humans who have stood up, wherever we could stand up, in defense of children, animals, the earth, and we have had ancestors before us who have done the same."[83] Walker identifies Muhammad Ali, "[t]hat fierce, indignant poet of words and fists," as an ancestor committed to standing up, and whose "courageous walk through a challenging life, and a battered but triumphant exit from it," inspired her initial title for the volume, "The Long Road Home."[84] Although she did not ultimately use that title, Walker paused to meditate on its continuing relevance to her work:

> I still like this idea—that to remain on that road 'home' to the truest self we can muster is a knockout in the ring of life. And to achieve, even to approach, or get on that road home! Maybe to actually get your whole self there . . . this would be bliss beyond imagining. For then we would surely join the immortals: those who laid out the path as best they could for us, by their example. Which, in so many instances, was all they had. Imagine. Owning only the example of one's behavior. When applied to our people and to so many peoples we are now discovering, we begin to see our inherited riches. Our inherited wealth. It is the road itself.[85]

She includes "The Long Road Home, *for Muhammad Ali*," as the first poem in the collection. "I am beginning to comprehend / the mystery / of the gift of suffering," Walker affirms in viewing Ali as the epitome of suffering that brings others to their feet and off their knees: "I have been weeping / all day / thinking of this. / The cloud of witness / the endless teaching/ the long road home."[86]

Her reflection on suffering to uplift leads to a major consideration in the book's poetic vision: the coexistence of wealth and poverty in the world. She expresses a need to understand both as contributing to what makes us human. Wealth, however, is not to be mistaken for money. Instead, she paints a visual sense of what it means to have wealth, riches as a person of color who is often without much in the way of monetary riches. "Owning the example of one's behavior" becomes a way of identifying the wealth of African Americans and so many other people of color in the larger world.

One realization of the true wealth that generations of people of color have shared over simply cooking food is paramount in "Making Frittatas," a poem for Walker's daughter Rebecca. She recalls her absent daughter who once taught her to make frittatas: "Ten years is a long time / and I have missed you. . . . time stops/when we are absent / . . . . And so, today. I think: it is all the simple / times of sharing simple things/ that we have missed. The mutual teaching and learning / that is, or should be, a daughter's and a mother's right."[87] The absence of simple sharing marks a mutual loss of wealth that cannot be calculated monetarily.

Owing the example of behavior is another of the aspects of wealth that allows Walker to enlarge the political messages inherent in her homage to Ali. In "Gather" (for Carl Dix and Cornel West), she laments: "It is still hard to believe / that millions of us saw Eric Garner die. / He died with what looked like a half-dozen / heavily clad / policemen / standing on his body, twisting and crushing / him / especially his head / and neck."[88] Thinking about that death of a "big man" with "clumsy midgets" dragging him down, she remembered the first lynching she heard about as a toddler, "mystified by pieces of something / called 'two by fours'" which men in robes and hoods used to beat the man to death, but grown up, she understood the weight and the heaviness of the wood for building houses or for hating Black men. The poet thinks, too, about all the men, Black, Brown, Red, Yellow, in all sizes whose very being drove the mentality of a lynch mob; however, when she considers the fate of Nat Turner, she issues a call: "*Gather.* / Come see what stillness / lies now / in the people's broken hearts. / It is the quiet force of comprehension, / of realization. / of the meaning / of our ancient / and perfect contrariness; / of what must now be understood / and done to honor / and cherish / ourselves."[89] Walker's message encodes the contrariness of Black people from the past in the present moment of uniting in love of self and moving forward yet again toward freedom. As a reminder that Garner's death and those others are not forgotten in "To the Po'lice," she emphasizes that "In case you are / wondering / the answer is yes; / you have hurt us. Deeply / just as you / intended." But Walker's ethical practice unites the poor weeping mothers who have lost their sons with "the poor, white, and dumb" who are being used "to do the deed," and places them together in a circle, while admonishing the police "within that enclosure / Naked to their grief / Is where you must center / If you are ever / To be freed."[90]

While enunciating her distinct thematic messages, the poems display the range of Walker's command over poetics. In long and short formal poems, she surveys the world and people in what is an unprecedented sustained political vision surveying the entire spectrum of her beliefs from the cushion she has claimed. She includes poems on South Africa, "Burnt Offerings" and "At the Door of Pollsmoor Prison," to contemplate what has happened to the nation after the treatment of Winnie Mandela and the death of Nelson Mandela. She muses on the gentrification in Oakland, as easily as memorializing Julian Bond and her youthful self in Atlanta "standing in / the Circle of Life / so long ago / holding hands / with those as fragile, / as determined, / as pure as you / waiting for the future / we would make / with just our circle / and our song."[91] And, she attends to the musicians who have been integrated into previous melodies in her poems, for example, Bob Marley and especially B. B. King who earns a special tribute: "The King Has Gone Away for Good: Long Live the King." But for Walker, the attention to women and children is paramount to her activist and international stance, as in "I Believe the Women" and "The Slain Children of Palestine Hold Council in Paradise." "Hope Is a Woman Who Has Lost Her

Fear," *for Sundus Shaker Saleh, Iraqi Mother, with my love*, however, proceeds "in the name of Peace" but ends with the warning that is Walker's signature message: "Without justice, we will never / be healed."[92]

Salamishah Tillet plays on Walker's statement, "called back to the world," in entitling her interview with Walker after the publication of *Taking the Arrow Out of the Heart*, which she cites "in many ways as a return for Walker."[93] Although Tillet refers to concerns in Walker's earlier books of poetry, the term "return" also signals the concept that Walker has made integral to her thinking and writing since her earliest work, and especially in *Meridian.* The willingness to return is apparent in her revisiting people, characters, and places that have been meaningful to her. "Is Celie Actually Ugly?" returns, for example, to another consideration of her central character from *The Color Purple*, but this time the references are actually to the Broadway musical, as the dedication to Cynthia Erivo who portrayed Celie announces. "It is Celie's designation / as 'nigger of the universe' / by the heartless sufferers around her / that makes her 'ugly' to them; / they who cannot see, until Love of Herself / lights the dreariness of Celie's existence, / that / the beauty of her / resilient spirit / has become one with the compassionate / loveliness / of / her face."[94] Celie's presence is a return to Walker's enervating the complacent acceptance of a high culture critique and energizing a broader spectrum of cultural practices in the analysis of literature as an accommodating space for the creation and production of art.

From the very beginning of her career, Alice Walker has invented her own "radically subjective politics" within a matrix of change in her art. Using what could have been a limited platform as a Black woman, she saw the expansive necessity of pluralism, intersectionality, and relativism. She read her Southern background and upbringing for what it could offer of positive values and modes of resistance. Rejecting nostalgia and sentimentalism, she claimed political relevance for her transformative positions and subversive ideologies, all the while insisting on her own vision, often idiosyncratic and subjective, but not fractured or paranoid. In beginning to write in the political and cultural upheaval of the 1960s, Walker envisioned both the importance of articulating her own Southern Black woman identity and the necessity of new formations and modalities—even while asserting the changing ground for all such formulations. In particular, she was able to foreground in her writing the damaging impact of segregationist practices, racism, sexism, and misogyny that combined with patriarchal authority, economic exploitation, and institutional power to oppress and subjugate. She has deliberately sought freedom for herself and others who suffer under restrictive mandates and dogmas. As a result, she has experienced reprisals, but she has not succumbed to lethargy or despair. Walker has, instead, produced work projecting her truth and a womanist identity that is neither fragmentary nor contradictory despite its fluid boundaries. She has acknowledged personal pain, while also reading the harm, often systemic and deliberate, inflicted on vulnerable human beings and on the earth itself. She has persisted in writing, witnessing, and testifying to what she sees and understands about the world. In her abundant publications, she continues on her journey as an artist, as a seer, as a visionary, as a poet affirming life, proselytizing human rights, mediating anguish, celebrating joy, and encouraging love. Without compromise, she has made her full raced and gendered self visible in her work, and in the electronic age, she shares her most recent personal offerings, causes, and photographs, including those capturing her special reconciliation with her daughter and grandson on Alice Walker: The Official Website and alicewalkersgarden.com.

Prolific and acknowledged as a major US writer, Walker has maintained a broad international readership. Her work has been translated into more than two dozen languages, and her books have sold worldwide over fifteen million copies. Flying in the face of contemporary wisdom as she so often has throughout her career, she has retained an unrelenting stance of rebellion and revolution in ever-evolving terms, but always with the constant of "the hunger for freedom and dignity" in the hearts of every human being that she accepts as a basic artistic and philosophical truth extrapolated early on from her reading of Camus and her reflection on the experiences of African Americans in the South. Hers is an amazing record of contribution and achievement.

Encompassing the diasporic and global, Walker's prose and poetry reverberate with a cluster of themes recapitulated and modulated over the course of her long career. Among the most prominent are: spiritual survival, individual identity, familial heritage, racial justice, gender equity, earth conservancy, freedom, power, and vision. Vision, in all of its actual and symbolic manifestations, has remained a primary trope in Walker's texts because it allows her to see the interconnection of all living things in her quest for a more equitable, just, and truthful relationship to all humanity and all nature. She recognized as much starting out in "Saving the Life That Is Your Own: The Importance of Models in the Artist's Life," when stating that the writer must acquire "a sense of essence, of timelessness, and of vision."[95] From her individual and collective experiences, from her personal and racial memory, she has concluded that "the gift of loneliness is sometimes a radical vision of society or one's people that has not previously been taken into account." Walker persists in seeking enlightenment, joy, and love, and she remains faithful and fearless in her way of living and seeing. Her canon flows from the often-dark interior, which once refracted takes shape in the literal, the externality of physical places, people, voices, and institutions, all reflections of the visions conjured out of a soul's struggle to actualize its existence concretely in discrete moments that must be shared. Those moments transmuted become the action and events, the mythologies of multiple spaces and selves readily dispensed in ever-imaginative ways in Walker's poetry, fiction, and meditations.

NOTES

Chapter 1

1. See "Alice Walker's Family Tree," Evelyn C. White, *Alice Walker: A Life* (New York: W. W. Norton, 2004), xvi–xvii.

2. Alice Walker, "Three Dollars Cash," *Revolutionary Petunias & Other Poems* (New York: Harcourt, 1973, 6; rpt. in *Her Blue Body Everything We Know: Earthling Poems, 1965–1990* (New York: Harvest, 1996), 161.

3. Quoted in White, *Alice Walker*, 40.

4. Alice Walker, "Beauty: When the Other Dancer Is the Self," in *In Search of Our Mothers' Gardens: Womanist Prose* (New York: Harvest, 1983), 366.

5. Alice Walker, Interview with John O'Brien, *Interviews with Black Writers* (1973; rpt. In *The World Has Changed: Conversations with Alice Walker*, ed. Rudolph P. Byrd (New York: The New Press, 2010), 35.

6. White, *Alice Walker*, 44–48.

7. "Beauty: When the Other Dancer Is the Self," 367.

8. White, *Alice Walker*, 44.

9. Walker, "The Black Writer and the Southern Experience," 17.

10. Walker, "Acknowledgments," *In Search of Our Mothers' Gardens*, xviii.

11. Mary Helen Washington, "Alice Walker: Her Mother's Gifts," *Ms. Magazine*, June 1982, 38.

12. "Beauty: When the Other Dancer Is the Self," 370.

13. Ibid.

14. Kevin Everod Quashie, *Black Women, Identity, and Cultural Theory: (Un)Becoming the Subject* (New Brunswick, NJ: Rutgers University Press, 2004), 19. Walker's essay frames his first chapter "The Other Dancer as Self: Notes on Girlhood Selfhood" (13–41) and informs his theorizing throughout the book.

15. "A Conversation with Howard Zinn at City Arts & Lectures (1996)," in Byrd, *The World Has Changed*, 148.

16. Ibid., 149.

17. "For My Sister Molly Who in the Fifties," in *Revolutionary Petunias*, 16–19.

18. Interview with John O'Brien, 38.

19. Alice Walker, *Once: Poems* (New York: Harcourt Brace Jovanovich, 1968), 16.

20. "The Ballad of the Brown Girl," in *Once*, 73.

21. Interview with John O'Brien, 41.

22. "A Talk: Convocation 1972," in *In Search of Our Mothers' Gardens*, 38.

23. Ibid., 39.

24. Ibid., 38, 39.

25. Ibid, 38.

26. Ibid.

27. Interview with John O'Brien, 39.

28. Ibid.

29. Rudolph P. Byrd, "Introduction," *The World Has Changed: Conversations with Alice Walker,* 9.

30. "The Black Writer and the Southern Experience," 16.

31. Ibid., 21.

32. Ibid.

33. "Regarding the Seasons," in *In Search of Our Mothers' Gardens,* 224.

34. Winson Hudson's book would not appear until 2002, when it was published as *Mississippi Harmony: Memoirs of a Freedom Fighter* with the assistance of Constance Curry and a foreword by the legal scholar Derrick Bell.

35. "'But Yet the Cotton Gin Kept on Working. . .'," in *In Search of Our Mothers' Gardens,* 31.

36. "The Unglamorous but Worthwhile Duties of the Black Revolutionary Artist, Or Of the Black Writer Who Simply Works and Writes," in *In Search of Our Mothers' Gardens,* 138.

37. "One Child of One's Own: A Meaningful Digression Within the Work(s)," in *In Search of Our Mothers' Gardens,* 392.

38. Alice Walker, "'I know what the earth says,'" Interview by William Ferris, *Southern Cultures* (Spring 2004), 12; reprinted in Byrd, *The World Has Changed,* 229.

39. Walker, Interview with O'Brien, 44.

40. Maria Lauret, *Alice Walker* (2000; 2nd Ed. New York: Palgrave Macmillan, 2011), 43–50.

41. Alice Walker, *The Third Life of Grange Copeland* (New York: Harcourt Brace Jovanovich, 1970), 112.

42. Ibid.

43. Ibid. 78.

44. Ibid., 227.

45. Ibid., 179. See Walker's definitions of "Womanist" in her opening epigraph to *In Search of Our Mothers' Gardens,* xi–xii.

46. *The Third Life of Grange Copeland,* 210.

47. Ibid.

48. Ibid., 126.

49. See Marcellus Blount and George P. Cunningham, eds. *Representing Black Men* (New York: Routledge, 1996); Marlon B. Ross, "In Search of Black Men's Masculinities," in *Feminist Studies,* 24.3 (Autumn, 1998): 599–626; and GerShun Avilez, *Radical Aesthetics and Modern Black Nationalism* (Champaign: University of Illinois Press, 2016).

50. *The Third Life of Grange Copeland,* 145, 153–54.

51. See Melissa Walker, *Down from the Mountaintop: Black Women's Novels in the Wake of the Civil Rights Movement, 1966–1989* (New Haven, CT: Yale University Press, 1991); and Madhu Dubey, *Black Women Novelists and the Nationalist Aesthetic* (Bloomington: Indiana University Press, 1994).

52. *The Third Life of Grange Copeland,* 225.

53. Ibid., 104.

54. Ibid., 107.
55. Ibid., 193.
56. Ibid., 214.
57. Ibid., 247.
58. Walker, Interview with O'Brien, *In Search of Our Mothers' Gardens,* 249.
59. Peter Erickson, "'Cast Out Alone/ to Heal/ and Re-create/ Ourselves': Family-Based Identity in the Work of Alice Walker," in *CLA Journal,* 23, no. 4 (September 1979); rpt. In *Modern Critical Views: Alice Walker,* ed. Harold Bloom (New York: Chelsea House, 1989), 5.
60. Alice Walker, "Diary of an African Nun," in *In Love & Trouble: Stories of Black Women* (New York: Harcourt Brace Jovanovich, 1973), 118.
61. Ibid.
62. "Roselily," in *In Love & Trouble,* 8.
63. "'Really, *Doesn't* Crime Pay?'" in *In Love & Trouble,* 11.
64. Ibid., 15. Walker's italics.
65. Ibid., 18.
66. Ibid., 16. Walker's italics.
67. See Hortense J. Spillers' insightful reading of "The Child Who Favored Daughter," in "'The Permanent Obliquity of an In(pha)llibly Straight': In the Time of the Daughters and the Fathers," in *Changing Our Own Words: Essays on Criticism, Theory, and Writing by Black Women,* ed. Cheryl A. Wall (New Brunswick, NJ: Rutgers University Press, 1989), 127–49.
68. "The Revenge of Hannah Kemhuff," in *In Love and Trouble,* 67.
69. Ibid., 68.
70. Ibid., 70–72.
71. Ibid., 73.
72. Ibid., 80.
73. "Everyday Use," in *In Love and Trouble,* 48.
74. Ibid., 49.
75. Barbara T. Christian, "Introduction," *Alice Walker, "Everyday Use"* (New Brunswick, NJ: Rutgers University Press, 1994), 3.
76. Barbara T. Christian, "The Black Woman as Wayward Artist," in *Alice Walker, "Everyday Use,"* 128.
77. June Jordan, personal letter to Alice Walker, quoted in Walker, *Revolutionary Petunias,* 67. Walker's italics.
78. "Reassurance," in *Revolutionary Petunias,* 33.
79. "Revolutionary Petunias," in *Revolutionary Petunias,* 29.
80. Ibid.
81. "Burial," in *Revolutionary Petunias,* 14. Walker's italics.
82. Ibid., 15.
83. "The Girl Who Died #2" and "Nothing Is Right," in *Revolutionary Petunias,* 46, 36.

Chapter 2

1. Elliott Butler-Evans, *Race, Gender, and Desire: Narrative Strategies in the Fiction of Toni Cade Bambara, Toni Morrison, and Alice Walker* (Philadelphia: Temple University Press, 1989), 139.

2. John Fiske, "Cultural Studies and the Culture of Everyday Life," in *Cultural Studies,* eds. Lawrence Grossberg, Cary Nelson, and Paula Treichler (New York: Routledge, 1992), 162.

3. Walker, "Women," in *Revolutionary Petunias,* 5.

4. Alice Walker. *Meridian* (New York: Harcourt Brace Jovanovich, 1976), 4.

5. Ibid.

6. Ibid., 12.

7. Barbara T. Christian, "Alice Walker: The Black Woman Artist as Wayward," 1984; rpt. in Barbara T. Christian, ed. *Alice Walker, "Everyday Use"* (New Brunswick, NJ: Rutgers University Press, 1994), 134–35.

8. Walker, *Meridian,* 19.

9. Ibid., 47.

10. Ibid., 52.

11. Ibid., 53.

12. Karla Holloway, *Moorings and Metaphors: Figures of Culture and Gender in Black Women's Literature* (New Brunswick, NJ: Rutgers University Press, 1992), 37.

13. "Alice Walker on Finding Your Bliss: Interview by Evelyn C. White," *Ms. Magazine*, September/October 1998: 42–50.

14. Ibid, 50.

15. Walker, *Meridian,* 34.

16. Ibid., 38.

17. Ibid., 39.

18. Ibid., 227.

19. Ibid.

20. Ibid., 236.

21. Ibid., 221.

22. Ibid., 12. My italics.

23. Ibid., 21. Walker's italics.

24. Ibid., 236.

25. Ibid., 227.

26. Alice Walker, *Anything We Love Can Be Saved: A Writer's Activism* (New York: Random House, 1997), 46.

27. Alice Walker, Dedication, "On Refusing to Be Humbled by Second Place in a Contest You Did Not Design: A Tradition by Now," in *I Love Myself When I Am Laughing and Then Again When I Am Looking Mean and Impressive: A Zora Neale Hurston Reader* (New York: The Feminist Press, 1979), 2.

28. Walker, Afterword, "Looking for Zora," in *I Love Myself,* 307.

29. Walker, *Meridian,* 42.

30. Ibid.

31. Ibid.

32. Alice Walker, "Acknowledgments," in *In Search of Our Mothers' Gardens: Womanist Prose* (New York: Harcourt Brace Jovanovich, 1983), xviii.

33. Alice Walker, "Father," in *Living by the Word: Selected Writings, 1973–1987* (San Diego: Harcourt Brace Jovanovich, 1988), 9.

34. Walker, *Anything We Love Can Be Saved,* xiv.

35. Alice Walker, "Did This Happen to Your Mother? Did Your Sister Throw Up a Lot?" in *Good Night, Willie Lee, I'll See You in the Morning* (New York: The Dial Press, 1979), 3.

36. "Confession," in *Good Night, Willie Lee,* 10.
37. "At First," in *Good Night, Willie Lee,* 15.
38. "Janie Crawford," in *Good Night, Willie Lee,* 18.
39. Combahee River Collective Statement, in Zillah Eisenstein, *Capitalist Patriarchy and the Case for Socialist Feminism* (1978).
40. "On Stripping the Bark from Myself," in *Good Night, Willie Lee,* 24.
41. "Forgive Me If My Praise," in *Good Night, Willie Lee,* 35.
42. Ibid.
43. "Malcolm," in *Good Night, Willie Lee,* 38.
44. Walker, *Meridian,* 74.
45. "facing the way," in *Good Night, Willie Lee,* 44–45.
46. "talking to my grandmother who died poor (while hearing Richard Nixon declare 'I am not a crook.')," in *Good Night, Willie Lee,* 47.
47. "Good Night, Willie Lee, I'll See You in the Morning," in *Good Night, Willie Lee,* 53.
48. Alice Walker, "Nineteen Fifty-Five," in *You Can't Keep a Good Woman Down* (San Diego: Harcourt Brace Jovanovich, 1981), 20.
49. Walker, *Meridian,* 54.
50. "Source," in *You Can't Keep a Good Woman Down,* 141.
51. Ibid., 151.
52. Ibid.
53. Ibid.
54. Deborah E. McDowell, "Reading Family Matters," in *Changing Our Own Words: Essays on Criticism, Theory, and Writing by Black Women,* ed. Cheryl A. Wall (New Brunswick, NJ: Rutgers University Press, 1989), 88.
55. "Source," in *You Can't Keep a Good Woman Down,* 152.
56. Ibid., 154f.
57. Ibid., 156.
58. Ibid., 157.
59. Ibid., 165.
60. Ibid., 166.
61. Ibid, 167.
62. Ibid., 166.

Chapter 3

1. Walker, "A Talk: Convocation 1972," in *In Search of Our Mothers' Gardens,* 37.
2. Walker, "Writing *The Color Purple,*" in *In Search of Our Mothers' Gardens,* 357.
3. Ibid., 360.
4. Alice Walker, *The Color Purple* (New York: Harcourt Brace Jovanovich, 1982), 11.
5. See Wendy Wall, "Lettered Body and Corporeal Texts in *The Color Purple,*" in *Alice Walker: Critical Perspectives Past and Present,* eds. Henry Louis Gates, Jr., and K. A. Appiah (New York: Amistad, 1993), 261–74.
6. Mae G. Henderson, "*The Color Purple:* Revisions and Redefinitions," in *Changing Our Own Words: Essays on Criticism, Theory, and Writing by Black Women,* ed. Cheryl A. Wall (New Brunswick, NJ: Rutgers University Press, 1989), 67.
7. Elliott Butler-Evans, *Race, Gender, and Desire: Narrative Strategies in the Fiction of Toni Cade Bambara, Toni Morrison, and Alice Walker* (Philadelphia: Temple University Press, 1989), 164.

8. Salamishah Tillet, *In Search of* The Color Purple: *The Story of an American Masterpiece* (New York: Abrams Press, 2021), xi.

9. *The Color Purple,* 20.

10. Ibid., 19.

11. Ibid.

12. Ibid., 177.

13. Ibid., 178.

14. Deborah E. McDowell, "Reading Family Matters," in *Changing Our Own Words,* 75–96.

15. See Jacqueline Bobo, "Black Women's Responses to *The Color Purple,*" *Jump Cut: A Review of Contemporary Media,* 33 (February 1988), 43–51; and Rachel Lister, "The Conception and Reception of *The Color Purple,*" in *Alice Walker* The Color Purple: *A Reader's Guide to Essential Criticism* (New York: Palgrave Macmillan, 2010), 7–26.

16. *The Color Purple,* 249.

17. Lister, *Alice Walker* The Color Purple, 74–88, 123–40.

18. Walker, *The Color Purple,* 14.

19. Alice Walker, Preface to *The Same River Twice: Honoring the Difficult: A Meditation on Life, Spirit, Art, and the Making of the Film* The Color Purple *Ten Years Later* (New York: Scribner, 1996), 13.

20. Ibid.

21. Alice Walker, "Edwidge Danticat, The Quiet Stream," in *The Cushion in the Road: Meditations and Wanderings as The Whole World Awakens to Being in Harm's Way* (New York: The New Press, 2013), 162–63.

22. *The Same River Twice,* 286–87.

23. White, *Alice Walker*, 462–63. White quotes Walker as saying at the ceremony on 9 February 1994, "Whatever the word Tallulah means in itself, to me it means 'restored' in me.'" . . . "The work Kate means 'remembered' in me" (462f).

24. See Melanie L. Harris, *Gifts of Virtue, Alice Walker, and Womanist Ethics* (New York: Palgrave/Macmillan, 2010) for a comprehensive analysis of "Womanism" in Black religion and ethics.

25. Alice Walker, "In Search of Our Mothers' Gardens," in Alice Walker, *In Search of Our Mothers' Gardens: Womanist Prose* (New York: Harcourt Brace Jovanovich, 1983), 233.

26. See Houston A. Baker and Charlotte Pierce-Baker, "Patches: Quilts and Community in Alice Walker's 'Everyday Use,'" *The Southern Review* 21 (Summer 1985): 706–20.

27. "In Search of Our Mothers' Gardens," 239.

28. Ibid., 240.

29. "The Unglamorous but Worthwhile Duties of the Black Revolutionary Artist, or Of the Black Writer Who Simply Works and Writes," in *In Search of Our Mothers' Gardens*, 135. Walker's italics.

30. Ibid., 128.

31. See Thadious M. Davis, "Alice Walker Matters: The Fruits of Gendered Space," in *Southscapes: Geographies of Race, Region, and Literature* (Chapel Hill: University of North Carolina Press, 2011), 334–74.

32. Alice Walker, *Her Blue Body Everything We Know: Earthling Poems 1965–1990 Complete* (San Diego: Harcourt Brace and Company, 1991), 311.

33. Alice Walker, "Preface," in *Living by the Word: Selected Essays, 1973–1987* (San Diego, Harcourt Brace Jovanovich, 1988), xx.

34. "In the Closet of the Soul," in *Living by the Word,* 79, 85.

35. Ibid., 92.

36. "Everything Is a Human Being," in *Living by the Word,* 142.

37. "The Universe Responds: Or, How I Learned We Can Have Peace on Earth," in *Living by the Word,* 192.

38. Alice Walker, "How Poems Are Made / A Discredited View," in *Horses Make a Landscape Look More Beautiful: Poems* (San Diego: Harcourt Brace Jovanovich, 1984), 17.

39. "Mississippi Winter II," in *Horses Make a Landscape,* 20.

40. "These Days," in *Horses Make a Landscape,* 75. The friends for whom the world must be saved are Belvie Rooks, Robert Allen, Elena, Susan Kirschner, Sheila, Gloria Steinem, Rebecca Walker, and John, Yoko, and Sean Lennon.

41. Walker, Dedication, *Horses Make a Landscape,* vii–ix.

42. "Remember?" in *Horses Make a Landscape,* 1.

43. Ibid., 2.

44. "Songless," in *Horses Make a Landscape,* 27.

45. Ibid., 28–29.

46. "Family Of," in *Horses Make a Landscape,* 48.

47. Alice Walker, "We Have a Beautiful Mother," in *Her Blue Body Everything We Know: Earthling Poems, 1965–1990 Complete* (San Diego: Harcourt Brace Jovanovich, 1991), 409. Walker's italics.

48. Ibid., 410. Walker's italics.

49. "Poem at Thirty-Nine," in *Her Blue Body,* 352.

50. "I Said to Poetry," in *Her Blue Body,* 355.

51. "My Heart Has Reopened," in *Her Blue Body,* 411.

52. Ibid., 413.

53. Ibid.

54. Ibid., Walker's inserted untitled poem "O landscape of my birth," 413–15.

55. Jean Toomer, "Song of the Son," in Jean Toomer, *Cane,* 1922; Norton Critical Edition, ed. Darwin T. Turner (New York: W. W. Norton, 1988), 14.

56. "Once, Again," in *Her Blue Body,* 463.

57. Ibid., 189.

58. Alice Walker, *The Temple of My Familiar* (New York: Harcourt Brace Jovanovich, 1989), 123.

59. Ibid., 182.

60. Ibid., 52.

61. Walker, "Turquois and Coral: The Writing of *The Temple of My Familiar,*" in *Anything We Love Can Be Saved,* 118, 115–16.

62. Walker quoted in "'The Richness of the Very Ordinary Stuff': A Conversation with Jody Hoy (1994)," in Rudolph Byrd, *The World Has Changed,* 130.

63. Alice Walker, *Possessing the Secret of Joy* (New York: Simon and Schuster, 1992), 3.

64. Ibid., 5.

65. Ibid., 275.

66. Ibid., 279.

67. Ibid., 180.

68. Ibid.

69. "'The Richness of the Very Ordinary Stuff': A Conversation with Jody Hoy," in Byrd, *The World Has Changed,* 130–31.

70. *Possessing the Secret of Joy,* 274.

71. Ibid., 277–78.

72. Ibid., 279.

73. Ibid., 28.

74. "Looking for Jung: Writing *Possessing the Secret of Joy,*" in *Anything We Love Can Be Saved,* 125.

75. Ibid., 126.

76. Muriel Rukeyser, "The Place in the Ways," in Alice Walker, *Anything We Love Can Be Saved: A Writer's Activism* (New York: Random House, 1997), ix.

Chapter 4

1. Alice Walker, *By the Light of My Father's Smile* (New York: Random House, 1998), 4.

2. Ibid., 30.

3. Ibid., 194, 210.

4. Pamela B. June, "Subverting Heteronormativity: Another Look at Alice Walker's *By the Light of My Father's Smile,*" *Women's Studies* 40, no. 5 (July–August 2011): 610.

5. Walker, *By the Light of My Father's Smile,* 58, 171.

6. "Longing to Die of Old Age," in *Living by the Word,* 36.

7. *By the Light of My Father's Smile,* 217.

8. Ibid, 219.

9. "Father," in *Living by the Word,* 9–10.

10. Alice Walker, "Preface," *Absolute Trust in the Goodness of the Earth: New Poems* (New York: Random House, 2003), xi.

11. Ibid., xii.

12. Ibid.

13. Ibid., xii–xiii.

14. Ibid., xiv.

15. "Projection," in *Absolute Trust,* 134.

16. Ibid., 120 (Walker's italics).

17. "New House Moves," in *Absolute Trust,* 33–36.

18. "My Ancestors' Earnings," in *Absolute Trust,* 130.

19. "If They Come to Shoot You," in *Absolute Trust,* 211.

20. "Bring Me the Heart of Maria Sabina," in *Absolute Trust,* 220.

21. Ibid., 228–29.

22. Alice Walker, "Preface," *The Way Forward Is with a Broken Heart* (New York: Random House, 2000), xiv.

23. "The Ruin," in *The Way Forward,* 51.

24. Ibid.

25. Ibid.

26. "Kindred Spirits," in *The Way Forward,* 65.

27. Ibid., 66.

28. Ibid.

29. "Coddling," in *The Way Forward,* 86.

30. "Preface," *Absolute Trust in the Goodness of the Earth,* xi.

31. "A Name Is Sometimes an Angel Saying Hi, I'm With You," in *Living by the Word,* 97.

32. "Lying Quietly," in *Absolute Trust,* 205.

33. Alice Walker, *Now Is the Time to Open Your Heart* (New York: Random House, 2004), 11.

34. Ibid., 75.

35. Ibid., 122.

36. Ibid., 164.

37. Ibid., 194.

38. Alice Walker, *We Are the Ones We Have Been Waiting For: Inner Light in a Time of Darkness, Meditations* (New York: The New Press, 2006), 1, Walker's italics.

39. Ibid., vii.

40. "Acknowledgments," *In Search of Our Mothers' Gardens,* xvii.

41. "Introduction," *We Are the Ones,* 4.

42. See Walker, "Looking to the Side, and Back," in *In Search of Our Mothers' Gardens,* 316–19.

43. Cheryl A. Wall, "On Women, Rights, and Writing: June Jordan and Alice Walker," in *On Freedom and the Will to Adorn: The Art of the African American Essay* (Chapel Hill: University of North Carolina Press, 2018), 216.

44. Introduction, *We Are the Ones,* 4.

45. "Three Fates," in *We Are the Ones,* 21.

46. "The Day You Are Born," poem in "Three Fates," in *We Are the Ones,* 28.

47. Alice Walker, *Overcoming Speechlessness: A Poet Encounters the Horror in Rwanda, Eastern Congo, and Palestine/Israel* (New York: Seven Stories Press, 2010), 8–9.

48. Ibid., 9.

49. Ibid., 10.

50. Ibid., 53–54.

51. Ibid., 54.

52. Ibid.

53. Ibid., 56.

54. Ibid., 57.

55. Ibid., 58.

56. Ibid., 67.

57. Ibid., 60.

58. Alice Walker, "Preface: Learning to Dance," in *Hard Times Require Furious Dancing (New Poems)* (Novato, CA: New World Library, 2010), xv.

59. "Lost," in *Hard Times Require Furious Dancing,* 25, 26.

60. "Meeting You," in *Hard Times Require Furious Dancing,* 92, 94.

61. Preface, in *Hard Times Require Furious Dancing* xv-xvi. See also "Sisterloss," in *The Cushion in the Road: Meditation and Wandering as the Whole World Awakens to Being in Harm's Way* (New York: The New Press, 2013), 154–59.

62. "Preface: Learning to Dance," in *Hard Times Require Furious Dancing,* xvi.

63. "Yes, I Know," in *Hard Times Require Furious Dancing,* 8.

64. "Morning *For Kaleo,*" in *Hard Times Require Furious Dancing,* 159.

65. Alice Walker, *A Poem Traveled Down My Arm: Poems and Drawings* (New York: Random House, 2003).

66. Alice Walker, "On Raising Chickens: A Conversation with Rudolph P. Byrd," in *The World has Changed,* 322.

67. Ibid.

68. Ibid.

69. See Susan Sontag, *On Photography* (1977; New York: Picador/Farrar, Straus and Giroux, 2001).

70. Alice Walker, *The World Will Follow Joy: Turning Madness in to Flowers: New Poems* (New York: The New Press, 2013), xiv.

71. "What Makes the Dalai Lama Lovable?," in *The World Will Follow Joy,* 7–8.

72. "Going Out to the Garden," in *The World Will Follow Joy,* 189.

73. Walker, Introduction, *The Cushion in the Road,* 2.

74. Ibid., 2–3.

75. See Nagueyalti Warren, *Alice Walker's Metaphysics: Literature of Spirit* (New York: Rowan and Littlefield Publishers, 2019.

76. "Encountering the Unknown Brazil," in *The Cushion in the Road,* 355.

77. Ibid., 356.

78. "Getting as Black as My Daddy," in *Anything We Love Can be Saved,* 156–57.

79. Alice Walker, "A Note about the Translator," in *Taking the Arrow Out of the Heart: Poems* (New York: 37INK ATRIA Books, 2018), xx.

80. Ibid., xix.

81. Walker, "Introduction," *Taking the Arrow Out of the Heart,* xvi.

82. Ibid., xv.

83. Ibid.

84. Ibid.

85. Ibid., xvi.

86. "The Long Road Home," in *Taking the Arrow Out of the Heart,* 3.

87. "Making Frittatas," in *Taking the Arrow Out of the Heart,* 209.

88. "Gather," in *Taking the Arrow Out of the Heart,* 205.

89. Ibid., 207.

90. "To the Po'lice," in *Taking the Arrow Out of the Heart,* 223.

91. "Julian" *Julian Bond, 1940–2015,* in *Taking the Arrow Out of the Heart,* 61, 63, 65.

92. "Hope Is a Woman Who Has Lost Her Fear," in *Taking the Arrow Out of the Heart,* 161.

93. Salamishah Tillet, "'Called Back to the World': An Interview with Alice Walker," *The New York Review of Books,* October 1, 2018.

94. "Is Celie Actually Ugly?" in *Taking the Arrow Out of the Heart,* 29, 31.

95. "Saving the Life That Is Your Own: The Importance of Models in the Artist's Life," in *In Search of Our Mothers' Gardens,* 8.

SELECTED BIBLIOGRAPHY

Works by Alice Walker

NOVELS

The Third Life of Grange Copeland. New York: Harcourt Brace Jovanovich, 1970.

Meridian. New York: Harcourt Brace Jovanovich, 1976.

The Color Purple. New York: Harcourt Brace Jovanovich, 1982.

The Temple of My Familiar. New York: Harcourt Brace Jovanovich, 1989.

Possessing the Secret of Joy. New York: Simon and Schuster, 1992.

By the Light of My Father's Smile: A Story of Requited Love, Crossing Over, and the Sexual Healing of the Soul. New York: Random House, 1998.

Now Is the Time to Open Your Heart. New York: Random House, 2004.

NONFICTION

I Love Myself When I Am Laughing and Then Again When I Am Looking Mean and Impressive: A Zora Neale Hurston Reader. Ed. Alice Walker. Old Westbury, NY: Feminist Press, 1979.

In Search of Our Mothers' Gardens: Womanist Prose. New York: Harcourt Brace Jovanovich, 1983.

Living by the Word: Selected Writings, 1973–1987. San Diego: Harcourt Brace Jovanovich, 1988.

(With Pratibha Parmar) *Warrior Marks: Female Genital Mutilation and the Sexual Blinding of Women.* New York: Harcourt, 1993.

The Same River Twice: Honoring the Difficult: A Meditation of Life, Spirit, Art, and the Making of the Film, The Color Purple, *Ten Years Later.* New York: Scribner's, 1996.

Anything We Love Can Be Saved: A Writer's Activism. New York: Random House, 1997.

Sent by the Earth: A Message from the Grandmother Spirit After the Bombing of the World Trade Center and the Pentagon. New York: Seven Stories Press, 2001.

We Are the Ones We Have Been Waiting For: Light in a Time of Darkness. New York: The New Press, 2006.

Overcoming Speechlessness: A Poet Encounters the Horror in Rwanda, Eastern Congo, and Palestine/Israel. New York: Seven Stories Press, 2010.

The Cushion in the Road: Meditation and Wandering as the Whole World Awakens to Being in Harm's Way. New York: The New Press, 2014.

POETRY

Once: Poems. New York: Harcourt, Brace & World, 1968.

Five Poems. Detroit, MI: Broadside Press, 1972.

Revolutionary Petunias & Other Poems. New York: Harcourt Brace Jovanovich, 1973.
Good Night, Willie Lee, I'll See You in the Morning. New York: Dial, 1979.
Horses Make a Landscape Look More Beautiful: Poems. San Diego, CA: Harcourt Brace Jovanovich, 1984.
Her Blue Body Everything We Know: Earthling Poems, 1965–1990. San Diego, CA: Harcourt Brace Jovanovich, 1991.
Absolute Trust in the Goodness of the Earth: New Poems. New York: Random House, 2003.
A Poem Traveled Down My Arm: Poems and Drawings. New York: Random House, 2003.
Hard Times Require Furious Dancing: New Poems. Novato, CA: New World Library, 2010.
The World Will Follow Joy: Turning Madness into Flowers (New Poems). New York: The New Press, 2013.
Taking the Arrow Out of the Heart: Poems. New York: 37INK Aria, 2018.

SHORT FICTION

In Love & Trouble: Stories of Black Women. New York: Harcourt Brace Jovanovich, 1973.
You Can't Keep a Good Woman Down: Stories. New York: Harcourt Brace Jovanovich, 1981.
The Way Forward Is with a Broken Heart. New York: Random House, 2000.

CHILDREN'S BOOKS

Langston Hughes, American Poet. New York: Harper & Row, 1974.
To Hell with Dying. New York: Harcourt Brace Jovanovich, 1988.
Finding the Green Stone. Orlando, FL: Harcourt Brace & Company, 1991.
There Is a Flower at the Tip of My Nose Smelling Me. New York: HarperCollins, 2006.
Why War Is Never a Good Idea. New York: HarperCollins, 2007.

BLOG

Alice Walker: The Official Website alicewalkersgarden.com.

ARCHIVE, PAPERS, AND RECORDS

Alice Walker Papers, ca. 1930–2014, Emory University, Stuart A. Rose Manuscript, Archives, and Rare Book Library, Atlanta, Georgia.
rose.library@emory.edu
http://pid.emory.edu/ark:/25599/900jh

Selected Secondary Sources

Babb, Valerie. *Workings of the Spirit: The Poetics of Afro-American Women's Writing*. Chicago: University of Chicago Press, 1991.
Baker, Houston A., Jr., and Charlotte Pierce-Baker. "Patches: Quilts and Community in Alice Walker's 'Everyday Use.'" *The Southern Review* 21 (Summer 1985): 706–20.
Banks, Erma Davis, and Keith Byerman. *Alice Walker: An Annotated Bibliography*. New York: Garland, 1989.
Bass, Margaret Kent. "Alice's Secret." *CLA Journal* 38, no.1 (September 1994): 1–10.

Bates, Gerri. *Alice Walker: A Critical Companion.* Westport, CT: Greenwood Press, 2005.

Berlant, Lauren, "Race, Gender, and Nation in *The Color Purple.*" *Critical Inquiry* 14 (Summer 1988): 831–59.

Bloom, Harold, ed. *Alice Walker: Modern Critical Views.* New York: Chelsea House, 1989.

Bobo, Jacqueline. "Shifting Through the Controversy: Reading *The Color Purple.*" *Callaloo* 12 (Spring 1989): 332–42.

Boyd, Valerie, ed. *Gathering Blossoms Under Fire: The Journals of Alice Walker.* Atria/37INK, Simon & Schuster Digital, 2020.

Brown, Joseph A., SJ. "All Saints Should Walk Away': The Mystical Pilgrimage of Meridian." *Callaloo* 12 (Spring 1989): 310–20.

Buncombe, Marie H. "Androgyny as Metaphor in Alice Walker's Novels." *CLA Journal* 30 (June 1987): 419–27.

Butler, Robert James. "Making a Way out of No Way: The Open Journey in Alice Walker's *The Third Life of Grange Copeland.*" *Black American Literature Forum* 22 (Spring 1988): 65–79.

Butler-Evans, Elliott. *Race, Gender, and Desire: Narrative Strategies in the Fiction of Toni Cade Bambara, Toni Morrison, and Alice Walker.* Philadelphia: Temple University Press, 1989.

Byerman, Keith. "Desire and Alice Walker: The Quest for a Womanist Narrative." *Callaloo* 12 (Spring 1989): 321–31.

———, and Erma Banks. "Alice Walker: A Selected Bibliography, 1968–1988." *Callaloo* 12 (Spring 1989): 343–45.

Byrd, Rudolph P. "Spirituality in the Novels of Alice Walker: Models, Healing, and Transformation, or When the Spirit Moves So Do We." In *Wild Women in the Whirlwind: Afra-American Culture and the Contemporary Literary Renaissance*, edited by Joanne M. Braxton and Andree Nicola McLaughlin, 363–78. New Brunswick, NJ: Rutgers University Press, 1990.

———, ed. *The World Has Changed: Conversations with Alice Walker.* New York: The New Press, 2010.

Callahan, John F. "The Hoop of Language: Politics and the Restoration of Voice in *Meridian.*" In *The African-American Grain: The Pursuit of Voice in Twentieth-Century Black Fiction.* John F. Callahan, 217–55. Urbana: University of Illinois Press, 1988; 2nd Ed. 1990.

Chambers, Kimberly R. "Right on Time: History and Religion in Alice Walker's *The Color Purple.*" *CLA Journal* 31 (1987): 44–62.

Cheung, King-Kok. "Don't Tell: Imposed Silences in *The Color Purple* and *The Woman Warrior.*" *PMLA* 103 (1988): 162–74.

Christian, Barbara. "Alice Walker," In *Dictionary of Literary Biography: Afro-American Writers After 1955.* V. 33, edited by Thadious M. Davis and Trudier Harris. Detroit: Gale Research, 1984.

———. "Alice Walker: The Black Woman Artist as Wayward." In *Black Women Writers (1950–1980): A Critical Evaluation*, edited by Mari Evans, 457–77. Garden City: Anchor Press, 1984.

———, ed. *Alice Walker, "Everyday Use."* New Brunswick, NJ: Rutgers University Press, 1994.

Davis, Thadious M. "Alice Walker." In *Dictionary of Literary Biography: American Novelists Since World War II*. V. 6. Ed James Kibler. Detroit: Gale Research, 1980.

———. "Alice Walker Matters: The Fruits of Gendered Space." In *Southscapes: Geographies of Race, Region, and Literature*. Thadious M. Davis, 334–74. (Chapel Hill: University of North Carolina Press, 2011).

———. "Alice Walker's Celebration of Self in Southern Generations." In *Women Writers of the Contemporary South*, edited by Peggy Whitman Prenshaw, 160–76. Jackson: University Press of Mississippi, 1984.

———. "Poetry as Preface to Fiction: Alice Walker's Recurrent Apprenticeship." *Mississippi Quarterly* 44 (Spring 1991): 133–42.

———. "The Polarities of Space: Segregation and Alice Walker's Intervention in Southern Studies." In *Towards an Intellectual History of Black Women*, edited by Mia Bay, Farah J. Griffin, Martha S. Jones, and Barbara D. Savage, 160–76. Chapel Hill: University of North Carolina Press, 2015.

Dieke, Ikenna, ed. *Critical Essays on Alice Walker.* Westport, CT, and London: Greenwood Press, 1999.

Early, Gerald. "*The Color Purple* as Everybody's Protest Art." *Antioch Review* 44 (Summer 1986): 261–75.

Erickson, Peter. "'Cast Out Alone/ To Heal/ And Re-Create Ourselves': Family-Based Identity in the Work of Alice Walker." *CLA Journal* 23 (September 1979): 71–94.

Fifer, Elizabeth, "The Dialect and Letters of *The Color Purple*." In *Contemporary American Women Writers: Narrative Strategies*, edited by Catherine Rainwater and William J. Scheick, 155–71. Lexington: University Press of Kentucky, 1985.

Floyd-Thomas, Stacey M. *Deeper Shades of Purple: Womanism in Religion and Society.* New York: New York University Press, 2006.

Fontenot, Chester. "Alice Walker's 'Diary of an African Nun' and DuBois' Double Consciousness." In *Sturdy Black Bridges: Visions of Black Women in Literature*, edited by Roseann Bell, Bettye Parker, and Beverly Guy-Sheftall, 150–56. Garden City: Anchor, 1979.

Gates, Henry Louis, Jr., and K. A. Appiah, eds. *Alice Walker: Critical Perspectives Past and Present*. New York: Amistad, 1993.

George, Olakunle. "Alice Walker's Africa: Globalization and the Province of Fiction." *Comparative Literature* 53, no. 4 (Autumn, 2001): 354–72.

Gourdine, Angeletta K. M. "Postmodern Ethnography and the Womanist Mission: Postcolonial Sensibilities in *Possessing the Secret of Joy*. *African American Review* 30, no. 2 (1996): 237–44.

Gwin, Minrose. *The Woman in the Red Dress: Women, Gender, and Reading.* Urbana: University of Illinois Press, 2002.

Harris, Melanie L. *Gifts of Virtue, Alice Walker, and Womanist Ethics*. Palgrave MacMillan, 2010.

Harris, Trudier. "On *The Color Purple*, Stereotypes and Silence." *Black American Literature Forum* 18 (Winter 1984): 155–61.

———. "Tiptoeing Through Taboo: Incest in 'The Child Who Favored Daughter.'" *Modern Fiction Studies* 28 (Autumn 1982): 495–505.

———. "Violence in *The Third Life of Grange Copeland*." *CLA Journal* 19 (December 1975): 238–47.

———. "From Victimization to Free Enterprise: Alice Walker's *The Color Purple*." *Studies in American Fiction* 14 (Spring 1986): 1–17.

Hellenbrand, Harold. "Speech. After Silence: Alice Walker's *The Third Life of Grange Copeland.*" *Black American Literature Forum* 20 (Spring–Summer 1986), 113–28.

Henderson, Mae G. "*The Color Purple*: Revisions and Redefinitions." *Sage* 2 (Spring 1985), 14–18; rpt. in *Speaking in Tongues and Dancing Diaspora: Black Women Writing and Performing.* Mae G. Henderson, 22–34. New York: Oxford University Press, 2014.

Hernton, Calvin C. "Who's Afraid of Alice Walker: *The Color Purple* as Slave Narrative." In *The Sexual Mountain and Black Women Writers: Adventures in Sex, Literature, and Real Life.* Calvin C. Hernton, 1–36. New York: Doubleday/Anchor, 1987.

Hite, Molly. "Romance, Marginality, and Matrilineage: *The Color Purple* and *Their Eyes Were Watching God.*" In *Reading Black, Reading Feminist: A Feminist Anthology*, edited by Henry Louis Gates Jr., 431–53 New York: Meridian, 1990.

Hogue, Lawrence. "History, the Feminist Discourse, and Alice Walker's *The Third Life of Grange Copeland.*" *MELUS* 12 (Summer 1985): 45–62.

Holloway, Karla F. C. *Moorings and Metaphors: Figures of Culture and Gender in Black Women's Literature.* New Brunswick, NJ: Rutgers University Press, 1992.

hooks, bell. "Writing the Subject: Reading *The Color Purple.*" In *Reading Black, Reading Feminist,* edited by Henry Louis Gates Jr., 454–70. New York: Meridian, 1990.

Howard, Lillie P., ed. *Alice Walker and Zora Neale Hurston: The Common Bond.* London: Greenwood Press, 1993.

Jenkins, Candice M. "Queering the Black Patriarchy: The Salvific Wish and Masculine Possibility in Alice Walker's *The Color Purple.*" *Modern Fiction Studies* 48.4 (2002): 969–1000.

June, Pamela B. "Subverting Heteronormativity: Another Look at Alice Walker's *By the Light of My Father's Smile.*" *Women's Studies* 40, no. 5 (July–August 2011): 600–19.

King, Lovalerie. "African American Womanism: From Zora Neale Hurston to Alice Walker." In *The Cambridge Companion to the African American Novel,* edited by Maryemma Graham, 233–52. Cambridge, United Kingdom: Cambridge University Press, 2004.

Kirschner, Susan. "Alice Walker's Nonfictional Prose: A Checklist, 1966–1984." *Black American Literature Forum* 18 (Winter 1984): 162–63.

Lauret, Maria. *Alice Walker.* New York: Palgrave Macmillan, 2000; 2nd Ed. 2011.

Lister, Rachel. *Alice Walker* The Color Purple*: A Reader's Guide to Essential Criticism.* New York and London: Palgrave Macmillan, 2010.

McDowell, Deborah E. *"The Changing Same": Black Women's Literature, Criticism, and Theory.* Bloomington: Indiana University Press, 1995.

———. "Reading Family Matters." In *Changing Our Own Words: Essays on Criticism, Theory, and Writing by Black Women*, edited by Cheryl A. Wall, 75–97. New Brunswick, NJ: Rutgers University Press, 1989.

———. "The Self in Bloom: Alice Walker's *Meridian.*" *CLA Journal* 24 (March 1981): 262–75.

McGowan, Martha J. "Atonement and Release in Alice Walker's *Meridian.*" *Critique* 23, no. 1 (1981): 25–36.

Mason, Theodore O., Jr. "Alice Walker's *The Third Life of Grange Copeland*: The Dynamics of Enclosure." *Callaloo* 12 (Spring 1989): 297–309.

Melancon, Trimiko. *Unbought and Unbossed: Transgressive Black Women, Sexuality and Representation.* Philadelphia: Temple University Press, 2014.

Moore, Geneva Cobb, and Andrew Billingsley. *Maternal Metaphors of Power in African American Women's Literature: From Phillis Wheatley to Toni Morrison*. Columbia: University of South Carolina Press, 2017.

Nadel, Alan. "Reading the Body: Alice Walker's *Meridian* and the Archeology of Self." *Modern Fiction Studies* 34 (1988): 55–68.

O'Brien, John. "Alice Walker." In *Interviews with Black Writers*. Ed. John O'Brien. New York: Liveright, 1973, pp. 185–212. Reprinted in part, "From an Interview." In *In Search of Our Mothers' Gardens*. Alice Walker, 244–72. San Diego: Harcourt Brace Jovanovich, 1983.

Parker-Smith, Bettye J. "Alice Walker's Women: In Search of Some Peace of Mind." In *Black Women Writers, 1950–1980*, edited by Mari Evans, 478–93. Garden City, NY: Doubleday/Anchor, 1984.

Petry, Alice Hall. "Walker: The Achievement of the Short Fiction." In *Alice Walker Critical Perspectives Past and Present*, edited by Henry Louis Gates Jr. and K. A. Appiah, 193–210. New York: Amistad, 1995.

Plant, Deborah G. *Alice Walker: A Woman for Our Times*. Santa Barbara, CA: ABC-CLIO, 2017.

Pollock, Kimberly Joyce. "A Continuation of Pain: A Woman's Legacy in Alice Walker's *Possessing the Secret of Joy*." In *Women of Color: Mother-Daughter Relationships in 20th Century Literature*, edited by Elizabeth Brown-Guillory, 38–56. Austin: University of Texas Press, 1996.

Pratt, Louis H., and Darnell D. Pratt. *Alice Malsenior Walker: An Annotated Bibliography, 1968–1986*. Westport, CT: Meckler, 1988.

Quashie, Kevin Everod. *Black Women, Identity, and Cultural Theory: (Un)becoming the Subject*. New Brunswick, NJ: Rutgers University Press, 2004.

Richards, Mary Margaret. "Alice Walker." In *African American Writers*, edited by Lea Baechler and A. Walton Litz, 441–58. New York: Charles Scribner's Sons, 1991.

Ross, Daniel W. "Celie in the Looking Glass: The Desire for Selfhood in *The Color Purple*." *Modern Fiction Studies* 34 (Spring 1988): 69–84.

Royster, Philip M. "In Search of Our Fathers' Arms: Alice Walker's Persona of the Alienated Darling." *Black American Literature Forum* 20 (1986): 347–70.

Sadoff, Dianne F. "Black Matrilineage: The Case of Alice Walker and Zora Neale Hurston." *Signs* 11 (Autumn 1985): 4–26.

Shelton, Frank W. "Alienation and Integration in Alice Walker's *The Color Purple*." *CLA Journal* 28 (June 1985): 382–92.

Simcikova, Karla. *To Live Fully, Here and Now: The Healing Vision in the Works of Alice Walker*. Lanham, MD: Lexington Books, 2007.

Spillers, Hortense J. "'The Permanent Obliquity of an In(pha)llibly Straight': In the Time of the Daughters and the Fathers." In *Changing Our Own Words: Essays on Criticism, Theory, and Writing by Black Women*, edited by Cheryl A. Wall, 127–49. New Brunswick, NJ: Rutgers University Press, 1989.

Stein, Karen F. "*Meridian*: Alice Walker's Critique of Revolution." *Black American Literature Forum* 20 (Spring–Summer 1986): 129–41.

Steinem, Gloria. "Do You Know This Woman? She Knows You-A Profile of Alice Walker." *Ms. Magazine*, 10 (June 1982): 35–37.

Tate, Claudia. "Alice Walker." In *Black Women Writers at Work*, edited by Claudia Tate, 175–87. New York: Continuum, 1983.

Tavormina, M. Teresa. "Dressing the Spirit: Cloth-working and Language in *The Color Purple*." *Journal of Narrative Technique* 16 (Fall 1986): 220–30.

Tillet, Salamishah. "'Called Back to the World': An Interview with Alice Walker." *New York Review of Books,* October 1, 2018.

———. In *Search of* The Color Purple*: The Story of an American Masterpiece.* New York: Abrams Press, 2021.

Walker, Robbie Jean. "Implications for Survival: Coping Strategies of the Women in Alice Walker's Novels." *Explorations in Ethnic Studies* 10 (January 1987): 9–27.

Wall, Cheryl. "Living by the Word: June Jordan and Alice Walker's Quest for a Redemptive Art and Politics." In *Towards an Intellectual History of Black Women*, edited by Mia Bay, Farah J. Griffin, Martha S. Jones, and Barbara D. Savage, 214–32. Chapel Hill: University of North Carolina Press, 2015.

———. "On Women's Rights and Writing: June Jordan and Alice Walker." In *On Freedom and the Will to Adorn: The Art of the African American Essay*. Cheryl A. Wall, 176–216. Chapel Hill: University of North Carolina Press, 2018.

Wall, Wendy. "Lettered Bodies and Corporeal Texts in *The Color Purple*." *Studies in American Fiction* 16 (Spring 1988): 83–97.

Walsh, Margaret. "The Enchanted World of *The Color Purple*." *Southern Quarterly* 25 (Winter 1987): 89–101.

Warren, Nagueyalti. *Alice Walker's Metaphysics: Literature of Spirit*. Lanham, Maryland: Rowan and Littlefield Publishers, 2019.

Washington, J. Charles. "Positive Black Male Images in Alice Walker's Fiction." *Obsidian II* 3 (Spring 1988): 23–48.

Washington, Mary Helen. "Alice Walker: Her Mother's Gifts," *Ms. Magazine,* 10 (June 1982): 38.

Walker, Melissa. *Down from the Mountaintop: Black Women's Novels in the Wake of the Civil Rights Movement, 1966–1989*. New Haven, CT: Yale University Press, 1991.

Weisenburger, Steven C. "Errant Narrative and *The Color Purple*." *Journal of Narrative Technique* 19 (Fall 1989): 257–75.

Werner, Craig. "Alice Walker." In *Black American Women Novelists: An Annotated Bibliography*. Pasadena, CA: Salem Press, 1989, pp. 238–58.

Weston, Ruth D. "Inversion of Patriarchal Mantle Images in Alice Walker's *Meridian*." *Southern Quarterly* 25 (Winter 1987): 102–7.

White, Evelyn C. *Alice Walker: A Life*. New York: W.W. Norton, 2004.

Willis, Susan. "Alice Walker's Women." *New Orleans Review*, 12 (Spring 1985): 33–41.

Winchell, Donna Haisty. *Alice Walker*. New York: Twayne, 1992.

Winchell, Mark Royden. "Fetching the Doctor: Shamanistic Housecalls in Alice Walker's 'Strong Horse Tea.'" *Mississippi Folklore Register* 25, no. 2 (Fall 1981): 97–101.

INDEX

Absolute Trust in the Goodness of the Earth (Walker), 124; and aging, 115–16; death in, 110–11; environmentalism in, 99, 109–10; forgiveness in, 110–11, 113, 117; healing in, 108; location in, 109–10; peace in, 108–9, 116–17; spirituality in, 114, 116–17

activism, 118–19; in *Living by the Word,* 80; in *Once,* 6; in *Revolutionary Petunias,* 30–31; in *Taking the Arrow Out of the Heart,* 130, 132–33; in Walker's works, 1, 62, 96–97, 99–100

African diaspora, 53; in *Color Purple,* 64–65, 71; in *Goodnight, Willie Lee,* 51; in *Possessing the Secret of Joy,* 90–96; in *Temple of My Familiar,* 86–89

aging, 115–16, 127

Aidoo, Ama Ata, 53

Algebra Project, 30

Ali, Muhammad, 130–31

Alice Walker, "Everyday Use" (Christian), 28

Alice Walker, The Color Purple (Lister), 71

"The Alice Walker Calendar for 1986," 61

Allen, Robert, 72, 78, 80, 96

Amadi, Elechi: *The Concubine,* 21–22

American Book Award, 69

The American Scholar, 10

animals: in *Once,* 7; in *Poem Traveled Down My Arm,* 124; in *Possessing the Secret of Joy,* 91; in *Taking the Arrow Out,* 130; in *Temple of My Familiar,* 88–91; in *World Has Changed,* 124–25, 127; in *World Will Follow Joy,* 99, 127

Anything We Love Can Be Saved (Walker), 50, 62, 95–97

autobiography, 1, 32–34; in *Color Purple,* 65; in *Horses Make a Landscape,* 81, 85, 99; in *Now Is the Time,* 99; in *Once,* 7, 9; in *Revolutionary Petunias,* 29–31; in *Way Forward,* 111–12, 114–15; in *You Can't Keep a Good Woman Down,* 55–56

Autobiography of an Ex-Colored Man (Johnson), 58

Avilez, GerShun, 18

Awiakta, Marilou: "Motheroot," 78

Baldwin, James, 74

"Ballad of a Brown Girl" (Walker), 7–8

"Beauty" (Walker), 1, 5–6

Beloved (Morrison), 49, 118

Best American Short Stories (Foley), 28

The Best Short Stories by Negro Writers (Hughes), 11, 20

Black Elk Speaks (Neihardt), 34

Black Macho and the Myth of the Superwoman (Wallace), 69

Black Nationalism, 18, 35–36

Black Power movement, 34–36

"The Black Writer and the Southern Experience" (Walker), 9

Blount, Marcellus, 18

blues: men, 17–20; music, 53–54, 67; singers, 53, 67–68

The Bluest Eye (Morrison), 118

Bond, Julian, 132

Bradford, Perry, 53

Bread Loaf Writers' Conference, 10

Brother, I'm Dying (Danticat), 73

Buddha, 120, 124
Butler-Baker High School, 4
Butler-Evans, Elliott, 35, 64
Byrd, Rudolph P., 124–26
By the Light of My Father's Smile (Walker), 99; death in, 101–2, 104, 106–7; location in, 101–3; maimed bodies in, 104–5; myth in, 104–5, 107; violence in, 103

California Institute of Integral Studies, 120
Camus, Albert, 72–73; *De l'envers et l'endroit,* 9–10; *The Rebel,* 29
Cane (Toomer), 21, 23, 84
Cannon, Katie G., 75
Castro Ruz, Fidel, 127
The Chicken Chronicles (Walker), 124, 125
Children of Mississippi Program, 11
Children's Defense Fund, 10
Chopin, Kate, 77
Christ, 51
Christian, Barbara T., 38; *Alice Walker, "Everyday Use,"* 28
civil rights movement, 121; in *Goodnight, Willie Lee,* 49; in *In Love & Trouble,* 12–14; in *Meridian,* 34–38, 45; in *Once,* 7; in *Revolutionary Petunias,* 29–32, 45; in *Third Life of Grange Copeland,* 12–14, 17–18; and *Walker,* 6, 10–12
"The Civil Rights Movement" (Walker), 10
Clifton, Lucille, 118
The Color Purple (Walker), 2, 61, 120; African diaspora in, 64–65, 71; characters from in later works, 87, 88, 90; criticism of, 68–74, 97; fathers in, 62, 65–66, 70, 87; feminism in, 65, 68, 71; healing in, 52, 72; and "Is Celie Actually Ugly?," 133; letter writing in, 62–63, 71; love in, 63, 65, 67–68, 70–71; mothers in, 31, 66, 70; patriarchy in, 15, 62–63, 66–67, 69, 70; sexual assault in, 15, 66, 69, 70; sexuality in, 67–69; spirituality in, 62–63, 67–68, 71, 100; storytelling in, 65–66
Combahee River Collective, 51, 68
commencement addresses, 119–21
The Concubine (Amadi), 21–22
Cooper, Jane, 8
Cortez, Jayne, 118
Crazy Horse, 39
Create Dangerously (Danticat), 73
creativity: in *Color Purple,* 88; Hurston as model of, 49; in *In Search of Our Mothers' Gardens,* 74–77; in *Now Is the Time,* 115–17; in *Same River Twice,* 72–74; in *Temple of My Familiar,* 87–88; in *Way Forward,* 112–13; and women, 12–13, 49, 75–77, 118–19; in *You Can't Keep a Good Woman Down,* 54–55
Crenshaw, Kimberlé, 36
The Cushion in the Road (Walker), 100, 125, 127–30

Dalai Lama, 126–27
Danticat, Edwidge, 73
Davis, Miles, 127
death: in *Absolute Trust,* 110–11; in *By the Light,* 101–2, 104, 106–7; in *Horses Make a Landscape,* 83; in *Possessing the Secret of Joy,* 91–92, 95; in *Revolutionary Petunias,* 30–31; in *Temple of My Familiar,* 101
De l'envers et l'endroit (Camus), 9–10
Descartes, 23
Dessa Rose (Williams), 118
Dickens, Charles: *A Tale of Two Cities,* 118
Dix, Carl, 131
dreams: in *Absolute Trust,* 109–10; in *In Love & Trouble,* 26; in *Possessing the Secret of Joy,* 91, 94–95; in *Temple of My Familiar,* 89–90
Dust Tracks on a Road (Hurston), 47

Earth Mother, 41; in *Absolute Trust,* 109–10; in *Cushion in the Road,* 129; in *Horses Make a Landscape,* 84–85; in *Now Is the Time,* 114; in *Taking the Arrow Out,* 130
Ebert, Roger, 70
Edelman, Marian Wright, 10
Edgar, Joanna, 53

Ellison, Ralph: *Invisible Man,* 18, 36
Emecheta, Buchi, 53
Emory University, 4
environmentalism: in *Absolute Trust,* 109–10; in *Hard Times Require Furious Dancing,* 123; in *Horses Make a Landscape,* 80–81; in *Living by the Word,* 78–80; in *Taking the Arrow Out,* 130; and Walker, 1, 6, 83–84, 100–101, 134
Erickson, Peter, 20
Erivo, Cynthia, 133
Evers, Medgar, 45
"Exercises on Themes of Life" (Walker), 7
Experiment in International Living, 7

"Family Romance" (Freud), 14
fathers: in *Anything We Love,* 50; in *By the Light,* 101–7; in *Color Purple,* 62, 65–66, 70, 87; in *Good Night, Willie Lee,* 49, 52; in *Horses Make a Landscape,* 83–84; inadequate protection by, 32, 51; in *In Love & Trouble,* 25; in *In Search of Our Mothers' Gardens,* 50; in *Meridian,* 35, 39–41; in *Now Is the Time,* 115; in *Possessing the Secret of Joy,* 95; in *Temple of My Familiar,* 87–89; in *Third Life of Grange Copeland,* 14–15, 19; in *Way Forward,* 112, 114; in *You Can't Keep a Good Woman Down,* 20
Faulkner, William, 77
Fauset, Jessie, 58
feminism, 36, 51, 118–19; in *By the Light,* 105; in *Color Purple,* 65, 68, 71; in *Goodnight, Willie Lee,* 50–51; in *Horses Make a Landscape,* 80; and identity, 62; in *In Search of Our Mothers' Gardens,* 74; in *Meridian,* 37; in *Revolutionary Petunias,* 32; in *Temple of My Familiar,* 86; in *Third Life of Grange Copeland,* 12, 18; and Walker, 1, 9, 12–13, 18, 29, 53, 62; in Walker's writing, 46–47; in *Warrior Marks,* 96–97; in *You Can't Keep a Good Woman Down,* 52–53
Fiske, John, 36
flashbacks: in *Meridian,* 35, 46; in *Possessing the Secret of Joy,* 91, 93; in *Third Life of Grange Copeland,* 16. *See also* memory
Foley, Martha: *Best American Short Stories,* 28
folklore, 11, 15, 46–47
for colored girls who have considered suicide . . . (Shange), 68
forgiveness: in *Absolute Trust,* 110–11, 113, 117; in *Color Purple,* 52; in *Cushion in the Road,* 129; in *Meridian,* 46, 52; in *Way Forward,* 112–13
"For My Sister Molly Who in the Fifties" (Walker), 6
Freud: "Family Romance," 14
From A Native Daughter (Trask), 41

Garcia Verdecia, Manuel, 130
Garner, Eric, 132
genital mutilation, 2, 92–97
Geronimo, 39
Giffords, Gabrielle, 126
Gilman, Charlotte Perkins, 28
Give Birth to Brightness (Williams), 118
"Good Country People" (O'Connor), 24
Goodnight, Willie Lee, I'll See You in the Morning (Walker), 49–52, 60
Grant, Nettie Lee, 65
Grosvenor, Verta Mae, 29
Guggenheim Fellowship, 46
Gurdjieff, George, 58–59

haiku, 8
Hamer, Fannie Lou, 30, 37
Harcourt Brace Jovanovich, 61
Hard Times Require Furious Dancing (Walker), 99, 123–24
Hathor, 105
Head, Bessie, 53
Head Start Friends of the Mississippi Program, 11
healing: in *Absolute Trust,* 108; in *By the Light,* 104; in *Color Purple,* 72; in *Cushion in the Road,* 129; and dancing, 123; in *Horses Make a Landscape,* 80, 81; in *Living by the Word,* 78–79; in *Meridian,* 46, 52; and

healing (*continued*)
poetry, 80, 108; in *Possessing the Secret of Joy,* 90–91, 93, 98; in *Same River Twice,* 73; and storytelling, 86, 90; in *Temple of My Familiar,* 86–87, 98; and Walker, 41, 97–98
Henderson, Mae G., 63
Her Blue Body Everything We Know (Walker), 62, 80, 82–85
Hesse, Hermann: *Siddhartha,* 60
Hiawatha, 39
Holloway, Karla, 40
Horses Make a Landscape Look More Beautiful (Walker), 62, 80–83
Hudson, Winson, 11, 30
Hughes, Langston, 33; *The Best Short Stories by Negro Writers,* 11, 20
Hunt, Charlotte, 47
Hurston, Zora Neale, 33, 103; "Characteristics of Negro Expression," 75; *Dust Tracks on a Road,* 47; and feminism, 53; grave of, 47–48; *I Love Myself When I Am Laughing . . .,* 46–47; influence of on Walker, 21, 25, 46–47, 114; as model of creativity, 49; *Mules and Men,* 26, 47; *Their Eyes Were Watching God,* 15, 18, 50–51

I Love Myself When I Am Laughing . . . (Hurston), 46–47
Imitation of Life, 58
In Love & Trouble (Walker): as autobiography, 29; civil rights movement in, 12–14; intra-family relationships in, 20; mental decline in, 24–25; oppression in, 21–24, 56; poverty in, 21, 56; racism in, 22, 28, 56, 58; revenge in, 25–27; rural South in, 21, 27–28
In Search of Our Mothers' Gardens (Walker), 37, 50, 74–78, 118; success of, 61, 97
"In Search of Our Mothers' Gardens" (Walker), 21, 49
In Search of The Color Purple (Tillet), 71
Institute for the Harmonious Development of Man, 58
International Women's Day, 121
intertextuality, 21
Invisible Man (Ellison), 18, 36

Jackson, George, 30
Jackson State University, 12
Jeffers, Trellie, 4–5
"Johann" (Walker), 7
Johnson, James Weldon: *Autobiography of an Ex-Colored Man,* 58
Jonah's Gourd Vine (Hurston), 47
Jones, Quincy, 72
Jordan, June, 29, 118–20
journal entries, 21, 23, 79, 128
joy: in *Anything We Love,* 97; in *Chicken Chronicles,* 124; in *Cushion in the Road,* 128; in *In Love & Trouble,* 22; in *Meridian,* 48; in *Third Life of Grange Copeland,* 17; Walker's encouragement of search for, 4, 6, 8, 32, 78, 100–101, 134; in *World Will Follow Joy,* 126–27
June, Pamela B., 105
Jung, Carl, 86, 90, 92, 96

King, B. B., 132
King, Coretta Scott, 130
King, Martin Luther, Jr., 51, 112

Larsen, Nella, 21, 58; *Passing,* 56
Larson, G. Kaleo, 124, 126
Lauret, Maria, 14
Law Students Civil Rights Research Council, 10
Leaves of Grass (Whitman), 85
Leopard Clan, 7
Leopold, King, 120–21
Lester, Julius, 29
Letters to a Young Poet (Rilke), 8, 22, 30
letter writing: in *Color Purple,* 62–63, 71; in *Cushion in the Road,* 128; in *Possessing the Secret of Joy,* 90–92, 95; in *Temple of My Familiar,* 89
Leventhal, Melvyn R., 10, 13–14, 21, 30, 46, 111–12
Levine, Suzanne Braun, 53
Lewis, John, 34
Lilith, 105
Lister, Rachael: *Alice Walker,* The Color Purple, 71

Little, Rachel, 65
Liuzzo, Viola, 45
Living by the Word (Walker), 50, 62, 78–80
location, 1, 100; in *Absolute Trust,* 109–10; in *Anything We Love,* 95–96; in *By the Light,* 101–3; in *Meridian,* 36–37; in *Overcoming Speechlessness,* 120–22; in *Possessing the Secret of Joy,* 90–94; in *Temple of My Familiar,* 86–89; in *Way Forward,* 111; in *You Can't Keep a Good Woman Down,* 58–59
"Looking for Zora" (Walker), 47
Lorde, Audre, 118, 122
love: in *Absolute Trust,* 109, 111; in *Anything We Love,* 97; in *By the Light,* 103–6; in *Color Purple,* 63, 65, 67–68, 70–71; in *Cushion in the Road,* 128–29; in *Goodnight, Willie Lee,* 49–51; in *Hard Times Require Furious Dancing,* 123–24; in *Horses Make a Landscape,* 83–85; in *In Love & Trouble,* 23–24, 28; in *Living by the Word,* 78, 80–81; in *Meridian,* 41, 43, 45–46; in *Now Is the Time,* 114, 116; in *Overcoming Speechlessness,* 121–22; in *Possessing the Secret of Joy,* 91, 94; in *Revolutionary Petunias,* 30; in *Taking the Arrow Out,* 132–34; in *Temple of My Familiar,* 16, 87–89; in *Third Life of Grange Copeland,* 16, 19–20; in "To Hell with Dying," 20; in *Way Forward,* 112–13; in *World Will Follow Joy,* 126–27; in *You Can't Keep a Good Woman Down,* 53, 56, 59

MacDowell Colony, 10, 33
Malcolm X, 51
Mandela, Nelson, 132
Mandela, Winnie, 115, 132
Marley, Bob, 126, 132
McCloud, Shiloh, 123
McDowell, Deborah E., 57, 69
memory, 125, 134; in *Absolute Trust,* 109–10; in *Anything We Love,* 97; in *Cushion in the Road,* 127–28; in *Good Night, Willie Lee,* 49; in *Horses Make a Landscape,* 83–84; in *In Love & Trouble,* 25, 28; in *In Search of Our Mothers' Gardens,* 78; in *Meridian,* 35, 40, 46; in *Possessing the Secret of Joy,* 91–92; in *Revolutionary Petunias,* 31; in *Temple of My Familiar,* 86, 89; and Walker's fiction, 125; in *Way Forward,* 111–12. *See also* flashbacks
mental illness: in *Color Purple,* 70; in *In Love & Trouble,* 23–25; in *Possessing the Secret of Joy,* 93, 95; in *Temple of My Familiar,* 90–93, 95; in *World Will Follow Joy,* 126; in *You Can't Keep a Good Woman Down,* 58
Meridian (Walker): civil rights movement in, 34–38; flashbacks in, 46; forgiveness in, 52; motherhood in, 34, 35–38, 48; poetry in, 44–45; protest in, 43; return to South in, 35, 39, 45–46, 71, 133; and sacredness of all life, 38–40, 42; sacrifice in, 38–39, 52, 82; slavery in, 41–42; spirituality in, 38–41, 43, 60, 114; themes of, 114; transfiguration in, 45–46, 114; women's rights in, 35–38
Merrell Lynd, Helen, 8, 9
Merritt Monument Company, 47
mind-body dualism, 23
Minnehaha, 39
monologues, 21, 64, 90–92
Morgan, Marlo: *Mutant Message Down Under,* 115
"Mornings" (Walker), 7
Morrison, Toni, 29, 118; Beloved, 49
Moses, Bob, 30
Moses Man of the Mountain (Hurston), 47
"Motheroot" (Awiakta), 78
mothers: in *Absolute Trust,* 116–17; in *Anything We Love,* 97; and artistic creativity, 12–13, 75–77; in *By the Light,* 103, 105; in *Color Purple,* 31, 66, 70; in *Good Night, Willie Lee,* 52; in *Hard Times Require Furious Dancing,* 123; in *Horses Make a Landscape,* 80, 84; influence of, 4–5, 11, 32–33, 37, 48, 74; in *In Love & Trouble,* 23, 27–28; in *Meridian,* 34–35, 37–38, 43–44, 48, 52, 82; in *Now Is the Time,* 115; oppression of, 19, 31, 35–38, 48; in

mothers (*continued*)
Same River Twice, 73; in *Taking the Arrow Out,* 131–33; in *Temple of My Familiar,* 86–89, 91, 93–95; in *Third Life of Grange Copeland,* 13–16, 31
Ms. Magazine, 41, 46, 52–53, 69
Mules and Men (Hurston), 26, 47
Mutant Message Down Under (Morgan), 115
myth: in *Absolute Trust,* 116–17; in *By the Light,* 104–05, 107; in *Temple of My Familiar,* 88–89
"The Myth of Black Macho" (Staples), 69

NAACP Legal Defense and Educational Fund, 10
National Book Award, 1–2
National Endowment for the Arts award, 12
Native Americans, 35, 39–42, 55
Naylor, Gloria: *The Women of Brewster Place,* 68
Neihardt, John G.: *Black Elk Speaks,* 34
New York City Department of Welfare, 10
Ngugi, Wa Thiong'o, 53
9/11, 108–09
Now Is the Time to Open Your Heart (Walker), 41, 99, 114–15

Obama, Barack, 128
O'Connor, Flannery, 21, 28, 77; "A Good Man Is Hard to Find," 16; "Good Country People," 24
Office of Economic Opportunity, 11
Once (Walker), 6–9, 49, 126
"One Child of One's Own" (Walker), 12–13
oppression, 100, 133; in *By the Light,* 106; in *Color Purple,* 70; in *Cushion in the Road,* 128; in *Horses Make a Landscape,* 81–82, 84; in *In Love & Trouble,* 21–24; of mothers, 19, 31, 35–38, 48; in *Third Life of Grange Copeland,* 18–19
Overcoming Speechlessness (Walker), 100, 120–22

Parmar, Pratibha: *Warrior Marks,* 96–97
Passing (Larsen), 56
patriarchy, 20, 133; in *By the Light,* 102, 105, 107; in *Color Purple,* 15, 62–63, 66–67, 69–70; in *Her Blue Body Everything We Know,* 83; in *Meridian,* 44; in *Now Is the Time,* 117; in *Taking the Arrow Out,* 117; in *Third Life of Grange Copeland,* 12–13, 15–16, 19
p'Bitek, Okot, 53
peace, 1, 99, 100–101; in *Absolute Trust,* 108–9, 116–17; in *By the Light,* 104; in *Cushion in the Road,* 128; in *Horses Make a Landscape,* 83–85; in *Living by the Word,* 79–80; in *Now Is the Time,* 114; in *Taking the Arrow Out,* 133; in *World Will Follow Joy,* 127; in *You Can't Keep a Good Woman Down,* 56, 60
The Peacock Poems (Williams), 118
photography, 125–27
Pinkie, 58
"The Place in the Ways" (Rukeyser), 97
"Poems of a Childhood Poetess" (Walker), 4
A Poem Traveled Down My Arm (Walker), 99, 124
poetry, 1–2, 99; and activism, 130; and gender, 8–9; and healing, 80, 108; and memory, 125; in *Meridian,* 44–45; and suicide, 7–8; Walker on, 80, 82, 108; Walker's early writing of, 4–5
political messages, 6, 29, 118–21; in *Absolute Trust,* 109–11; in *Color Purple,* 71; in *Cushion in the Road,* 128; in *Hard Times Require Furious Dancing,* 123; in *Horses Make a Landscape,* 82; in *In Search of Our Mothers' Gardens,* 74, 78; in *Meridian,* 34–41, 44, 46, 114; in *Now Is the Time,* 114; in *Once,* 9; in *Overcoming Speechlessness,* 120–22; in *Revolutionary Petunias,* 31–32; in *Same River Twice,* 72; in *Taking the Arrow Out,* 131–32; in *Temple of My Familiar,* 86, 93; in *Third Life of Grange Copeland,* 12, 14; of Walker, 1–2, 11, 62, 73–75, 80, 99–100, 125,

133; in *Warrior Marks,* 96–97; in *World Will Follow Joy,* 127; in *You Can't Keep a Good Woman Down,* 53
Porter, Katherine Anne, 28
Possessing the Secret of Joy (Walker), 62; African diaspora in, 90–96; death in, 91–92, 95; healing in, 90–91, 98; psychotherapy in, 90–92
poverty, 100, 133; in *Absolute Trust,* 109–10; in *Color Purple,* 70; and economics, 40, 43–44; in *Good Night, Willie Lee,* 52; in *Hard Times Require Furious Dancing,* 123; in *In Love & Trouble,* 21, 56; in *Meridian,* 35–36, 40; in *Once,* 9; in *Revolutionary Petunias,* 29; in *Taking the Arrow Out,* 131; and Walker, 3, 5, 32
Presley, Elvis, 54
Proust, Marcel: *Remembrance of Things Past,* 125
psychotherapy, 86, 90–92
Pulitzer Prize, 1–2, 69
Push (Sapphire), 71

Quashie, Kevin Everod, 5
quilting, 27–28; in "Everyday Use," 76–77

racism, 2–3, 11–13, 25, 32, 48, 100, 133; in *Absolute Trust,* 110; in *By the Light,* 106; and economics, 40, 43–44; in *Good Night, Willie Lee,* 50; in *Horses Make a Landscape,* 81; in *In Love & Trouble,* 22, 28, 56, 58; in *In Search of Our Mothers' Gardens,* 74–75, 77; in *Meridian,* 35, 37–40, 44–45; in *Once,* 9; in *Revolutionary Petunias,* 28; in *Same River Twice,* 73; in *Third Life of Grange Copeland,* 16; in *Way Forward,* 113–14
Radcliffe Institute, 20–21, 33
Rainey, Gertrude "Ma," 53
The Rebel (Camus), 29
Remembrance of Things Past (Proust), 125
Revolutionary Petunias & Other Poems (Walker), 21; civil rights movement in, 29–32, 45; sacrifice in, 82
Riggs, Marcia Y., 75
Rilke, Rainer Maria: *Letters to a Young Poet,* 8, 22, 30
Rosenthal Award, 28
Ross, Marlon B., 18
Rukeyser, Muriel, 8; "The Place in the Ways," 97

sacrifice, 38–39, 52, 82
Saleh, Sundus Shaker, 133
The Same River Twice (Walker), 62, 72–74, 78
Sanchez, Sonia, 118
Sánchez Manduley, Celia, 127
Sapphire: *Push,* 71
Sarah Lawrence College, 7–8, 10, 61–62
Sartre, Jean-Paul, 13
"Saving the Life That Is Your Own" (Walker), 134
Sembene, Ousmane, 53
Sent by the Earth (Walker), 100
sexism, 48, 100, 133; in *Color Purple,* 68; and economics, 40, 43–44; in *In Love & Trouble,* 56; in *Meridian,* 35, 40; in *Same River Twice,* 73; and women artists, 75–76
sexual assault: in Absolute Trust, 117; in By the Light, 105; in Color Purple, 15, 66, 69–70; in *Meridian,* 36; in *Temple of My Familiar,* 89; in *Way Forward,* 113; in *You Can't Keep a Good Woman Down,* 53
sexuality, 62, 78, 100; in *Absolute Trust,* 116–17; in *By the Light,* 101–7; in *Color Purple,* 67–69; in *Meridian,* 36–37, 45; in *Possessing the Secret of Joy,* 94–95; in *Temple of My Familiar,* 86, 91; in *Way Forward,* 113–14
Shange, Ntozake, 29; *for colored girls who have considered suicide . . . ,* 68
shape shifting, 89
Siddhartha (Hesse), 60
Silko, Leslie Marmon, 28
"The Sisterhood," 29
Sitting Bull, 39
slavery, 41–42, 85, 103
Smith, Bessie, 53–54
Smith, Mamie, 53
Smith College, 21

Sojourner Truth, 114
Song of Solomon (Morrison), 118
"Song of the Son" (Toomer), 84–85
Sontag, Susan, 125
Southern Regional Council, 34
Spelman College, 6
Spielberg, Steven, 68–70, 72
spirituality: in *Absolute Trust,* 114, 116–17; in *Color Purple,* 62–63, 67–68, 71, 100; in *Cushion in the Road,* 128–29; in *Goodnight, Willie Lee,* 60; in *Living by the Word,* 79–80; in *Meridian,* 38–41, 43, 60, 114; in *Temple of My Familiar,* 89–90; and *Walker,* 99–100; in *You Can't Keep a Good Woman Down,* 60
Staples, Robert: "The Myth of Black Macho," 69
Steinem, Gloria, 46, 53, 81, 126
Stone, Oliver, 70
storytelling: in *Color Purple,* 65–66; and healing, 86; in *Possessing the Secret of Joy,* 90; in *Temple of My Familiar,* 86–87, 90
stream of consciousness, 21
Student Nonviolent Coordinating Committee (SNCC), 30
suicide, 4, 7–8
Sula (Morrison), 118

Taking the Arrow Out of the Heart (Walker), 99, 130–34
A Tale of Two Cities (Dickens), 118
"A Talk" (Walker), 61
The Temple of My Familiar (Walker), 62, 85; creativity in, 87–88; death in, 101; family in, 87, 89; healing in, 98; and memory, 125; mythic in, 88–89; spirituality in, 89–90; storytelling in, 86–87, 90
Their Eyes Were Watching God (Hurston), 15, 18, 47, 50–51
The Third Life of Grange Copeland (Walker), 10–11; abuse in, 15–16, 18–19; civil rights movements in, 14, 17–18; dedication to, 13–14; intergenerational bonding in, 14, 16–18, 20; return to South in, 16, 45; rural Black South in, 12, 14; women in, 12, 14–16, 18–19, 31
Thornton, Willie Mae "Big Mama," 54
Tillet, Salamishah, 133; *In Search of* The Color Purple, 71
time travel, 86, 89
"To Die Before One Wakes Must Be Glad" (Walker), 7
"To Hell with Dying" (Walker), 11, 20
Toomer, Jean, 33, 47, 58–59, 112; *Cane,* 21, 23, 84; "Song of the Son," 84–85
Tougaloo College, 12, 21
Townes, Emilie M., 75
transfiguration: in *Color Purple,* 64–65, 70–71; in *Meridian,* 45–46; in *Now Is the Time,* 115
transformation, 1, 101, 119, 133; and civil rights movement, 6, 12; in *Color Purple,* 63–64, 66, 70; in *Horses Make a Landscape,* 81; in *In Love & Trouble,* 29; in *Meridian,* 35, 37, 44–45; in *Possessing the Secret of Joy,* 90–91, 95, 96; and search for joy, 4; in *Temple of My Familiar,* 85, 88; in *Third Life of Grange Copeland,* 16, 19; of Walker, 2, 4, 13–14, 32, 60; in *You Can't Keep a Good Woman Down,* 56–57
Trask, Haunani-Kay: *From A Native Daughter,* 41
Tubman, Harriet, 75
Turner, Nat, 132

Uncle Remus tales, 18
University of Massachusetts, 20

Van Vechten, Carl, 47
Voter Education Project, 34
voter rights, 10–11

Walker, Alice, 1, 133–35; awards received by, 1, 2, 12, 28, 69; on *Color Purple,* 72; divorce of, 21, 46; and healing, 97–98; influences on, 2, 4–5, 8, 11–13; injury to, 2–5, 32, 49, 125; as lecturer, 11–12, 20–21; literary influences on, 21, 25, 29, 33, 46–48, 114. *See also* individual works

Walker, Annie Ruth, 2, 53, 123
Walker, Curtis Ulysses, 2–3, 5, 49
Walker, Gaye, 4
Walker, Henry Clay, 115–16
Walker, James Thomas, 2, 49
Walker, Kate Nelson, 65, 114–16
Walker, Minnie Lee, 2
Walker, Minnie Tallulah Grant "Lou," 2–5, 13, 49–50, 72–74, 78
Walker, Rachel, 31
Walker, Rebecca Grant, 5, 30–31, 80, 97, 102, 111; birth of, 12–13; estrangement of, 123, 131; and reconciliation, 134
Walker, Robert Louis "Bobby," 2–3, 49
Walker, William Henry "Bill," 2, 4, 49
Walker, Willie Fred, 2, 49
Walker, Willie Lee, 2–3, 21, 49–50, 83
Wall, Cheryl A., 119
Wall, Wendy, 63
Wallace, Michelle: *Black Macho and the Myth of the Superwoman,* 69
wandering: in *Cushion in the Road,* 128; in *Meridian,* 39; in *Now Is the Time,* 114–17; in *Temple of My Familiar,* 88; and Walker, 114, 127–28
Wangari, 7, 127
war, 1, 100; in *Absolute Trust,* 108–9; in *Cushion in the Road,* 128; in *Hard Times Require Furious Dancing,* 123; in *Living by the Word,* 80
Wards Chapel, 2, 31
Warren, Nagueyalti, 128
Warrior Marks (Walker and Parmar), 96–97
Washington, Mary Helen, 5
The Way Forward Is with a Broken Heart (Walker), 99, 111–14
We Are the Ones We Have Been Waiting For (Walker), 100, 117–20
Webb, Constance, 13
Weems, Renita, 75
Wellesley College, 20
West, Cornel, 131
West, Traci C., 75
Whitman, Walt: *Leaves of Grass,* 85
Williams, Sherley Anne, 118
Winfrey, Oprah, 126
womanism, 62, 74–75, 127, 133
The Women of Brewster Place (Naylor), 68
The World Has Changed (Walker), 125
The World Will Follow Joy (Walker), 99, 125–27
Wright, Richard, 13

You Can't Keep a Good Woman Down (Walker): Black women artists in, 54–55; family in, 20; feminism in, 52–53; race in, 55–60

Zen epigrams, 8
Zinn, Howard, 6, 9
"Zora Neale Hurston" (Walker), 33